NORWEGIAN NIGHTMARES

Traditions in World Cinema

General Editors
Linda Badley (Middle Tennessee State University)
R. Barton Palmer (Clemson University)

Founding Editor
Steven Jay Schneider (New York University)

Titles in the series include:

Traditions in World Cinema
Linda Badley, R. Barton Palmer and Steven Jay Schneider (eds)

Post-beur Cinema: North African Émigré and Maghrebi-French Filmmaking in France since 2000
Will Higbee

New Taiwanese Cinema in Focus: Moving Within and Beyond the Frame
Flannery Wilson

International Noir
Homer B. Pettey and R. Barton Palmer (eds)

Films on Ice: Cinemas of the Arctic
Scott MacKenzie and Anna Westerståhl Stenport (eds)

Nordic Genre Film: Small Nation Film Cultures in the Global Marketplace
Tommy Gustafsson and Pietari Kääpä (eds)

Contemporary Japanese Cinema Since Hana-Bi
Adam Bingham

Chinese Martial Arts Cinema: The Wuxia Tradition (Second edition)
Stephen Teo

Slow Cinema
Tiago de Luca and Nuno Barradas Jorge

Expressionism in the Cinema
Olaf Brill and Gary D. Rhodes (eds)

French-language Road Cinema: Borders, Diasporas, Migration and 'New Europe'
Michael Gott

Transnational Film Remakes
Iain Robert Smith and Constantine Verevis

Coming-of-Age Cinema in New Zealand
Alistair Fox

New Transnationalisms in Contemporary Latin American Cinemas
Dolores Tierney

Celluloid Singapore: Cinema, Performance and the National
Edna Lim

Short Films from a Small Nation: Danish Informational Cinema 1935–1965
C. Claire Thomson

B-Movie Gothic: International Perspectives
Justin D. Edwards and Johan Höglund (eds)

Francophone Belgian Cinema
Jamie Steele

The New Romanian Cinema
Christina Stojanova (ed) with the participation of Dana Duma

French Blockbusters: Cultural Politics of a Transnational Cinema
Charlie Michael

Nordic Film Cultures and Cinemas of Elsewhere
Anna Westerståhl Stenport and Arne Lunde (eds)

New Realism: Contemporary British Cinema
David Forrest

Contemporary Balkan Cinema: Transnational Exchanges and Global Circuits
Lydia Papadimitriou and Ana Grgić (eds)

Mapping the Rockumentary: Images of Sound and Fury
Gunnar Iversen and Scott MacKenzie

Images of Apartheid: Filmmaking on the Fringe in the Old South Africa
Calum Waddell

Greek Film Noir
Anna Poupou, Nikitas Fessas, and Maria Chalkou (eds)

Norwegian Nightmares: The Horror Cinema of a Nordic Country
Christer Bakke Andresen

Please see our website for a complete list of titles in the series
www.edinburghuniversitypress.com/series/TIWC

NORWEGIAN NIGHTMARES
The Horror Cinema of a Nordic Country

Christer Bakke Andresen

EDINBURGH
University Press

Edinburgh University Press is one of the leading university presses in the UK.
We publish academic books and journals in our selected subject areas across the
humanities and social sciences, combining cutting-edge scholarship with high editorial
and production values to produce academic works of lasting importance. For more
information visit our website: edinburghuniversitypress.com

© Christer Bakke Andresen, 2022, 2024

Edinburgh University Press Ltd
The Tun – Holyrood Road
12(2f) Jackson's Entry
Edinburgh EH8 8PJ

First published in hardback by Edinburgh University Press 2022

Typeset in 10/12.5 pt Sabon by
Cheshire Typesetting Ltd, Cuddington, Cheshire, and
printed and bound by CPI Group (UK) Ltd,
Croydon, CR0 4YY

A CIP record for this book is available from the British Library

ISBN 978 1 4744 5784 2 (hardback)
ISBN 978 1 4744 5785 9 (paperback)
ISBN 978 1 4744 5786 6 (webready PDF)
ISBN 978 1 47445 787 3 (epub)

The right of Christer Bakke Andresen to be identified as the author of this work
has been asserted in accordance with the Copyright, Designs and Patents Act 1988,
and the Copyright and Related Rights Regulations 2003 (SI No. 2498).

CONTENTS

List of Figures	vi
Acknowledgements	viii
Traditions in World Cinema	x
Foreword	xii
1. Introduction to Norwegian Nightmares	1
2. The Source of Horror	18
3. The Slashers of Norway	35
4. Open Bodies in Rural Nightmares	53
5. Norwegian Psychological Horror	71
6. Healing Power	85
7. Fantastic Horror Hybrids	106
8. Dead Water	124
9. The Norwegian Apocalypse	142
Filmography	159
Bibliography	165
Online Resources	171
Interviews Conducted	173
Index	174

FIGURES

1.1	'The Water Sprite' ('Nøkken'), a fantastic creature from Norwegian folklore peeking out of a dark lake, by the artist Theodor Kittelsen in 1904. (Creative Commons, Public domain)	6
2.1	Liljan Werner at the edge of the *Lake of the Dead*. (Screenshot)	28
2.2	Television producer Gunnar contemplates the dead body in the lake, while Lasse, left, and Per watch in the background. (Screenshot from *Dark Woods*)	30
3.1	Jannicke slumping in the snow, having become the exhausted final girl of the first true Norwegian slasher story. (Screenshot from *Cold Prey*)	40
3.2	Ingunn in the terrible place, wounded, doomed and desperate. (Screenshot from *Cold Prey*)	43
3.3	The Mountain Man, Jannicke's slasher film nemesis and a transnational icon of horror. (Screenshot from *Cold Prey*)	45
4.1	Jannicke fixes her eyes on the mountains in the distance, resolving to end the terror of the Mountain Man at whatever cost to herself. (Screenshot from *Cold Prey II*)	61
5.1	John sits down opposite Kim, on the surreal stage where Norway's first modern psychological horror film reaches its terrible climax. (Screenshot from *Next Door*)	79
6.1	Anna and Helge communicate with the dead via baby monitor. (Screenshot from *The Monitor*)	88

FIGURES

6.2	The empty windows of suburban Oslo stare out at Anna as she investigates the source of sounds on her baby alarm. (Screenshot from *The Monitor*)	90
6.3	Thelma crawls from the lake and regurgitates a blackbird, shortly after her father spontaneously combusts and dies in the cold water. (Screenshot from *Thelma*)	95
6.4	Ben and Anna's trial face-off in the woods in Eskil Vogt's supernatural thriller, foreshadowing the final showdown. (Screenshot from *The Innocents*)	100
7.1	Norway's biggest secret, quite literally, is revealed to be the Jötunn troll, itself a mountain in the mountains of Dovre. (Screenshot from *Troll Hunter*)	109
7.2	Hans the troll hunter, underplayed by comedian Otto Jespersen. (Screenshot from *Troll Hunter*)	110
7.3	'The troll that ponders how old it is' ('Trollet som grunner på hvor gammelt det er'), by artist Theodor Kittelsen in 1911, is one of the significant templates for the modern visualisation of trolls. (Public domain)	111
7.4	A Nazi zombie emerges from the Arctic snow. (Screenshot from *Dead Snow*)	115
7.5	Feeding on fossil fuel, in a rare socio-political satire depicting Norwegians as helpless oil junkies. (Screenshot from *Dark Souls*)	118
7.6	It could have been a Hollywood dinosaur, but it is the CGI Midgard Serpent of Norse mythology. (Screenshot from *Ragnarok*)	121
8.1	The contemporary Norwegian gothic castle. (Screenshot from *Dark Woods 2*)	126
8.2	Lillian and her twin brother ponder their separation in a boat on the lake, in the film's traumatising past event. (Screenshot from *Lake of Death*)	140

ACKNOWLEDGEMENTS

I thank Gillian Leslie at Edinburgh University Press for such genuine enthusiasm for this project and for shepherding the book along. Richard Strachan and Sam Johnson, also at EUP, for swift and faultless help to the author whenever needed. Series editors Linda Badley and R. Barton Palmer for encouraging this book to become a part of *Traditions in World Cinema*. I am grateful for the opportunity that you all have given me.

I am indebted to Gunnar Iversen for steering me into the field of Norwegian horror many years ago, and for sticking with me ever since. If I 'keep cool' just a fraction of how well you do it, I will consider myself well taught.

Rikke Schubart for reading and discussing drafts of the book along the way. Your insight and passion have been invaluable, and our talks are always a highlight of my day.

Anne Gjelsvik for always being supportive of my research, my ideas, and my teaching. If you only knew how often I hear your voice in my head: 'Baby steps.'

Friends, colleagues and students at the Department of Art and Media Studies, NTNU.

Luis Rocha Antuñes and Lorna Piatti-Farnell for generous input, inspiration and direction at various points of my research into Norwegian horror.

Jakub Sebastian Konefal at the University of Gdansk and *Panoptikum* for providing the first opportunity to publish my research in English, in their issue 17 on Nordic film and television (see Andresen 2017a). The *Journal of*

ACKNOWLEDGEMENTS

Scandinavian Cinema for allowing me to explore some of my ideas, in their volume 7 issue 3 and volume 9 issue 2 (see Andresen 2017b and 2019). Also, Karsten Meinich and Lars Ole Kristiansen at Montages.no for letting me have a critical go at a varied selection of popular, and less popular, Norwegian movies upon their release.

Trond-Atle Farestveit for a steady eye and calm hand in correcting and editing my text, and for constructive content discussions to go with it.

Sven Østgaard for essential help with the technicalities of the screenshot.

The filmmakers who gave generously of their time to discuss their genre work during my research: Pål Øie, Roar Uthaug, Martin Sundland, Pål Sletaune, Astrid Thorvaldsen and Eskil Vogt. Also, Joachim Trier for the uplifting residence visit to our department at NTNU in 2017, and Severin Eskeland for uncompromising dedication to horror genre filmmaking.

First and last, my wife Line Solberg Ohnstad for patience and support.

TRADITIONS IN WORLD CINEMA

General editors: **Linda Badley and R. Barton Palmer**
Founding editor: **Steven Jay Schneider**

Traditions in World Cinema is a series of textbooks and monographs devoted to the analysis of currently popular and previously underexamined or undervalued film movements from around the globe. Also intended for general interest readers, the textbooks in this series offer undergraduate- and graduate-level film students accessible and comprehensive introductions to diverse traditions in world cinema. The monographs open up for advanced academic study more specialised groups of films, including those that require theoretically-oriented approaches. Both textbooks and monographs provide thorough examinations of the industrial, cultural, and socio-historical conditions of production and reception.

The flagship textbook for the series includes chapters by noted scholars on traditions of acknowledged importance (the French New Wave, German Expressionism), recent and emergent traditions (New Iranian, post-Cinema Novo), and those whose rightful claim to recognition has yet to be established (the Israeli persecution film, global found footage cinema). Other volumes concentrate on individual national, regional or global cinema traditions. As the introductory chapter to each volume makes clear, the films under discussion form a coherent group on the basis of substantive and relatively transparent, if not always obvious, commonalities. These commonalities may be formal, stylistic or thematic, and the groupings may, although they need not, be popularly identified as genres, cycles or movements (Japanese horror, Chinese martial arts cinema, Italian Neorealism). Indeed, in cases in which a group of films is not already commonly identified as a tradition, one purpose of the volume is to establish its claim to importance and make it visible (East Central European Magical Realist cinema, Palestinian cinema).

Textbooks and monographs include:

- An introduction that clarifies the rationale for the grouping of films under examination
- A concise history of the regional, national, or transnational cinema in question
- A summary of previous published work on the tradition
- Contextual analysis of industrial, cultural and socio-historical conditions of production and reception
- Textual analysis of specific and notable films, with clear and judicious application of relevant film theoretical approaches
- Bibliograph(ies)/filmograph(ies)

Monographs may additionally include:

- Discussion of the dynamics of cross-cultural exchange in light of current research and thinking about cultural imperialism and globalisation, as well as issues of regional/national cinema or political/aesthetic movements (such as new waves, postmodernism, or identity politics)
- Interview(s) with key filmmakers working within the tradition.

FOREWORD

Norway is a very small country, and public funding has long been necessary to maintain a national cinema. Against this background, commercial film genres (with the sole exception of the comedy) had never taken permanent hold at any point in Norway's cinema history, until shortly after 2000. Since then, popular genres like the action film, the romantic comedy and the war film have proliferated in Norway. Norwegian horror fiction also came to a massive turning point in 2003: that year saw the release of *Dark Woods*, the first clear-cut and successful Norwegian horror film to hit cinemas since *Lake of the Dead* in 1958. For the past two decades, genre entertainment has reached unprecedented popularity in Norwegian cinema, including the previously shunned horror film. In fact, Norway has become the only Nordic country to cultivate a regular output of horror, both in underground moviemaking as well as the mainstream cinema which is the focus of the present book.

Besides *Dark Woods* by director Pål Øie, my book will give particular attention to the *Cold Prey* trilogy of slasher films that started with Roar Uthaug's *Cold Prey* in 2006; the psychological horror films *Next Door* (2005) and *The Monitor* (2011) by Pål Sletaune, and Joachim Trier's *Thelma* (2017); as well as the horror-related genre hybrids *Troll Hunter* (2010) by André Øvredal, and *Ragnarok* (2013) by Mikkel Brænne Sandemose. These films are major works of commercial and artistic importance in Norway's horror cinema tradition, although many others will be discussed along the way. I will also chart the changes and continuities that are discernible in the development of Norwegian horror from the original *Lake of the Dead* by Kåre Bergstrøm in 1958 to the modern re-adaptation of the same source novel, Nini Bull Robsahm's *Lake of Death* in 2019.

This book follows on from my PhD research into popular Norwegian cinema, a project which was designed to serve the need for a closer look at how and why horror became a mainstay in Norwegian national cinema, and how this tradition relates to the major global force of Hollywood genre cinema. Genre entertainment, including horror fiction, enjoys great popularity in Norway these days. The book will aim to explain why a coherent Norwegian horror cinema did not exist prior to 2000, and how horror became a trend after that point. One might assume that Norway was fertile soil for this kind of national tradition, bearing in mind that the closely related crime genre has a peculiar history in this country.

In March 1923, publishers Gyldendal took out a ground-breaking ad to hype their latest crime novel, *The Train to Bergen Was Robbed Last Night* (*Bergenstoget plyndret i natt*). The book was co-written by poet Nordahl Grieg and translator Nils Lie, under the pseudonym Jonathan Jerv (which translates as Jonathan Wolverine), and the publisher's inventive approach to marketing consisted of a front-page ad in the newspaper *Aftenposten*, among others, which read 'The Train to Bergen Was Robbed Last Night!'. The ad was designed to look like a newspaper headline, many people mistook it for an actual headline, and this created quite the intended uproar. Once the wilful act of misguidance was revealed, the book sold like hot cakes around the time of the 1923 Easter holidays.

With a formal tradition of taking a minimum of five days off at Easter, Norwegians have seen fit to use this time for visits to mountain or seaside cabins. This national pastime of recreation in nature is effortlessly combined with reading fairly light thrillers and crime novels, something that literature marketing has not failed to exploit. In Norway, enjoying peace and quiet comes with a certain dose of murder and mystery, and the proper literature is easily adaptable to radio as well. As television became more and more common, including in remote cabins, this Easter reading and listening tradition morphed into an Easter viewing tradition, with British detectives like P. D. James' Dalgliesh and Agatha Christie's Poirot gaining great popularity in Norway. So ingrained in Norwegian culture are the Easter holiday traditions that one of the greatest public outrages of the 2020 pandemic lockdown was aimed at the ban on travelling to remote cabins at Easter. Taking this annual cabin vacation away from Norwegians was controversial enough for the government to not even consider such a ban during the second year of the pandemic in 2021.

The 1923 publishing coup related above might be called the 'seed of the Easter crime phenomenon' (Folkvord 2018), at least in terms of marketing and possibly in terms of reading habits, a phenomenon that seems curiously particular to Norway. Throughout the twentieth century Norwegian crime literature grew steadily into a strong and coherent tradition, and when we fast forward to the 1990s, closer to the post-2000 horror boom in Norwegian cinema, we find the start of the truly massive output of crime and thriller fiction from Norwegian authors that we are now accustomed to. However, horror films being popular with Norwegian audiences did not automatically translate into this same type of fiction becoming a trend in domestic film production. Indeed, horror film has only quite recently become a solid national tradition in Norway, a fact which is a main issue of discussion in this book.

The relevance of the Easter crime tradition to the question of Norwegian horror cinema is obvious when one considers the settings of two of the earliest films in the genre: *Dark Woods* (the Norwegian title *Villmark* literally translates as *Wilderness*) takes place in the woods around a mountain lake, far from the city, and *Cold Prey* stages its action in and around a mountain lodge, which is plopped down in the middle of an Easter-like snowy desolation. The question of why Norwegians like to spend their holidays devouring crime fiction can be extended to asking why such a seemingly peaceful and happy country, in a peaceful and happy Nordic region of Europe, produces horror movies at all. This is another main topic of the book.

The interest in Norwegian horror from abroad does not represent something completely new or truly unique. The post-2000 popularity of the literature, film and television crime fiction known collectively as Nordic noir is a strong example of dark and troublesome entertainment from the Scandinavian and Nordic countries that strikes a global nerve, not necessarily by being very original in terms of plots and stories, but through the particularities of their melancholic settings. Modern Norwegian crime literature and the recent wave of horror cinema are not alone in having a global reach, for the aesthetics of horror have generally made for strong cultural exports from Norway to the world: from the scary folktales of the 1800s to the black metal music scene that grew globally influential in the 1990s, horror motifs and tropes in Norwegian popular culture have since coalesced into the modern horror cinema of Norway. With the non-artistic and sinister sideshows of church burnings and murders heightening a sense of international infamy, some elements of the early black metal scene took its relation to horror culture way too far. Even so, an aesthetic of dread and terror in the presentation of Nordic rock music no doubt communicates very well across borders. Recently, the Norwegian heavy metal band Vreid released the album *Wild North West* and accompanied the music with a long-form video filmed in the same woods where the Norwegian horror cinema ground-breaker *Dark Woods* was shot nearly two decades ago.

Horror and its related genres are thriving in Norway at the time of writing. The producers of *Dark Woods* are currently in post-production with the psychological horror film *The Nightmare* and are also preparing a television series called *Norwegian Horror Kit* that will combine folktales and horror in a contemporary setting. The producers of *Cold Prey*, on the other hand, have shifted their focus from horror to disaster films, of which *The North Sea* is the latest example. Several more horror films and horror-related genre hybrids are in the works in Norway, the horror tradition in Norwegian cinema still going strong. It is my hope that the present book will illuminate its past, its major works, and also its possible future.

Christer Bakke Andresen
Trondheim, Halloween 2021

1. INTRODUCTION TO NORWEGIAN NIGHTMARES

On 1 November 2019, the weekend of Halloween, a Norwegian horror movie premiered in cinemas across the country. The title of the movie was *Lake of Death* (*De dødes tjern*), and it was loosely based on a 1942 novel by the esteemed Norwegian poet and crime author André Bjerke. At the time of its release, this adaptation by director Nini Bull Robsahm was the latest addition to the popular horror cinema tradition that had flourished in Norway since the turn of the millennium.

The film was also the second adaptation of Bjerke's novel, the first incarnation being the only full-blooded pre-2000 Norwegian horror film: Kåre Bergstrøm's *Lake of the Dead* (*De dødes tjern*) in 1958. While such a genre movie had been one-of-a-kind in the 1950s, a generic anomaly in a national cinema that rarely indulged popular Hollywood-related genres except for the comedy, the horror film had become so common and proliferating in post-2000 Norwegian cinema that the new adaptation barely registered in the national press. A lot had changed in the film and media landscape of Norway in the preceding twenty years, and the coming and consolidation of a national horror cinema was one of the results.

Robsahm's *Lake of Death* tells the story of a group of young people who venture into the wilderness of Norway to spend time together in a remote house in the woods. Here they will ostensibly help the film's central character Lillian (Iben Akerlie) overcome the lingering trauma of losing her twin brother. As is common for many types of horror tales, things are not quite as they seem: the lost brother returns, and the deep secrets of his disappearance and subsequent reappearance force their way back to the surface. The return of the repressed, overwhelmingly often staged in and around dark waters or desolations of snow and ice, is an aesthetic hallmark of Norwegian horror cinema.

This book concerns itself with three main topics. First, why did Norway begin to produce horror movies regularly after 2000 and not before? Second, what types of horror have been the prevalent subgenres in Norwegian cinema, and how do these Norwegian films relate to the Anglo-American cinema that seems to be their chief inspiration? Third, what are the identifiable hallmarks of a specifically Norwegian brand of the transnational horror genre? I will start my inquiry by describing the country where it happened and the people who are the makers of, as well as the principal audience for, this national genre tradition.

Norway and Norwegians

Each year Norwegians can look at international rankings and find that their country, Norway, is among the best countries in the world to live in, sometimes even topping the list as the very best nation on the planet in which to spend one's life. The official United Nations indicators ranked Norway highest as recently as 2020 (UN Development Programme 2020). Norway scores consistently well in terms of health and life expectancy, income and education, peace and stability. Crime rates are low, and affluence is high. There is no death penalty, although lifetime incarceration is possible, and the guiding principle of the judicial system is rehabilitation rather than revenge. People in Norway have a remarkable level of trust in their government and institutions, and they are generally optimistic about the future. The World Bank and the World Economic Forum confirm the positive state of affairs in reports that gauge wealth per capita and the level of economic inclusion, naming Norway the wealthiest and most inclusive country in the world (Corrigan 2017; Berglund 2018). Life in Norway, however, has only become this good quite recently.

The Kingdom of Norway is a small European country with a population of about 5,400,000. Norway's extensive coastline stretches from the Arctic Ocean in the north to the North Sea area of the Atlantic Ocean in the south, and the country shares mainland borders with Sweden, Finland and Russia. Together with Sweden and Denmark, Norway makes up the cultural region known as Scandinavia, which is part of the Nordic region that also includes Finland, Iceland, Greenland and the Faroe and Åland islands. The Norwegian language is a type of North Germanic, similar to but distinct from Swedish and Danish.

Norway is a social-democratic welfare state, like all of its Nordic neighbours, meaning that within an essentially capitalist framework there exists a strong regulatory state and a well-established tradition for promoting and securing social and economic equality through democratic processes, strong labour unions, and universal health care. As such, Norway is widely perceived as an affluent and peaceful nation state, where there is a high degree of income redistribution and very little social unrest. The country is also marked by its cultural, political and military bonds with Great Britain and the United States of America in the west, as well as its geographical close proximity to Russia in the east.

For most of its history, Norway has been a poor country, but this changed with the discovery of oil and gas along its coast in the 1960s. Indeed, even those who know next to nothing about Norway and its people are likely to associate the country with Vikings, trolls and oil. Respectively, these concepts represent Norway's iconic past, its mythical wilderness, and its current status as one of the richest countries in the world.

Norway became a relatively unified kingdom under King Harald I Fairhair in the late AD 800s (Sørensen 1998). The Viking Age, generally considered to be the period from about AD 800 to about AD 1050, brought Norwegian expansion through conquest, trade and settlements in Europe as well as North America. A period of peace and stability in Norway was followed by civil war over contested and unclear succession laws from 1130 to 1240, before a renewed period of unification and prosperity was achieved by King Håkon IV Håkonsson in the mid-1200s. Under his rule the Crown of Norway included Iceland and Greenland in its domain, and the foundations for the later myth of a medieval Norwegian empire were thus laid down (Bomann-Larsen 2004: 235–6). However, in 1349 and 1350 the plague known as the Black Death decimated the Norwegian population, and this led to a recession that precipitated a long period of unions with Denmark and Sweden.

Norway remained in a union with Denmark for more than 430 years, until the end of the Napoleonic wars in 1814. At that point Denmark was forced to cede mainland Norway to Sweden as part of a peace treaty, and Norway thus entered a personal union with Sweden despite also declaring independence and creating the Norwegian constitution that same year. The country maintained its independence in all matters of state except foreign policy, but ultimately broke out of the union in 1905 and became the sovereign nation state of modern Norway. The country chose to remain a constitutional monarchy rather than become a republic, which was significant to power relations in a Europe dominated by monarchies, and then elected prince Carl of Denmark through national referendum to become King Haakon VII of Norway (Ibid.: 300–12, 412, 441). This sequence of events in 1905 established the country's new royal family as national symbols of unity and independence, in whose line the grandson of Haakon VII is now King Harald V of Norway.

The first few decades of the 1900s saw an effort to differentiate Norway, not from continental Europe or the United States of America, but from Sweden and

Denmark. Essential to this was a romantic view of Norway and Norwegians, the historical fallacy of assuming that certain traits, traditions and objects are more authentically and uniquely Norwegian than others (Bryn 1993: 39). The creation and perpetuation of the myth of national authenticity was, and still is, decisive. On the one hand, is the Norwegian national costume authentically Norwegian, when it was certainly created with influences from abroad? On the other hand, when does a hamburger become a typically Norwegian meal? In the romantic view, the costume is authentically Norwegian, while the fast-food item is an Americanised intrusion, precisely because the two are divided by the establishing period of national romanticism.

The national-romantic reconstruction of a fully independent Norway at the dawn of the 1900s, and the reframing of traits and traditions of *Norwegian-ness* took place in politics, literature, painting and also in the cinema. What Anne Marit Myrstad (1997) has labelled the national breakthrough of Norwegian cinema in the 1920s was essentially a bid to reclaim Norway's rural landscapes and national literature from Swedish filmmakers. In the early years of cinema, successful Swedish motion pictures like *A Man There Was* (*Terje Vigen*, Victor Sjöström, 1917) and *Synnöve Solbakken* (John W. Brunius, 1919) were based on Norwegian poetry and literature, and the latter was even filmed on location in Norway, something that many Norwegians took as a national insult at the time. This natural and cultural heritage, landscapes and literature perceived as authentically Norwegian, would be brought back home in the Norwegian cinema of the 1920s and 1930s, when many literary dramas were adapted for the screen and filmed in the national-romantically appropriate settings of the Norwegian countryside and wilderness (Iversen 2011: 32–8).

Norway and Norwegians are concepts that necessarily take shape against some notion of *otherness* (Bryn 1992: 79). The particulars of Norway as a country and Norwegians as a people were formed in opposition to Sweden and Denmark, because the national-romantic sense of Norway's uniqueness was built on perceived, and ultimately exaggerated, contrasts to the other Scandinavian countries. Sabine Henlin-Strømme (2012) has pointed out how the rural farmer personified this image of Norway, and how the distance to Sweden and Denmark was highlighted by fjords and mountains in the reconstruction of Norway in the early decades of the 1900s. Certain contrasts were readily identified. Where Denmark was flat, Norway was mountainous. While Sweden was urban, Norway was rustic. A large part of the population of Norway lived and worked in and with nature, and the country's farmers and working-class folk made for a clear, if partly contrived, ideological contrast to Sweden's urban aristocracy.

National romanticism was essential in defining the nation state of Norway in the 1800s and the early 1900s, and it also played a major part in shaping the early Norwegian cinema. Somewhat paradoxically, Norwegian films in the 1920s and 1930s were often stylistically close to the globally dominant Hollywood cinema, as they strove to establish the cinema of Norway as an alternative to the popular cinema of Sweden. Classical Hollywood style and narrative were a major influence on the most important Norwegian director of the era: Tancred Ibsen, grandson of the internationally acclaimed Norwegian authors and playwrights Bjørnstjerne Bjørnson and Henrik Ibsen. The latter's stage plays had in turn been important to the foundation of classical Hollywood cinema, and his grandson studied the craft of filmmaking in Hollywood before returning to direct feature films in Norway. Tancred Ibsen's 1937 movie *Gypsy* (*Fant*) would become one of the most important Norwegian films of all time due to its stylistic and narrative assuredness and its popularity with contemporary audiences and critics. Gunnar Iversen has written about Tancred Ibsen's significance to Norwegian film history that 'for the first time a Norwegian film director completely mastered that much-imitated [Hollywood] style', and that *Gypsy* 'resembled any film from Hollywood, but still contained something Nordic' (1997: 112–13).

As I will discuss in Chapter 2, the question of how to apply something specifically Norwegian to transnational genres, and a kind of love/hate relationship with the style and storytelling of popular Hollywood cinema, would be decisive in the turn to genre filmmaking in Norway after 2000. At certain points in time, Norwegian cinema has aimed to align itself more closely with the aesthetics of Hollywood cinema, and the concept of cultural *Americanisation* is pertinent, being the presumed movement away from something original towards something American (Bryn 1992: 19, 1993: 119). On the other hand, as this book will show, the Norwegian approach to genre filmmaking has often hinged on exploiting national history, landscapes and traditions in a conscious effort to create something that differs from American templates while still sticking close enough to tried and tested genre formulas.

However, the national-romantic application of rustic Norwegian nature and culture, whether in the political project of differentiating the newly independent Norway, or in the Hollywood-inspired shaping of early Norwegian cinema, is actually at odds with national folklore. The positive and regenerative qualities with which national romanticism imbues the Norwegian countryside, the fetishizing of nature and wilderness, seems to ignore the much scarier roots of woods, mountains and waters. After all, the wild nature of Norwegian folktales is filled with trolls, goblins and hulders: supernatural creatures that can and will harm you. Getting lost in the woods is dangerous, nature is a force far stronger than humans, and this folkloric vision of Norway is certainly much closer to the post-2000 horror film treatments than the national romanticism of the 1800s and 1900s.

The films of the Norwegian horror cinema clearly borrow their generic framework from other places, chiefly from popular American cinema. Still, they

Figure 1.1 'The Water Sprite' ('Nøkken'), a fantastic creature from Norwegian folklore peeking out of a dark lake, by the artist Theodor Kittelsen in 1904. (Creative Commons, Public domain)

feature landscapes, themes and creatures that can be considered specifically Norwegian in ways that will be discussed in the following chapters. What Mette Hjort (2016) has outlined as the parameters of Danish cinema is equally true for Norway: the population is too small to sustain a private sector film industry, the language is primarily understood within the country's borders, and American cinema is the dominant force in the marketplace. Within these parameters the largely publicly funded cinema of Norway negotiates the volatile oppositions of commercial popularity and artistic ambition, existing in a state of friction that has informed the emergence of a horror cinema tradition in a wealthy and prosperous Nordic country where, on the surface, everything seems fine.

A darkly paradoxical truth is the fact that suicide rates in Norway doubled from the late 1960s to the late 1980s, the same period in which oil riches set Norway on course towards the top of international rankings describing the wealth and health of nations, and the numbers have remained at this historical high ever since (Ekeberg and Hem 2019). Although precise answers to this are hard to find, it is a fact that young Norwegians in the age bracket from 18 to 24 have reported an increasing sense of unhappiness, loneliness and a lack of everyday meaning in recent years (Nes et al 2021). The suicide rates have proven tragically hard to lower during the same era that Norwegian crime literature and horror cinema have also laboured to expose the potential dark side of the allegedly best country in the world.

The last 100 years have brought two instances of utter darkness to Norway. The Nazi invasion and occupation during the Second World War, in the years 1940 to 1945, brought hardship of a kind Norwegians had never known. However, Norwegians' sense of national identity would ultimately be strengthened by the Allied victory and the fact that Norway was on the side of the Allies in the war, and King Haakon VII would become the object of immense national pride. The King and his government spent the war years in exile after refusing to give in to German demands for a Nazi-friendly administration, returning to a liberated Norway in the spring and summer of 1945. These events have been fundamentally important in shaping the image of Norway and Norwegians, both at home and abroad.

After prosperous post-war decades of rebuilding, in which the Norwegian social democracy and its welfare state flourished, darkness descended once again on 22 July 2011. The Oslo bombing and the Utøya massacre on that day were the worst displays of criminal violence the country had seen since the war. A right-wing extremist set off a bomb in the government quarter in Oslo and attacked a Labour Party youth camp at the Utøya Island with semi-automatic weapons. A total of seventy-seven people, most of them teenagers, were killed and many more injured in the two sequential terror attacks. Although the title of this book could hardly be more appropriate for such a national trauma, the complexities involved in the discussion of 22 July lie outside the purview of the present work. I will, however, make note of the fact that the killer infiltrated the Utøya camp by posing as a police officer.

It is a curious fact that we will only find one single Norwegian horror movie in which a law enforcement officer is a villain. In Severin Eskeland's debut feature film *Detour (Snarveien*, 2009), the principle bad guy is a police officer. However, this man and his badge are Swedish, not Norwegian. The absence of Norwegian law enforcement villains in the country's horror cinema points to a hallmark of the social-democratic Norwegian welfare state: a high level of trust in police institutions. The crime rate in Norway has been in steady decline for decades (Statistics Norway 2019), and police officers are mostly unarmed. This means that they carry firearms under lock in their vehicles, but not at the hip unless the situation demands it. There is a broad political consensus in Norway that unarmed police officers are important to reaching peaceful resolutions in heated situations, and research suggests a clear correlation between the lack of firearms and the low number of shootings in countries like Norway and Great Britain (Knutsson 2014). This trust level makes bad guys with badges significantly less viable in Norwegian horror cinema than they are in justifiably more paranoid American thrillers like *Kiss the Girls* (Gary Felder, 1997), although there are examples of such villains in Norwegian crime literature.

The golden age of Norwegian crime and horror fiction coincides strikingly with a time when the citizens of Norway are wealthier and, by most accounts, healthier than at any other point in history. In light of this fact, what is the stuff that Norwegian nightmares are made of? What horror do Norwegians fear? Is there a dreadful dark side of the social-democratic utopia that serves dark storytelling in a way that appeals to audiences both in Norway and abroad? Indeed, Norway is the home of internationally acclaimed author Jo Nesbø, whose novels about hard-boiled detective Harry Hole are among the most globally well-known and commercially successful crime literature of the subgenre labelled *Nordic noir*. Despite the wealth, despite the peaceful and prosperous existence at the top of UN and World Bank rankings: in the world of fiction, Norway is a place of terrifying crime and horror.

Nordic noir and Nordic horror cinema

The term Nordic noir is fairly new. It was probably first used in mainstream media, and possibly coined, by critic Laura Miller of *The Wall Street Journal* in a January 2010 article titled 'The Strange Case of the Nordic Detectives'. This was followed that same year by further media coverage like *The New York Times* article 'Nordic Noir and the Welfare State' and the *BBC* documentary 'Nordic Noir: The Story of Scandinavian Crime Fiction'. Ove Solum has pointed out that, just like its semi-namesake *film noir*, the term itself was created by people looking in from the outside (2016a: 109, 115–18).

By that point the United States and Europe had long been exposed to a wave of Nordic crime literature that the Germans had already labelled *Scandi krim*. The roots of Nordic noir as a crime subgenre are often traced to the Swedish novels featuring detective Martin Beck, published by Maj Sjöwall and Per Wahlöö from 1965 to 1975. Swedish authors of major significance in the 1990s and 2000s include Henning Mankell, known for the detective character Kurt Wallander, Håkan Nesser and his novels about detective Van Veeteren, and Stieg Larsson, who wrote the *Millennium* trilogy about journalist Mikael Blomqvist and hacker Lisbeth Salander. In recent years, the series of novels featuring detective Joona Linna by Lars Kepler (a pseudonym for Alexander Ahndoril and Alexandra Coelho Ahndoril) has been met with international acclaim and massive commercial success, and the crime fiction of Danish author Jussi Adler-Olsen is also among the most popular Nordic literature in the years after 2000. Deadly crime and troubled detectives in Scandinavia and the Nordic countries would capture imaginations around the world, contrasting the upper-class mysteries of British crime solvers like Agatha Christie's Poirot by venturing into the dark side of contemporary and ostensibly classless social-democratic societies.

INTRODUCTION TO NORWEGIAN NIGHTMARES

This Nordic detective tradition, exploiting the shock value of uncovering violence and death in a seemingly peaceful society, has deeper roots than one might think. While Edgar Allan Poe's short story 'The Murders in the Rue Morgue', published in 1841, is usually credited as the first modern detective story, there were others. One year earlier, in 1840, Norwegian author Maurits Hansen had published his novel *The Murder of Engine Maker Roolfsen (Mordet på maskinbygger Roolfsen)*, a book with several characteristics that would ultimately become hallmarks of detective fiction (Dahl 1993). About a hundred years later there would be more snippets of early Norwegian crime fiction that pointed ahead to Nordic noir, like Arthur Omre's *The Escape (Flukten)* in 1936 and André Bjerke's *Dead Men Disembark (Døde menn går i land)* in 1947.

Internationally acclaimed crime fiction from Norway in the age of Nordic noir includes the Konrad Sejer series by Karin Fossum, the Cato Isaksen series by Unni Lindell, the Varg Veum series by Gunnar Staalesen (who had been active as a crime author all the way back to the 1970s), and Jo Nesbø's novels about alcoholic detective Harry Hole, the latter of which spawned the Hollywood adaptation *The Snowman (Snømannen*, Tomas Alfredson) in 2017. A Norwegian precursor to the later film and television output of Nordic noir was the debut feature film from director Erik Skjoldbjærg, the detective thriller *Insomnia* in 1997. Alongside director Pål Sletaune's debut film *Junk Mail (Budbringeren*, 1997), *Insomnia* was selected for the 1997 Cannes Film Festival and inspired the short-lived term *Norwave* that purported to describe the new direction and influence of Norwegian cinema. *Insomnia* stood out as a detective story in the way that Skjoldbjærg utilised the perpetual daylight of a northern Norwegian summer, making a basic film noir premise literally light up with a tangible sense of Nordic authenticity. In fact, French critics called the movie a *film blanc*, and the road to a cinematic Nordic noir subgenre of crime fiction was opened (Engelstad 2006; Listmoen 2017: 34–8).

Indeed, the Nordic noir phenomenon would soon make the leap to feature films and television series. Some of these would be adaptations, like the Swedish films based on Larsson's *Millennium* trilogy, which was also turned into the Hollywood feature *The Girl with the Dragon Tattoo* (2011) by David Fincher, a director who had launched his strong genre reputation with the horror-related crime thriller *Seven* (1995). Other and more consistently popular projects have included the original Danish television series *The Killing* (2007–12) and the Danish and Swedish co-production *The Bridge* (2011–18), both of which have subsequently been remade in non-Nordic countries while sometimes, confusingly, retaining the Nordic noir label. There has also been the Icelandic series *Trapped* (2016–19) and the Finnish *Bordertown* (2016–20), adding to a collective body of Nordic work with significant international impact.

A key issue in Nordic noir is a leftist criticism of the modern Nordic society, utilising characters and stories that essentially reveal the dark side of paradise (Forshaw 2012: 16–18; Solum 2016b: 137–41). Social-democratic welfare states are not always as socially and economically equitable as they might appear on the surface, and the narratives of Nordic noir often aim to express a concern for how the Nordic welfare model is under duress in an age of globalised capitalism and New Public Management ideals. It is evident that even in the perceived Nordic utopia, the rich get richer and the poor stay poor. Utopia for some, but not for others. Nordic noir, as well as some of the Nordic horror cinema, stirs these waters.

Another hallmark of Nordic noir is the frequent spectre of a dark past, in particular the Second World War and a significant proclivity for Nazism in the Nordic countries at that time. If not for the German invasion in April 1940, Norway and Denmark might have chosen the path that Sweden did: an ostensible neutrality in the conflict playing into the hands of the violent Nazi aggressors, and ultimately coming to haunt the Swedes of the future. Indeed, Norway spent the war with a Nazi-friendly administration in the absence of the country's exiled legal government. The conflicts of this dark past are important to the background of Nordic noir stories like Larsson's *Millennium*, and they also feature in the backstory to the Norwegian *Dark Woods* (2003–15) horror duology by director Pål Øie.

The transnational cultural influence of the Nordic noir crime fiction is unprecedented in Scandinavian and Nordic history. Its books, films and television series have gained widespread international attention over the past couple of decades (Solum 2016b: 134–5; Toft and Waade 2017: 4–9). Kerstin Bergman has suggested many reasons for this export success. Among them are the works' reputation for quality storytelling, a non-metaphorical straightforward language, complexity in main characters, gender equality in character portrayals, social criticism of the ailing welfare state, brand marketing, and the perceived exoticism of the Nordic setting, which is Sweden in Bergman's case (2014: 135). The unique audio-visual aesthetic and sensory appeal of these works is an important part of their engagement with audiences, including the books, but what exactly is the Nordic aesthetic?

The books, films and television series of Nordic noir are characterised by landscapes, either urban or rural, that Anne Marit Waade (2017) has described as representative of a certain Nordic *melancholy*. The settings of these stories are the spaces of a cold and pale north on the edge of the Arctic, where there seems to be some sort of perpetual autumn or early spring, sometimes also deep winter. Summer barely exists. As the *BBC* described it in their 2010 documentary, this is 'a place of haunting natural beauty, a utopian society where beautiful people lead idyllic lives. It is the perfect place for murder. [. . .] An atmospheric setting where nights can last for days, with many lonely places

INTRODUCTION TO NORWEGIAN NIGHTMARES

to hide a body' (Solum 2016a: 118). Indeed, this tactile sense of melancholy, a kind of meditation on darkness, is evident in Norwegian music of many types, from the classical Romantic works of Edvard Grieg to the modern pop music of the band a-ha. The latter's song 'Sycamore Leaves', appearing on the 1990 album *East of the Sun, West of the Moon* (which takes its title from an old Norwegian folktale), ruminates on 'wet grounds, late September . . . the foliage of the trees', and the dreadful feeling that 'someone's lying covered by sycamore leaves'. This tree is not typically Nordic, but the song's mood certainly is, and much of a-ha's music can be described in terms of 'a chill, Nordic, and melancholy temper blowing through the songs' (Nilsson 2017), akin to the books, films and series that would later appear. In terms of film and television dramas in the Nordic noir crime subgenre, the décor and lighting will tend towards cold blue and grey colours to highlight this pensive mood of loneliness and melancholia, and the look is often accompanied by the equally bleak tones of music scores and introverted pop songs.

Despite such aesthetic characteristics, this kind of crime fiction was influenced in turn by American film and literature, and the genre label itself was partially lifted from the term *film noir*, which was coined by French critics in the post-war 1940s to describe the mood and style of a wave of American crime films that included *The Maltese Falcon* (John Huston, 1941), *Double Indemnity* (Billy Wilder, 1944) and *The Big Sleep* (Howard Hawks, 1946). These films were based on hard-boiled detective novels by authors Dashiell Hammett, James M. Cain and Raymond Chandler, respectively, the likes of whom would often provide the source materials that filmmakers turned into popular American movies. Film noir is essentially an audio-visual style applied to crime fiction. There is low-key chiaroscuro lighting and extensive use of shadows. There is cigarette smoke indoors, and fog and rain outdoors. The filmmakers create a dark and miserable urban frame and setting for murder mysteries investigated by jaded and troubled detectives, with an added touch of social criticism thrown into the mix as well. In retrospect, perhaps this sort of anti-heroic tale suited the Nordic mood and attitude quite well, that which British film and literary critic Barry Forshaw has summed up as 'difficult and proud' (2012: 96).

The visual characteristic of cold and gloomy landscapes is a feature that Nordic noir crime fiction has in common with the admittedly sporadic Nordic horror cinema. Although there has been much European horror cinema with considerable transnational significance, Gunnar Iversen has pointed out that there is 'no long and coherent horror tradition in the cinemas of the Nordic countries, and no large and consistent body of horror film production' (2016: 332). While Denmark and Sweden have produced horror films now and then as far back as the silent era, Iceland, Finland and Norway have contributed very few such genre pictures between them, until after 2000. The present book will outline the history of a coherent and relatively consistent Norwegian horror cinema in the years since 2003, but I will first briefly consider some examples of horror from other Nordic countries in recent decades, starting with the cinemas of Sweden and Denmark.

Sweden enjoys a proud art horror legacy through the works of legendary director Ingmar Bergman, whose films *The Seventh Seal* (1957), *The Virgin Spring* (1960) and *Hour of the Wolf* (1968) can be seen as precursors to later folk horror like the British movies *Witchfinder General* (Michael Reeves, 1968) and *The Wicker Man* (Robin Hardy, 1973), a tradition also exemplified by the recent Swedish-American co-production *Midsommar* (Ari Aster, 2019). Supernatural horror in the Nordics is also in large part the domain of Swedish cinema, and in the years after 2000, Swedish horror would have a particular preoccupation with vampires.

One of the most influential Nordic horror films of this era has been Tomas Alfredson's *Let the Right One In* (2008), an adaptation of the John Ajvide Lindqvist novel. The story is about 12-year-old Oskar, a boy who is bullied at school and ignored at home. One day he befriends the vampire girl Eli, and his life changes dramatically. The film, like the book, is both a social-realistic tale of young friendship and a vampire horror story, set in the bleak urban landscapes of a Swedish 1980s suburbia. Other Swedish films with vampire stories in the years after 2000 include *Frostbite* (Anders Banke, 2006), which sports the rather excellent tagline 'dawn is just a month away', and the less successful *Not Like Others* (Peter Pontikis, 2008). There is also the more recent psychological horror film *The Evil Next Door* (Tord Danielsson and Oskar Mellander, 2020), which treads the familiar path of a supernatural thriller, but *Let the Right One In* has been particularly convincing in demonstrating the applicability of transnational horror archetypes in a social-democratic Nordic setting.

Danish cinema reached two horror milestones in 1994. That year saw the release of Ole Bornedal's feature film *Nightwatch*, which was later remade in Hollywood by Bornedal himself, as well as Lars von Trier's influential television series *The Kingdom*. Von Trier would later add to his horror credentials with the psychological thrillers *Antichrist* (2009) and *The House That Jack Built* (2018), cementing the impression of Denmark's horror output as being largely inspired by arthouse cinema. His horror movies also depict nature as a negative force, characterised by chaos, dissolution and destruction. The traumatised couple at the centre of *Antichrist* experience a descent into hell that is made all the more horrific by the wild nature around them, a descent that ends in violence and death.

Danish filmmakers have mostly remained preoccupied with artistically ambitious and arguably less entertainment-oriented horror subgenres, including the psychological thriller *The Neon Demon* (2016) by Nicolas Winding Refn, an international co-production, and the surrealist horror *Koko-di Koko-da* (Johannes Nyholm, 2019), which was a Swedish-Danish co-production. However, both Denmark and Sweden have also occasioned a certain tradition for low-budget independent exploitation horror, films that would reach genre fans on DVD or streaming platforms and not necessarily play in cinemas. In a similar vein, Greenland, formally a Danish island in the North Atlantic Ocean, has also produced a horror film, the low-budget *Shadows in the Mountains* (2011) by Malik Kleist, which utilises the wild Arctic landscapes of Greenland to tell a horror story inspired by the country's mythology.

In the middle of the North Atlantic lies the island nation of Iceland. The land was settled by Norwegians in the early Viking Age and was a part of the Kingdom of Norway in the Middle Ages. Later, Iceland came under the rule of the Danish Crown, before gaining independence in 1918 and finally leaving the personal union with Denmark in 1944 to become a sovereign republic. There had been low-budget horror-related movies made for television in the 1970s and '80s, but Iceland's first properly cinematic horror film was the satirical body horror of Júlíus Kemp's *Reykjavik Whale Watching Massacre* in 2009. Set against the backdrop of Iceland's financial collapse in 2008, the film utilised well-established slasher movie conventions in telling the tale of a group of spoiled international tourists going on an ill-fated whale safari in the waters off the Icelandic coast.

When their boat breaks down, the tourists are seemingly saved by a family of Fishbillies in their old and rusty ship. However, the whaler Fishbillies have been put out of business by the combined forces of Greenpeace and the international financial crisis, and now they channel their energies into hunting and slaughtering unsympathetic tourists instead. The positive connotations of Icelandic nature are twisted to become a threateningly negative force, and the horror genre is used for a critical look at the country's social and economic situation. In the subsequent years, there have been a few additional horror films taking advantage of Iceland's melancholy settings, like the found footage thriller *Frost* (Reynir Lyngdal, 2012) and the horror mystery *I Remember You* (Óskar Thór Axelsson, 2017), the latter of which is an adaptation of the popular novel by Icelandic crime author Yrsa Sigurðardóttir.

There has also been Nordic horror coming from the woods and lakes of Finland. 2008 saw the release of the monster horror movie *Dark Floors* (Pete Riski), featuring the costumed rock band Lordi, and the historical psychological horror drama *Sauna* (also known as *Evil Rising*, Antti-Jussi Annila), which tells a story set during the conflict between Finland and Russia in the late 1500s. Some years later a slasher movie also appeared: *Bodom* (2016) by Taneli Mustonen. The film was based on the true story of the murders at Lake Bodom in 1960, when three teenagers on a camping trip were stabbed and beaten to death. The killer was never caught, and *Bodom* follows four young friends travelling to the lake on a morbid camping trip where they plan to reconstruct the 1960 events in hope of solving the mystery.

Sauna and *Bodom* are examples of Finnish filmmakers making use of two significant national symbols of Finland, the sauna and the lake, and putting them into horror tales. The connotations of cleansing and recreation are replaced by death and destruction, in much the same way that the positive forces of woods and mountains would be transformed in the horror cinema of Norway. However, all is not horrific in Finland: the fantastical and comedic *Rare Exports* (2010) by Jalmari Helander blends horror elements with a fantasy tale about Santa Claus, where he comes from, how scary he can truly be, and how he manages to cover all of the world in the course of just one single Christmas night. Genre hybridisation lends itself to the fusion of horror with comedy, and *Rare Exports*, an international co-production that also includes Norwegian money and actors, is a prime example.

It is possible to identify certain characteristics in the horror cinema of each Nordic country, even though this has indeed been a cursory glance. The suburban and sometimes vampiric horror films of Sweden are conspicuous, as are the psychological thrillers of Denmark. Meanwhile, Iceland, Finland and Norway all seem very much preoccupied with their respective nature and wilderness as sources and sites of horror stories. One thing that all Nordic countries have in common, however, is the fact that the small size of these nations makes it impossible to sustain a private sector film industry, and thus they are all dependent on public funding to maintain a national cinema. The relative absence of horror film in these countries until quite recently is a question of national film and censorship policies, among other things. As censorship rules have been liberalised, and as genre entertainment has gained a higher cultural status than before, the horror film has found a foothold in the Nordic countries, and in Norway especially.

About the book

This book contributes to the developing recognition of horror genre filmmaking in the Nordic countries, and Norway in particular. It is my ambition that the present work will provide insight into how and why Norway has become a country with a considerable horror genre tradition since the start of the millennium. The origins and nature of Norwegian nightmares, as they take form in Norwegian horror cinema, will be discussed in terms of national film policies, the emergence of key Norwegian filmmakers, and the aesthetic relation of Norwegian horror films to certain transnational subgenre traditions.

The selection of films in this book is based on the criteria that these are Norwegian horror movies or horror hybrids that have had a general cinema release in Norway. This means having regular screenings in cinemas in at least three of the country's four biggest cities: Oslo, Bergen, Trondheim and Stavanger. Most of the films in my selection have had cinema runs in all of these cities as well as many smaller cities and towns, even if some of them are independently funded and not reliant on public support through the Norwegian Film Institute's funding programmes.

In making this selection I am leaving out from my discussion short films as well as a group of low-budget independent feature films, the latter meaning films made without public funding and which have not been showcased in cinemas nationwide. Examples of this are some of the exploitation movies by director Reinert Kiil, films like *Whore* (*Hora*, 2009) and *Inside the Whore* (2012). Tanja Aas Hindrum discussed these less exposed films in her Norwegian-language MA thesis *From the Underground to the Surface: Norwegian Underground Horror* (2018), a rare academic study of the phenomenon where Hindrum positions the low-budget underground horror of Norway in aesthetic relation and opposition to the general cinema release horror corpus that I will treat in this book.

My reason for selecting what might reasonably be called the mainstream of Norwegian horror, at the expense of independent underground horror, is that Norwegian film politics and the mechanics of the publicly funded Norwegian cinema is of prime interest when tracing the emergence of Norwegian horror after 2000. With a population of only 5,400,000 at the time of writing, Norwegian film production is largely dependent on public funding. Political initiatives and priorities are therefore of great significance in directing the course of Norwegian cinema, including its horror genre.

The book has nine chapters. Chapter 1, 'Introduction to Norwegian Nightmares', has introduced Norway and Norwegians, and highlighted peculiarities of the nation's history and its population that informs my subsequent discussion of the Norwegian horror cinema. Crime and horror fiction have been prevalent in Norwegian literature and film in the early decades of the new millennium, and Norway is the only Nordic country with a steady output of horror cinema since 2000. The following chapters explore the reasons for this and discuss major works and subgenres of Norwegian horror cinema.

The starting point for Chapter 2, 'The Source of Horror', is the fact that Norwegian horror cinema uses woods and mountains as sources and sites of death and destruction to an overwhelming degree. Contrary to the national romanticising of nature that played an important part in shaping the image of Norway in the late 1800s and early 1900s, Norwegian horror cinema uncovers dread and death in the wild and rural. A subchapter called 'The Turn to Genre in Norwegian Cinema' discusses the cultural and political origins of the modern Norwegian horror tradition and points out the basic aesthetics that define Norwegian horror. Since the early forebear *Lake of the Dead* (*De dødes tjern*, Kåre Bergstrøm) in 1958, the horror of Norwegian cinema has been a horror from the deep. The consistent use of nature in Norwegian horror sets it apart from American and European traditions in the genre. I will argue that what is specific about Norway's horror wave is its origin in nature and its almost exclusively wild or rural settings. A subchapter called '"We should have stayed away from that lake": *Dark Woods*' builds on these observations and discusses the founding text of modern Norwegian horror, *Dark Woods* (*Villmark*, 2003) by Pål Øie, the movie that initiated a national genre tradition that would not have been possible at any other time in Norwegian film history.

Chapters 3 and 4, 'The Slashers of Norway' and 'Open Bodies in Rural Nightmares', discuss the slasher subgenre of Norwegian horror cinema, with a particular focus on the popular *Cold Prey* trilogy that started with Roar Uthaug's debut feature *Cold Prey* (*Fritt vilt*) in 2006. Carol J. Clover's concepts of this subgenre were fundamentally important in bringing about the conventional genre wisdom of Wes Craven's postmodern milestone *Scream* (1996) and subsequent slasher aesthetics. We shall see that the Norwegian slasher films shed new light on the assumed conventions of this transnational subgenre, including its gender issues. The archetypes of the slasher movie, the final girl and the masked killer, were never as clear-cut as popular convention presents them. Still, the Norwegian slasher films utilise highly generic modes of storytelling, while removing the action to the terrible places of Norway's countryside and wilderness, where archetypical characters and events are framed in a way that is unique in slasher history.

Chapters 5 and 6, 'Norwegian Psychological Horror' and 'Healing Power', discuss the other major subgenre of Norwegian horror cinema: the psychological horror film. Where the slasher focuses on physical threats and bodily harm, the psychological horror tale looks inside the mind to reveal dark and deadly secrets. Even in a seemingly serene society, such things exist. However, this is also where we find Norwegian horror stories that culminate in spiritual redemption and healing. These chapters will focus on the horror movies of Pål Sletaune, *Next Door* (*Naboer*, 2005) and *The Monitor* (*Babycall*, 2011), and will also consider Joachim Trier's *Thelma* (2017) and Eskil Vogt's *The Innocents* (*De uskyldige*, 2021).

Chapter 7, 'Fantastic Horror Hybrids', discusses genre crossbreeds. The blending of horror with other genres has always been popular, and Norway has embraced hybrids when combining horror with dark humour in Tommy Wirkola's zombie-splatter-comedy *Dead Snow* (*Død snø*, 2009), broader comedy in André Øvredal's mockumentary *Troll Hunter* (*Trolljegeren*, 2010), and action adventure in Mikkel Brænne Sandemose's *Ragnarok* (*Gåten Ragnarok*, 2013). These commercially successful films pinpoint a peculiar void in Norwegian film history: the lack of monsters. Even the culturally significant trolls had not made an appearance in Norwegian live-action cinema before turning up in *Troll Hunter*.

Chapter 8, 'Dead Water', follows the Norwegian horror genre back to its point of origin, as Pål Øie revisits *Dark Woods* for a sequel. Like many other films in the canon of Norwegian horror cinema, *Dark Woods 2* (*Villmark 2*, 2015) shines a light on the shadow side of Norway, in this case including Norwegian war history. The chapter also discusses the variables and constants of Norwegian horror in a comparative analysis of the original *Lake of the Dead* and the recent re-adaptation *Lake of Death* (*De dødes tjern*, Nini Bull Robsahm, 2019), where my discussion arrives at the ultimate hallmark of our national horror tradition: its perpetual meditation on the deep and dark waters of personal and national pasts, and its treatment of a specifically Norwegian type of downfall. This leads into Chapter 9, 'The Norwegian Apocalypse', in which I also consider the horror-related Norwegian disaster films of recent years. All horror is to some extent the tale of the end of things as we know them, the opening of dark chests of secrets, and in this sense the Norwegian horror cinema has brought about the end of an innocent time when Norway and its nature was a safe and beautiful place.

The sublime dread and terror of Norwegian horror movies depends on the existence of dark forces of nature, and in particular the threatening invasion of dead water. Be it lakes, pools, rivers, or even the snow and ice into which water can transform, water is indeed the element of Norwegian horror. Dreadful horror from the deep can invade all aspects of mind and physical reality to wreak absolute destruction upon the known world. This gothic use of water in Norwegian horror signifies a national adaptation of a transnational genre. Norwegian horror cinema has created its own kind of apocalypse through the recasting of nature as a force of evil, staging the end of the world on the wild frontier of Nordic civilisation. The characters we follow either die out there, or they reach a point of no return where their previous lives are irrevocably over. Norwegian horror is a continuous tale of transformation and apocalypse, in which the image of Norway is twisted and turned in an effort to identify the dark essence of Norwegian nightmares.

2. THE SOURCE OF HORROR

Lasse and Per have gone fishing. They are television technicians on a team-building trip with would-be colleagues Elin and Sara, spending four days in the wild woods of western Norway under the leadership of ambitious television producer Gunnar. Now they need food and approach the lake in the woods with some trepidation. Being city dwellers, they lack faith in their own wildlife skills. While waiting for fish to hopefully take the bait, they discover an abandoned campsite by the waterside. A tent is erected there, cups and plates are sitting on the ground, but it appears that no one has been there for a long time. Returning to the site with their weary and grumpy producer, the boys find a fishing net submerged in the lake nearby. They pull it out slowly, revealing the naked dead body of a woman from the murky depths. As the initial shock wears off, the producer argues that they keep the discovery secret until they return to civilisation. The lake reclaims the body, pulling the net back down into the darkness. The team-building has already failed, conflict ensues, and evil has been unleashed.

These scenes are from the early parts of Pål Øie's *Dark Woods* (*Villmark*, 2003), the first film of the modern Norwegian horror cinema, and they constitute the inciting incident that sets the terrible drama in motion. For the cinematic tradition that Øie initiated, publicly funded Norwegian horror movies with general cinema distribution in their home country and considerable commercial success, the use of Norwegian nature as a source of evil and a site of dark contemplation has been all-important. The horror in Norwegian cinema emanates from water. It often rises up from the deep darkness of desolate lakes, the kind of water that philosopher Gaston Bachelard has described as 'blood which bears death' ([1942] 1983: 59), and it infects woods and mountains with its evil. In a country on the edge of the Arctic, the gothic curse of dead water dominates the horror genre and allows us to see a dark concept of the Nordic and the Arctic through the lens of Norwegian genre filmmaking.

The horror film festival Ramaskrik Oppdal is evidence of the current popularity of horror movies in Norway. Located not far south of Trondheim, in or near the woods and mountains that can be seen in André Øvredal's *Troll Hunter* (*Trolljegeren*, 2010), the Ramaskrik festival has showcased all sorts of horror features and short films from around the world since 2011. International and Norwegian filmmakers visit Ramaskrik with new and classic films, and the directors and producers of Norwegian horror are mainstays: Pål Øie premiered *Dark Woods 2* (*Villmark 2*) at Ramaskrik in 2015, and Roar Uthaug visited for a retrospective screening of his 2006 *Cold Prey* (*Fritt vilt*) debut in 2019. In 2018, *MovieMaker Magazine* named Ramaskrik one of the thirty best genre festivals in the world, and ticket sales for this particular experience of horror have grown steadily year by year.

The success of Ramaskrik indicates a maturation of the Norwegian horror audience and the insertion of the horror genre into the mainstream of Norwegian cinema. This chapter will delve into the questions of why now and why not before? What premises have been positioned to pave the way for Norwegian horror cinema in the period after 2000 that were not in place before? What led to the success of Pål Øie's *Dark Woods*? The answers include government film policies, professionalised education for filmmakers, the development of a genre-competent national audience, and general changes in societal attitudes towards genre entertainment. Ultimately, there is also the appropriation of transnational genre conventions and aesthetics into a specifically Norwegian brand of horror, with roots reaching all the way back to the gothic fiction that essentially created the horror film.

A brief history of horror

All genre films aim to please. The very concept of film genres is predicated upon delivering a viewer experience that matches expectations to a certain degree. We expect certain plots and settings from a western film, and we expect sounds of music and song from a musical. A genre is a framework of expectation, the contract for communication that exists between the filmmaker, the viewer, and the critic. It is a template for storytelling, a way in which to structure tales that ultimately determines meaning. Within the framework, however, there is always the opportunity to circumvent conventions, a potential for expanding the boundaries.

Fans of horror will debate, and more often than not *enjoy* debating, what constitutes the horror genre essentials. The admirably eclectic programming of the Ramaskrik festival is a case in point. Some will complain that *The Shape of Water* (Guillermo Del Toro, 2017) is not a horror film, and should not have been part of the 2017 festival program, while others will appreciate and applaud the inclusion of a wide variety of films that in different ways relate to an aesthetic of horror. As Cynthia A. Freeland once wrote, 'the genre is just slippery' (2000: 10), and it fluctuates hungrily from disgusting bodily destructions to tear-jerking romantic tragedies.

However, I will suggest a common trait: horror movies aim to scare, or at least to unsettle, in one way or another. Indeed, their guiding aesthetic principle is to create experiences of unease, tension, dread and terror for their audience, but also to facilitate the audience's enjoyment of such experiences (Hanich 2010). This goal of creating a certain audience experience is crucial to the definition of horror film, a definition that can be decided to a large degree by the external factor of audience expectations, rather than specific internal elements of iconography or action (Altman 1999: 84–86). Comedy is expected to make you laugh, and horror is expected to make you scared, even if both comedy and horror come in a variety of types, subgenres and genre hybrids. For instance, the pairing of the horrific and the romantic can be traced to an inescapable source for the development of horror cinema, and also for its Norwegian branch: the gothic literature of the 1700s and 1800s.

David Punter has defined the gothic as a set of oppositions, the most important being the opposition between the modern and the old-fashioned, the civilised and the barbaric, elegance and crudity (1980: 6). These conflicts, as well as the gothic tales' preoccupation with madness, death and decay, can also describe the horror film. The friction between the rational and the fantastic, a product of the eighteenth-century Enlightenment and the subsequent Romantic reaction, was a fertile ground for the pioneering works of authors like Horace Walpole, Anne Radcliffe, Mary Shelley, John Polidori, Edgar Allan Poe and H. P. Lovecraft (Cuddon [1976] 1998: 356; Botting 2014: 1–3). Their novels, poems and short stories provided a seemingly endless source of inspiration for the horror cinema that started developing early in the twentieth century in Europe and America.

From the very beginning, the potential for trickery and effects in the capture, editing and exhibition of moving pictures lent itself to the fantastic. In particular, Georges Méliès would be remembered as a film pioneer for whom the camera was 'a machine to register the world of dreams and the supernatural [. . .]' (Clarens 1967: 3). The silent era in Europe saw the rise of significant precursors to horror cinema. German expressionist cinema yielded the early classics *The Cabinet of Dr. Caligari* (Robert Wiene, 1920) and *Nosferatu* (F. W. Murnau, 1922), the latter of which was an unauthorised adaptation of Bram Stoker's gothic novel *Dracula* from 1897. In that same decade, French impressionist cinema also mined gothic literature with *The Fall of the House of Usher* (Jean Epstein, 1928), one of many adaptations of Poe's short story. The German silent horror cinema in particular would influence the American horror cycle that began in 1931 with Universal's *Dracula* (Tod Browning) and *Frankenstein* (James Whale). These same creatures of gothic literature would be the crux of the British Hammer horror movies that were launched in the late 1950s, sporting elaborate Technicolor production designs and a then-controversial abundance of bloody details.

The American horror film was usually considered a B-movie at best, with a low or moderate budget and little artistic or commercial prestige. This would change in the 1970s, when a string of high-profile and more expensive Hollywood productions put the horror genre firmly in the mainstream, including the much-coveted Oscar race. William Friedkin's *The Exorcist* (1973), Steven Spielberg's *Jaws* (1975), Richard Donner's *The Omen* (1976), Brian De Palma's *Carrie* (1976) and Ridley Scott's *Alien* (1979) all contributed to the growing esteem of the horror genre and would all have long-term influence on a new generation of filmmakers across the world, including Norway.

At the same time, a contrary trend was established in American cinema: the independent low-budget horror movies that exploited simple premises and the shock value of splatter effects. Among the most important movies of what came to be known as the slasher subgenre of horror were *The Texas Chain Saw Massacre* (Tobe Hooper, 1974), *Halloween* (John Carpenter, 1978), *Friday the 13th* (Sean S. Cunningham, 1980) and *A Nightmare on Elm Street* (Wes Craven, 1984). *Halloween* was the movie that made a huge amount of money on a very modest budget and thus inspired a long line of similarly constructed tales of stalking and slashing, often featuring killers who would ultimately become icons of the genre. Sequels, remakes and reboots would happen and happen again in the decades that followed, as audiences flocked to experience the predictable tension and release in stories about rampaging mass murderers like Michael Myers, Jason Voorhees and Freddy Krueger, and the resourceful young people who would narrowly escape them. Although the action had been removed from European nineteenth-century castles and mansions to the American suburbs and summer camps of the twentieth century, making the murderous threat of violence all the more horrific, the gothic opposition of the civilised against the barbaric was still clearly in evidence. It is largely against a backdrop of filmmakers' and audiences' familiarity with these Anglo-American horror cinema traditions and conventions that the coming of Norwegian horror must be considered and understood.

Within the broad range of horror movie subgenres, the Norwegian post-2000 wave of horror has to a large extent taken the shape of either slasher films or psychological thrillers, subgenres that Freeland would describe as respectively *graphic* and *uncanny* horror (2000: 215 and 241). The main difference between the two is that the threat in the slasher movie is one of physical violence to the body, while the psychological horror film in Norway deals with emotional and psychological disorientation. Arguably the most important filmmaker in the latter subgenre is Pål Sletaune, who has created two movies of this kind: *Next Door* (*Naboer*, 2005) and *The Monitor* (*Babycall*, 2011). These films stand firmly in a gothic tradition, being akin and comparable to such literary works as Poe's 'The Tell-Tale Heart' (1843) and Charlotte Perkins Gilman's 'The Yellow Wallpaper' (1892), stories that dwell on the gothic horror tropes of shutting something out or shutting oneself in, in an attempt to somehow escape from horrific realisation (Reiersen 2011; Andresen 2016: 165–6).

Pål Øie's *Dark Woods*, the launching point for modern Norwegian horror cinema, is just as clearly gothic, as is the sequel *Dark Woods 2*. In addition, both films are also quite specifically Nordic horror movies. They revel in the depiction of nature as an overwhelmingly sublime force, very much in the way that Freeland conceptualises her uncanny category, and yet they have much in common with the graphic slasher subgenre. The crossover between the graphic horror of physical violence and the uncanny presence of supernatural forces of nature is a significant hallmark of the Norwegian horror cinema that emerged after 2000.

The turn to genre in Norwegian cinema

Norway, a very small country, has historically produced somewhere between five and thirty feature films a year. This production has been largely dependent on public funding, these days organised through the programmes of the Norwegian Film Institute, and thus on government film policies. As a consequence, the film culture of the country has a tradition for debating the purpose and merits of Norwegian cinema as art or mass entertainment. There have been cycles of popular genres throughout Norwegian film history, like the different types of war films that have treated the German occupation of Norway during the Second World War. Other genres, like the biographical film and the crime film, have been experimented with at different points in time, but the comedy is the only major genre that has stayed prolific and popular throughout the history of Norwegian cinema (Iversen 2011: 145–155, 169–177, 191).

The popularity of Norwegian films as a gauge for success has been a contested issue at several points in history. Should a small Nordic country cultivate artistic and less commercial ambitions in its film policies and funding, or should it be an aim to attract as many people as possible to Norwegian cinematic features? After a period of social realism in the 1970s, which ultimately proved unpopular with critics and had little impact at the box office, Norwegian cinema took a commercial turn in the 1980s. Hollywood action films became the template for more immediately popular movies like *Orion's Belt* (*Orions belte*, Ola Solum, 1985) and *Pathfinder* (*Veiviseren*, Nils Gaup, 1987), as the government worked to increase private investment in Norwegian film production through tax incentives (Holst 1995: 58–61; Iversen and Solum 2010: 21–32). This period of action thrills that engaged larger audiences would prove to be brief, and the commercial value of Norwegian cinema would be debated again in the 1990s. However, the notion of looking to Hollywood for inspiration had steered Norwegian film production's early phases in the golden age of the 1930s, it had given Norwegian cinema a popularity boost in the 1980s, and it would return with force at the dawn of the new millennium.

As I touched upon in Chapter 1, the Hollywood-orientation in Norwegian cinema in the 1920s and 1930s was part of an effort to pry the national romantic Norwegian landscapes and Norway's literary heritage away from Swedish filmmakers. Norway's film production was to be established as independent from Sweden's and Denmark's, not necessarily as an aesthetic opposition to Hollywood cinema (Iversen 1997: 112–13; Myrstad 1997). Half a century later, the action films of the 1980s were certainly inspired by American genre filmmaking, but nevertheless featured sublime Nordic landscapes, as in *Pathfinder*, and also discussed the specific geopolitical situation of Norway in the Cold War, as in *Orion's Belt* and *After Rubicon* (*Etter Rubicon*, Leidulv Risan, 1987). It would therefore be erroneous to state unequivocally that these films represented an Americanisation of Norwegian cinema, since they could just as well be seen as a Norwegian appropriation of transnational genre patterns.

Opinions were divided on the merits of the 1980s action film wave in Norway. Some critics expressed dislike and concern over this new and commercial direction, while others applauded the effort to engage larger audiences, and still others claimed that these films did not go far enough in emulating the Hollywood action cinema of the period (Andresen 2016: 44). However, the look to America in the 1980s would not deliver a prolonged period of genre filmmaking in Norway. Certain factors or premises had to be developed for Norwegian genre cinema to become a bigger and more consistent phenomenon: more professionalised film and television education, the coming of age of a new generation of genre fans, and several specific policy decisions by cabinets and parliaments.

The Labour Government of Prime Minister Jens Stoltenberg presented new film policies in 2001 that were intended to improve audience support for Norwegian cinema by restructuring the funding system. The increased funding was split along two tracks: money would be granted either on the basis of a project's artistic ambitions, or by considering its commercial appeal and its potential to reach a wide audience. Inspired by the Danish Government's 1998 'Four-Year Plan' for developing Denmark's film production (Hjort 2000: 103), this market consideration was reinforced by the new 50/50 mechanism, a guarantee of 50 per cent funding if the first 50 per cent of the budget was secured from private sources. The aim was to encourage filmmakers to create more audience-friendly movies, and genre cinema has been consistently popular throughout film history. A consequence of this incentive was a stronger focus on crime fiction, romantic comedies and horror (St.meld. nr. 22 [2006–2007]; Iversen 2011: 294–5).

The policies worked as intended. Six Norwegian feature films played in cinemas in 2002, a number that rose to sixteen in 2003 (*Film & Kino* 2010: 53–5). Audiences increased considerably, as did the esteem of Norwegian cinema among the critics. This coincided with the 2000 and 2002 graduations of the first two classes of students from the newly established Norwegian Film School in Lillehammer, classes that included prolific future filmmakers like Sara Johnsen and Roar Uthaug. The systematic cultivation of talent along with the redirected government film policies would be important factors in maintaining the popularity of Norwegian cinema, which has consistently hovered at around 20 per cent of the domestic box office ever since, some years even reaching 24 to 25 per cent.

Prime Minister Stoltenberg's second Government, the Red-Green Coalition, followed up his first Government's film policies with the 'Pathfinder' white paper in 2007. This document evaluated the previous Stoltenberg Government's achievements and added several new suggestions that were geared towards a high output of Norwegian cinematic features and a solid structure of private production companies. The focus would continue to be firmly on expanding the popularity and commercial viability of Norwegian cinema, while also nurturing artistic talent that could provide the country with prestigious awards abroad (St.meld. nr. 22 [2006–2007]: 41–5).

It is important to note that a big part of the rationalisation behind spending public resources on developing the production of Norwegian film was the cultural significance with which cinema is imbued. In Denmark, the 'Four-Year Plan' had the stated aim of using cinema to 'express and sustain Danish culture, language, and identity' (Hjort 2000: 103). This was echoed in the Norwegian Government's 2007 'Pathfinder' document, where Norwegian cinema was considered essential to fostering 'Norwegian language, culture and storytelling traditions' (St.meld. nr. 22 [2006–2007]: 7). However debatable these concepts might be, government film policies in Norway were clearly primed to support much of what would shortly follow in terms of horror cinema.

In the time between Stoltenberg's two periods in charge, the second Government of Prime Minister Kjell Magne Bondevik, a Centre-Right coalition, had overseen a crucial liberalisation of censorship laws in 2004 that would have an impact on genre filmmaking in Norway. Authorities would no longer have the opportunity to ban films from being screened, and a new rating system was implemented which enabled filmmakers, distributors and exhibitors to depict and screen much more severe violence and explicit sexual content than before. This liberalisation reflected a general shift in society's perceptions of genre entertainment, as well as its attitudes towards censorship (Smith-Isaksen 2013: 211–3). The significance of violent imagery and soundscapes to the horror genre is obvious, and the new rating system contributed to opening the doors for films that would previously have been unthinkable in publicly funded Norwegian film production.

At this juncture, legislative reforms aligned with the coming of age of a generation of horror film fans that had been brought up on genre entertainment. Starting with the VHS and cable TV boom of the 1980s and moving into the information age of the DVD and the internet, horror cinema's target audience in Norway could be expected to be well versed in genre aesthetics and conventions by the turn of the millennium. Furthermore, films that are banned or controversial, movies that receive high ratings or negative media attention, will often have a corresponding drawing power over their young adult target audience, people in the 15 to 25 age-bracket. Horror movies have a natural place in youth counterculture, being interesting by virtue of not being accepted in the mainstream, along with certain types of music and clothing. The new Norwegian horror cinema of the 2000s, a horror wave unlike anything the country had previously experienced, was well positioned to cater to its core audience's need for group identity entertainment.

Of course, none of these premises would lead anywhere without a breakthrough film, one cinematic event that paved the way for others. All genre cycles come into being with the success of a single film, a pilot that is followed up by other similar films. In Norway, the horror cinema of the post-2000 period was triggered by Pål Øie's 2003 feature film debut, *Dark Woods*. It was clearly a horror movie, and it drew its deadly darkness from the depths of Norwegian nature.

'WE SHOULD HAVE STAYED AWAY FROM THAT LAKE': *DARK WOODS*

> Maybe the aesthetics I try to cultivate have certain parallels in the Norwegian climate and landscape? Slow, but massive. The mysteries. The riddles. The unspoken. Possibly somewhat cold and stylized.
> (Director Pål Øie, interviewed by the author [Øie 2015]).

Norway is a Nordic country, and also one of the eight countries that are geographically situated within the Arctic region, the 66 degrees North latitude cutting across the Nordland county a little north of the middle of Norway. Many parts of the country may be labelled subarctic due to local climates, and

Norway is dominated by landscapes that are often associated with the Arctic: vast empty spaces, desolate mountains, dark woods.

There are different ways to define the Arctic. It can be discussed as a geographical or geopolitical region, in terms of climate or aesthetics, among other things. The introduction to the anthology *Films on Ice: Cinemas of the Arctic* points out that 'moving images have been central to the very definition of the Arctic' and shows how this has influenced a cultural understanding of the region as '[frozen], inhospitable, static and sterile: techniques and tropes of mass audience visual representation from the nineteenth century onward cemented the view of the Arctic as an exemplar of sublime space overwhelmed by nature and as a point of desolation' (MacKenzie and Stenport 2015: 2–3).

Even if this understanding has been subject to scholarly critique, the experience of sublime space and desolation is nevertheless fundamentally important to the uniqueness of the Norwegian horror cinema, as suggested in the above quote by one of the genre's most important filmmakers, Pål Øie. The concept of the Arctic in Norwegian horror cinema is heavily geared towards the importance of spaces: sublime landscapes of Nordic dread and terror, nearly always nature and wilderness. If the history of the Arctic is *mythified*, as E. Carina H. Keskitalo argued in her 2009 essay on the nation state interests that have shaped the concept, the horror cinema of Norway also presents a *mythical landscape*, but one of death and decay. This is a countermyth to the national-romantic image of Norway, where the façade of safety and prosperity in a Nordic social democracy is torn apart, revealing the deadly darkness within. The threat of madness, death and destruction in these films is also inextricably linked to water, and in the case of Øie's horror films it literally seeps out from the dark depths of lakes and rivers. The deepest source of horror in Norwegian cinema is the gothic motif of dark and deadly water.

Norwegian nightmares seem to emanate from water. In particular they rise out of the deep darkness of desolate lakes, the kind of water that Bachelard has described as the gothic trope of *blood which bears death* ([1942] 1982). Of the approximately forty movies to date that this book categorises as the Norwegian horror cinema, only three utilise presumably Arctic settings: Mikkel Brænne Sandemose's action-adventure *Ragnarok* (*Gåten Ragnarok*, 2013), and Tommy Wirkola's *Dead Snow* (*Død snø*, 2009) and *Dead Snow 2* (*Død snø 2*, 2014). However, the concept of the Arctic, our notion of the far North, is defined by climate, weather and landscapes, not simply lines of latitude. Furthermore, as Luis Rocha Antuñes has stated, building on the research of historian Kenneth Coates (1994), 'Northern-ness' is not simply these objective definitions, not merely a case of 'what' and 'where', but 'a state of mind' (Antuñes 2016: 132). This certainly fits with the aesthetics that director Øie outlines in the quote at the start of this subchapter. In fact, all these points of definition are applicable to most of the Norwegian horror cinema, to the extent that the genre may be described as a set of films that regularly excavate the hidden evil of the rural and the wilderness, as narratives and audio-visual treatments that expose the Norwegian, Nordic and Arctic *state of mind*. The present book discusses the use of certain landscapes, and in particular certain types of waters, in Norwegian horror films that contemplate the nature of horror in a Nordic country. I will propose that the horror genre in Norway conceptualises Norway, the Nordic and the Arctic as places of deadly secrets, a realm of darkness beneath a glossy surface.

Bachelard wrote his essay under the title *Water and Dreams*. This more than implies, of course, water and nightmares. Indeed, one of Bachelard's chapters discussed the use of water in the works of gothic poet and author Edgar Allan Poe: '[His] favored substance is water or, more specifically, a special kind of water, a *heavy water* that is more profound, dormant, and still than any other deep, dormant, or still waters in nature' ([1942] 1983: 46). I suggest that a use of water resembling what Bachelard finds in his exploration of Poe's writing is a particular trait of Norwegian horror cinema. This is not because other nations' horror films do not use water in such ways, but because most of the Norwegian horror canon puts water at centre stage as both visual motif and thematic anchor.

The very first Norwegian horror movie, the psychological thriller *Lake of the Dead* (*De dødes tjern*), directed by Kåre Bergstrøm, foreshadowed the national horror genre tradition as early as 1958 and made the concept of what I will call *dead water* explicit. Based on a popular novel by the author André Bjerke, writing under the pseudonym of Bernhard Borge, the film tells the story of a group of friends who travel to a cabin in the woods for some relaxing summer days, but end up having to unravel the deadly mysteries of the nearby Blue Lake, which is said to be bottomless. One of the friends goes missing, and the rest are haunted by the potentially supernatural force of the lake. Could it be true that a ghost is luring people into the dark waters to disappear forever? The story ends on a slightly ambiguous note, appearing to wonder if the answer is safely psychoanalytic or uncannily supernatural.

From its very inception, the Norwegian horror cinema was preoccupied with what might be hiding in the deep, contemplating what secrets could be found in the dark and still waters of the country's wilderness. Whether the answers are physical, lodged in the mind or flowing from the existence of a spirit realm, the threat of the water is real. Such tales of horror subvert connotations of life and purity to give water the aesthetic quality that Bachelard finds in Poe: 'All living water is on the point of dying. Now, in *dynamic poetry*, things are not what they are, but what they are becoming' (Bachelard [1942] 1983: 47). The water in Norwegian horror cinema after 2000, either in its liquid form or as snow and ice, would always carry this potential for becoming death.

Figure 2.1 Liljan Werner at the edge of the *Lake of the Dead*. (Screenshot)

Kåre Bergstrøm would go on to direct the 1964 anthology film *Clocks by Moonlight* (*Klokker i måneskinn*), a collection of partly paranormal stories that lean in the direction of horror, although not as overtly or entertainingly as *Lake of the Dead*. The stories are exchanged by four men who have gathered for an evening of bridge. Arguing the merits of objective science against the power of superstition, they engage in a version of the campfire storytelling that characterises much classic horror in the vein of haunted houses and ghost stories. Director Bergstrøm and screenwriter André Bjerke indulge their interest in debating the psychology of women in particular, as they had previously done in *Lake of the Dead*. This time, however, unlike the ambiguous ending of *Lake of the Dead*, Bergstrøm and Bjerke allow the supernatural argument to carry the day. *Clocks by Moonlight* is a borderline crime and horror film, in itself remarkable at the time of its creation, although it spreads its narrative and stylistic intentions out wider than Bergstrøm's more disciplined 1958 horror classic, and thus remains obscure and less generically significant.

Much later, the 1990s saw a period of slightly horror-tinged crime thrillers in Norwegian cinema, including *Isle of Darkness* (*Mørkets øy*, Trygve Allister Diesen, 1997) and *Bloody Angels* (*1732 Høtten*, Karin Julsrud, 1998), none of which belong properly to the horror genre. There were also sporadic attempts at independent low-budget horror at the turn of the millennium, firmly outside of public funding and cinema distribution, including the urban slasher *22* (Pål Aam and Eystein Hanssen, 2001) and the Peter Jackson-inspired splatter film *Bread and Circus* (*Brød & Sirkus*, Martin Loke, 2003). However, the real breakthrough for Norwegian horror was about to happen on cinema screens. As genre moviemaking became much more common in Norway after 2000, Pål Øie (born 1961) created the film that ultimately built a bridge from the lake of the past to the water-related terrors of contemporary Norwegian horror cinema. *Dark Woods* may owe a debt to the 1999 horror movie *The*

Blair Witch Project by Daniel Myrick and Eduardo Sanchéz, particularly in its video-oriented visual style, but it is impossible in retrospect not to consider Øie's film as intimately connected to *Lake of the Dead*.

To make the point perfectly clear, Øie opens *Dark Woods* with a grainy video image of a lake in the woods, very much akin to the lake in the 1958 predecessor. As Øie's camera lingers on the black waters and the equally gloomy wood surrounding it, a voice-over intones: 'Are you there? [. . .] We were just looking for a real job. [. . .] We should have stayed away from that lake.' The voice belongs to Lasse (Kristoffer Joner), who is looking back at the events in which his friend Per (Marko Kanic) lost his life. The opening sequence of the film then juxtaposes images of the actual wilderness of the plot with images of Lasse, Per, Elin (Eva Röse) and Sara (Sampda Sharma) being interviewed for an upcoming reality television project produced by Gunnar (Bjørn Floberg). They are captured with a video camera, talking about their expectations and qualifications in front of the painted backdrop of woods, snowy mountains and a lake. Per's interview even namedrops national icons of Norway: Princess Märtha Louise and the actress and diva Wenche Foss.

Dark Woods marks the point in modern Norwegian cinema when conventionally positive symbols of national romanticism and healthy regeneration begin their horror genre transformation into threatening and ultimately deadly negatives (Iversen 2011: 304; Andresen 2016: 95). The sublime landscapes of the country become not merely the backdrop for horror tales, but a source of suffering and death. One of the ways in which Øie achieves this is by framing the approaching car of the television team from behind trees, looking out at them from within the forest and imbuing the landscape with a presence that is both unseen and threatening. However, the characters in Øie's movie are not yet aware of their peril.

The group of four young technicians and one middle-aged producer head into the woods to spend four days in a cabin, and hopefully to establish a bond that will facilitate the creation of a ground-breaking television program. After the boys' discovery of a dead body in the lake, which Gunnar insists on keeping secret from Elin and Sara, the relationship between the producer and Lasse in particular begins to unravel. Lasse suspects that Gunnar is losing his mind, an impression which Øie underscores by having Gunnar chop wood outside the cabin in the middle of the night and curiously tasting the resin from the exposed wound of the tree. Gunnar also hears, or more likely he remembers or imagines, the engine sounds of an airplane, as Øie cuts to a low angle of the nearby lake shrouded in mist. This is the only example of apparently subjective sound in the film. By this point, Gunnar has shared one piece of history with Lasse and Per: a German fighter plane crashed in the lake during the war in the 1940s, after that the lake never froze over, and he was forbidden from swimming there as a child. Øie creates a sombre mood in which the lake becomes a potent audio-visual symbol of the dark national past, and also a harbinger of an inescapably violent near future.

The most overt subversion of a national symbol in *Dark Woods* is found in a scene where Lasse investigates the abandoned tent by the waterside. He climbs inside and starts rummaging around in the luggage that is left behind, finding and stealing cigarettes and liquor. He also finds a book on Nazi Germany's air force, the Luftwaffe. Attached to its pages are private photos of soldiers and fighter planes. Suddenly a pair of hands reaches through the canvas and grabs Lasse by the throat. We only see this from inside the tent, not knowing who is choking him from outside, and when Lasse is finally let go, he climbs out of the collapsed tent to see nothing but the lake. The ultimate symbol of the freedom of movement in Norwegian recreational nature, the tent, is turned into a murderous agent of evil.

Shot on digital video, a cost-cutting measure that contributed to the feasibility of the project at a time when expensive analogue film still dominated cinema production (Nordås 2006), *Dark Woods* proved that technological advances were significant to the foundation of not only the independent underground of Norwegian horror, but also to its mainstream. At the same time, the coming of Norwegian horror was the result of a coordinated political and cultural project that aimed to increase the popularity of Norwegian cinema in general, an end that was justified by the argument that cinema is uniquely important to the propagation of Norwegian stories and experiences.

New film policies were certainly an important factor in facilitating genre filmmaking in Norway, as well as other Nordic countries, in the early 2000s

Figure 2.2 Television producer Gunnar contemplates the dead body in the lake, while Lasse, left, and Per watch in the background. (Screenshot from *Dark Woods*)

(Gustafsson and Käpää 2015: 4). However, Pål Øie maintains that genre aesthetics and commercial intentions were not at the creative base of *Dark Woods*. By the early 2000s, Øie and his team, including cinematographer Sjur Aarthun, had established a working relationship with the short films 'The Well' ('Brønnen', 1997), 'Tap Dance' ('Steppdans', 2001) and 'Stop' ('Stopp', 2001), and they felt ready to try their hands at a feature. *Dark Woods* was born out of the combination of two separate ideas: one about a couple who come across an empty tent at the waterside, and another about a TV crew on a team-building trip in the wilderness. 'None of us were thinking that we'll make a horror film because that's what the audience wants', Øie would tell the author, claiming that timing was simply on his side in terms of film policies and current trends (Øie 2015). Indeed, genre aesthetics entered the creative process through the cooperation with the feature film consultant at the Norwegian Film Institute, producer and director Karin Julsrud. 'She saw our potential and mentioned the word "horror" far into the screenwriting process', Øie remembers, adding that he was initially reluctant, but ultimately decided to pursue the genre angle (Ibid.).

Therein lay the start of the Norwegian horror wave. Genre had become a tool for the consultants in charge of choosing and cultivating publicly funded cinema features through the Norwegian Film Institute. Roar Uthaug would remember that the success of Øie's *Dark Woods* – 155,117 tickets sold (*Film & Kino* 2012: 37) – provided a good argument for his own debut feature *Cold Prey* to receive funding. To many readers this number will seem very low, so I should emphasise that the population of Norway at the time was just over 4,550,000. In this context, achieving 1,000,000 tickets sold would be of historical proportions, something that very few Norwegian films have ever done. *Dark Woods*, at just over 155,000, was a moderately budgeted genre picture with modest expectations of ticket sales. It proved that Norwegian horror, within strict budgetary limits, could be commercially viable. Uthaug and his producers could argue that an even more generically adapted film was likely to sell at least as many tickets as *Dark Woods*, probably more. In approaching the creation of *Cold Prey*, Uthaug would be 'very concerned about being clear with the film's generic expression, as I was specifically set on making a slasher movie' (Uthaug 2015).

Dark Woods may also arguably be placed in the slasher subgenre of horror, a category that its sequel more easily escapes. Still, both *Dark Woods* films emphasise the way in which Norwegian horror tends to combine the visceral thrills of the slasher tradition with the overwhelmingly sublime experience of Nordic landscapes. The definitive prototype of the slasher movie is the American classic *Halloween* (1978) by John Carpenter, and the setting for the terror in *Halloween* is a lazy suburbia. However, the suburb does not exist in the Norwegian slasher film, neither does the college campus, not even the summer camp, and least of all the urban cityscape. The site of terror in Norwegian slasher movies is almost exclusively the woods and mountains. At most the plots will venture into a rural small town, but by and large the characters in these films are in danger because they travel out there, into the wilderness, eschewing culture for nature and being stalked and killed for it.

It is always dangerous to go somewhere in horror movies, there is no safe place, and it is easy to understand the regret and resentment in Lasse's voice as he intones at the movie's conclusion: 'We should not have gone near that lake', almost repeating his opening line. Øie sets the pace for what is to come in the following two decades of horror in Norway. Indeed, water seems to be the connecting tissue that binds nearly every one of the Norwegian horror movies together. It is more prominent in some than others, and it sometimes takes the form of snow, but an essential narrative and stylistic trait of Norwegian horror cinema is the use of dead water in Bachelard's meaning of the term. The spectre of death in the water that haunted *Lake of the Dead* is given corporeal form in *Dark Woods* when the decaying corpse is pulled out of the deep. The darkness of the past has been repressed, but it literally returns to the surface. Gunnar's decision not to alert authorities leads not only to friction in the group, but also to death: one day, Per is found with his throat cut. Someone or something is out there in the woods, watching and waiting, and nerves become frayed.

Throughout the film, the characters continually come back to the dark and still water. In fact, escaping seems impossible: in whatever direction the characters set out from their cabin, they end up by the lake. When the apparent killer finally appears, a demented German tourist who is the husband of the drowned woman in the fishing net, some of the protagonists try to flee back to civilisation. This cannot be done. The raging water of a river running wild prevents them from escaping, and they have to return to the still and dead water of the lake to face the nightmare. As the story ends, the mystery is literally swallowed by the lake. Gunnar intervenes when the German killer holds Lasse, Elin and Sara at gunpoint, and a shotgun blast hits Gunnar in the stomach. He falls forward over the German, into the lake, pushing the killer under and thereby drowning him. The evil that came out of the water goes back into it, but Lasse suspects that something deeper and darker may still hide beneath the surface of the events that have unfolded.

'Something is not right here', Lasse thinks to himself. The police explain how the German tourist must have gone crazy while visiting the lake where his grandfather crashed a plane during the war, either killing or accidentally losing his wife. However, the tourists left a camera in their tent, and Lasse discovers a window reflection in one of the photographs: the picture was taken by a farmer who opened the gate for them when they first arrived in the wilderness at the start of the movie. Is he the real killer?

The thrills and mystery of *Dark Woods* met with critical approval and commercial success in Norway, and this was clear confirmation that Norwegian audiences were ready for their own brand of horror. It is, however, interesting to note that *Dark Woods* was still quite reserved in terms of eliciting emotions from its viewers. Even at its midpoint, the stage of the plot where tension is usually heightened considerably in horror movies, Øie keeps things at a relatively calm pace. Per is tied up and left alone in the woods as punishment for bringing his mobile phone, but the filmmakers keep building the mood slowly and meticulously rather than manipulating the viewer's reactions through the construction of emotion markers.

Greg M. Smith's term *emotion marker* can be applied to horror films to gauge how often and how precisely they seek to elicit strong emotional reactions from viewers (1999: 117–26). All the audio-visual cues that the filmmaker builds point the viewer in a specific direction of mood. In *Dark Woods* there are shadows, the dark water of the lake, eerie music, the rustling of leaves and, most ominously, the sound of an unknown person whistling somewhere in the darkness. These *mood cues* can be orchestrated into bursts of sound and picture: loud bangs or stings in the score, combined with swift camera movements, quick editing, and close-ups of scared faces. Many strong cues align to trigger a sudden experience of fear. Such *emotion markers* serve to confirm the mood of the viewer and encourage us to stay in the same frame of mind as we travel the fictional world of the film. Mood leads to bursts of emotion, which in turn maintains the mood.

The number of emotion markers can indicate the extent to which the filmmaker seeks to elicit strong bursts of emotion. Compared to American slasher films from around 2000, *Dark Woods* has a very low number of emotion markers, just eight up until the start of its frantic final act of confrontations. This is closer to the number that might be expected from a psychological horror film that relies more on mood than strong bursts of emotion. Indeed, Øie seems more preoccupied with the moody mysteries of wood and water than the generic plot mechanisms of slashers.

The significance of water is certainly not exclusive to Norwegian horror cinema. After all, the place of horror in the American slasher classic *Friday the 13th* is Camp Crystal Lake. Terror in or around the dark depths is also prevalent in other Nordic horror movies of the post-2000 period, like the Icelandic *Reykjavik Whale Watching Massacre* or the Finnish *Bodom*. However, what sets the Norwegian fascination with horrific waters apart is the consistent frequency of Norway's horror cinema output since 2003, and the fact that all but a few of these films feature important water motifs in the form of lakes, rivers, snow or ice.

By 2003, public funding policies had in effect encouraged filmmakers to *go genre*. The Film Institute helped guide *Dark Woods* in the direction of horror, and a genre-conscious domestic target audience greeted the film with enthusiasm. The pairing of horror with the nature and wilderness of Norway, in line with the double policy of creating popular cinema while also fostering Norwegian traits, had opened the floodgates: soon after Øie's ground-breaking *Dark Woods*, another team of filmmakers created the first proper Norwegian slasher, *Cold Prey*, in the snowy desolation of previously romantic Norwegian mountainscapes.

3. THE SLASHERS OF NORWAY

Jannicke is scared to death. Her friends have been killed, one by one, by the masked menace who hides in the mountain hotel where they have taken shelter. She is terrified and makes a desperate run for it, out into the freezing gloom of the brutal winter dusk. In a daze she stumbles through the door of the tool shed in the hotel yard. Breaking down on the floor, Jannicke finally begins to cry. Eyes closed, deep sobs, utter despair at the hopeless situation she finds herself in. Lying on her back, her sobs subsiding, she opens her eyes and sees a shotgun stowed under the ceiling. Jannicke loosens the gun from its rack and re-enters the hotel, where she knows there is a box of ammunition in the reception desk. The terrified girl gives way to another being, an angry woman about to avenge her friends and fight her way out of despair. She loads the shotgun and begins stalking her tormentor, armed and ready.

This is a scene from *Cold Prey* (*Fritt vilt*), the 2006 feature film debut of director Roar Uthaug. The main character Jannicke, portrayed by Ingrid Bolsø Berdal, goes through a moment typical of the slasher movie, a transition that turns a terrified girl into an angry woman. This subgenre archetype is removed to a Norwegian setting in *Cold Prey*, and Uthaug stages every beat of the character's development from initial innocence to ultimate showdown with the dark and deadly force personified by the masked killer (Clover 1992: 21–42).

Cold Prey was the movie that really set the Norwegian horror tradition in motion, taking its cue from *Dark Woods* (*Villmark*). The film was easily the most intense and graphic portrayal of physical violence in Norwegian cinema up to that point, and it enjoyed great popularity and commercial success. Uthaug's movie exploited the characteristics of the predominantly American slasher film and spawned two sequels, thus creating the first Norwegian horror movie franchise. This and the following chapter will examine the slasher subgenre and its particular emergence and resonance in Norwegian cinema post-2000.

Psychos and their victims: the slasher movie

The slasher subgenre of the horror movie usually tells the tale of a group of young people being stalked and murdered by a psychopathic killer. This psychopath, a man, tends to wear a mask and uses weapons of cutting, stabbing and slashing. After providing a spectacular series of violent attacks on the bodies of young victims, the killer is finally overthrown, sometimes killed, by the only person to survive his rampage: a young woman. At least this is the conventional subgenre wisdom that was given analytical frameworks in the ground-breaking research of Vera Dika (1990) and Carol J. Clover (1992), following the classic period of the American slasher movie in the late 1970s to mid-1980s.

Director Roar Uthaug has claimed that he modelled *Cold Prey* specifically on the American slasher, and producer Martin Sundland has stated that the filmmakers' aim was a horror genre picture that had not previously been attempted in Norwegian cinema (Sundland 2015; Uthaug 2015). Director and producer would highlight their ambition to adhere to a predominantly American subgenre, while at the same time infusing the model with something Norwegian. In doing so they built on a horror tradition that came into its own in the American cinema of the 1960s and 1970s.

Alfred Hitchcock's *Psycho* from 1960 is considered the most important precursor to the slasher subgenre. When Norman Bates (Anthony Perkins) kills a naked Marion Crane (Janet Leigh) in the shower, two of the most recognisable hallmarks of the slasher are formalised: the murder by stabbing and a sexual motif. Hitchcock himself made notes during the making of *Psycho* that highlighted the importance of the murder scene: 'An impression of a knife slashing, as if tearing at the very screen, ripping the film' (Spoto 1983: 419). The director wanted the knife to cut figuratively through the screen, and achieving this experience required a new brutality in staging and performance. Even if American censorship at the time would not permit Hitchcock to show the criminal deed in gory detail, Marion's blood being spilled in restrained black and white, the shock of stabbing and slashing would come to define the American slasher movie of the 1970s and 1980s.

Psycho was also a game changer in terms of settings. The major horror cycles to that point, such as the Universal monster movies in the 1930s and the gothic Hammer movies in the late 1950s, were dominated by the past. Stories were usually set in a vaguely defined period of the 1800s and took place in rural Europe. With *Psycho*, Hitchcock took horror to the contemporary United States. Steve Neale has written that *Psycho* 'is generally regarded as a turning point, as the beginning of something new: as the film which located horror firmly and influentially within the modern psyche, the modern world, modern relationships, and the modern dysfunctional family' (2000: 96). After the golden age of Hollywood, cinematic tales of horror were headed for a more recognisable here and now, a present-day setting which is almost exclusively the case in Norwegian horror cinema.

On 11 October 1974, two important films were released: Bob Clark's Canadian proto-slasher *Black Christmas*, and Tobe Hooper's United States classic *The Texas Chain Saw Massacre*. The latter was a low-budget film about a group of teenagers who get lost on a road trip in Texas and become victims of a family of slaughterhouse cannibals. The most iconic and brutal character in the movie is the masked son of the family, Leatherface (Gunnar Hansen), who wields a chainsaw and kills off the teenagers one by one. However, Sally (Marilyn Burns) escapes Leatherface and becomes the film's final girl.

Sally's sufferings have the universal appeal that Robin Wood describes as 'the authentic quality of a nightmare. I have had since childhood a recurring nightmare whose pattern seems to be shared by a very large number of people within our culture: I am running away from some vaguely terrible oppressors who are going to do dreadful things to me; I run to a house or a car, etc., for help; I discover its occupants to be precisely the people I am fleeing' (1986: 90). This aspect might be archetypical, but the film points ahead to the classic slasher in terms of gender: while there does exist a common misconception that horror film violence targets women more than men (Staiger 2005: 174), young women are certainly the main characters of the slasher subgenre, next to the iconic killer.

When director John Carpenter and producer Debra Hill were hired to stage a simple and visceral tale that took place during just one day, 31 October 1978, they ultimately created the breakthrough slasher movie that would inspire countless others, while also making an enormous amount of money relative to its small budget (Skal 2002: 155–61, Harper 2004: 12). *Halloween* follows the killing spree of escaped mental institution inmate Michael Myers (Nick Castle) as he stalks and murders teenagers in the fictional town of Haddonfield, Illinois. The killer's motives are unclear, with asylum psychiatrist Sam Loomis (Donald Pleasence) referring to Myers ominously as 'the Boogeyman', but he shows a particular and unexplained interest in Laurie Strode (Jamie Lee Curtis). On Halloween night Laurie is babysitting, while Myers is sneaking through Haddonfield and killing off Laurie's friends. As he closes in on Laurie, she faces the terror of her predicament and even fights and wounds him.

Doctor Loomis comes to the rescue, shooting Myers several times, and we see the killer fall from the first-floor veranda. Laurie Strode becomes the final girl of the story, but a sequel opening is provided: there is no body on the lawn. Michael Myers has disappeared.

Carpenter's *Halloween* was an independent production, a film made on a shoestring budget compared to Hollywood studio productions. When it became a commercial success, it effectively started an American cycle of slasher movies that imitated its low-budget exploitation of a simple premise and its focus on visceral shock value. The following years saw the releases of classic slashers like *Friday the 13th* (Sean S. Cunningham, 1980) and the inevitable sequels *Halloween II* (Rick Rosenthal, 1981) and *Friday the 13th Part II* (Steve Miner, 1981). Cynthia A. Freeland would come to define this subgenre of horror movies in properly narrow terms: 'I use the term "slasher" as a generic label for a movie with a psychopathic killer, usually a male, whose assumed blood lust drives him to a sort of extreme violence against women. Such violence, often eroticized, is showcased by the camera in increasingly graphic and disturbing ways' (2000: 161).

The slasher became a cultural phenomenon in the early 1980s, arguably culminating in the fantasy-styled reinvention of Wes Craven's *A Nightmare on Elm Street* in 1984. The question in these movies is not whether something terrible will happen to the characters, but when, where and how something terrible will happen to them. The building tension that gets released in the spectacle of the killing is the main attraction of such films, the orchestration of shocks that provides audience gratification (Dika 1990: 53–4; Andresen 2016: 79–81).

Dika also identified a repetitive plot structure in slasher movies, where action is divided into past and present events. The past event involves the killer experiencing a loss, either real or imagined. Consequently, he kills the member or members of the young community that he blames for his loss. The present event involves the reactivation of the killer's destructive force through a commemoration of the past, as in the celebration of Halloween, or the Valentine tradition that triggers the plot of *My Bloody Valentine* (George Mihalka, 1981). The killer then sets out to hunt and punish the young community again, only being stopped by the heroine. However, there is often an open question about whether or not the heroine is truly free at the end of the story (Dika 1990: 59–60).

In this chapter I will explore the issue of the slasher's perceived structure of morals and ideology, including questions of gender and archetypes, by reappraising it through the lens of its most accomplished Norwegian specimen. Does *Cold Prey* provide new insight into the subgenre, and what is the significance of Norway's appropriation of this chiefly American popular horror concept?

Death in the snow and ice: *Cold Prey*

Cold Prey takes place in February, but Norwegians will likely associate the setting with the Easter holidays, when skiing in the mountains is a popular national pastime. To illustrate this phenomenon's cultural importance: during the Coronavirus lockdown in early 2020, one of the biggest public outrages was caused when people were not allowed to visit their holiday homes during Easter. In *Cold Prey*, however, this snowy wilderness paradise leads to death and destruction, and the recreational nature of the country hides terrifying darkness and violence. In this respect the film follows in the footsteps of the 1958 forebear *Lake of the Dead* (*De dødes tjern*, Kåre Bergstrøm) and the 2003 genre kick-starter *Dark Woods*.

Roar Uthaug (born 1973) was among the first directors to be educated at the Norwegian Film School in Lillehammer. His student short film 'The Martin Administration' was nominated for the Student Academy Awards in the USA, and Uthaug quickly became an accomplished commercials director in Norway. Being a teenager in the 1980s, it is highly likely that Uthaug was also educated in the slasher subgenre by immersing himself in video entertainment. His debut feature is clearly conscious of its slasher aesthetics, and the most thoroughly conventional of all Norwegian slashers. Even though other films of the Norwegian horror tradition might have more artistic merit, *Cold Prey* is arguably the most memorable of them all. In commercial terms, the *Cold Prey* trilogy that Uthaug's film initiated is also the most successful in Norwegian horror cinema.

The film opens with a car ride. Five friends, the generic young community of the story, are making their way to the desolate mountains for downhill skiing. Jannicke (Ingrid Bolsø Berdal) and Eirik (Tomas Alf Larsen) are an established couple, but there is friction between them concerning whether or not they will move in together. Ingunn (Viktoria Winge) and Mikal (Endre Martin Midtstigen) are all but an item too, unable to keep hands and lips off each other. The fifth wheel is Morten Tobias (Rolf Kristian Larsen), uncomfortably single. Arriving in the wilderness of Jotunheimen, a real-world mountain range named after the Jötunn giants of Norse mythology, they set out from a high peak on skis and snowboards. As they pick up speed and negotiate treacherous terrain, Morten Tobias falls and breaks his leg open. With no chance of transporting their injured friend to a medical facility before nightfall, they decide to take shelter in an abandoned mountain lodge. The next morning, Eirik sets out to get help, while the others wait in the hotel.

Unbeknownst to them, it is already too late. The hotel is not as abandoned as it seems: Jannicke and Mikal discover that someone is living in a hidden room in the basement. There they also find a plethora of personal objects like clothes and sunglasses, as well as newspaper clippings that tell a disturbing

NORWEGIAN NIGHTMARES

story of the hotel's past. The place has been closed for thirty years, after the son of the hotel managers disappeared while playing in the snow. The parents themselves disappeared soon after, ostensibly while searching for their lost son. As Jannicke and Mikal uncover clippings much more recent than thirty years ago, as well as a box filled with engagement rings and wedding bands, they realise that something is horribly wrong.

Indeed, the masked menace that hides in the basement has already killed Ingunn the night before, and Eirik never gets more than a few yards from the hotel door before he is assaulted. The three remaining friends find only a pool of blood in the room where Ingunn stayed the night, and Eirik never returns with help. The hunt is on and the subgeneric psychopathic killer forces Jannicke and her friends to fight for their lives. Jannicke takes charge of the situation, but both her remaining friends get killed. She finally makes a desperate run for it, but she is intercepted by the murderous Mountain Man, his huge frame draped in thick winter clothing and his face obscured by ski goggles. In a confrontation on the edge of a deep crevasse, Jannicke drives a pick-axe into the Mountain Man's chest and sees him fall to his death. She is the final girl, victorious but alone in the glaring winter sunlight.

During the plot of *Cold Prey*, Jannicke goes through a three-stage transformation: she starts out as the reliable motherly leader figure of the group, then turns into a frightened and helpless girl, before finally becoming 'the image of an angry woman' (Clover 1992: 17). Jannicke exerts her violent revenge on the killer, and finally slumps alone in the snow as 'the one who did not die: the survivor, or Final Girl' (Ibid.: 35). She has won the fight, but she has lost everything. The final girl survives, but her sacrifice is massive. While some of her friends meet with quick deaths, having merely seconds to comprehend their plight, the final girl might suffer for hours, before she outsmarts and possibly

Figure 3.1 Jannicke slumping in the snow, having become the exhausted final girl of the first true Norwegian slasher story. (Screenshot from *Cold Prey*)

40

kills the killer in the end (Ibid.: 35–6). It is the inherent human qualities of the last survivor that makes her able to overcome the seemingly impossible. Jannicke in *Cold Prey* is this subgenre-defining character, but she is not a blueprinted copy of her American models. On several points she deviates from the classic character as described by Clover and others, as I will discuss shortly.

The group of friends that set out for an adventure at the beginning of *Cold Prey* is somewhat more one-dimensionally sketched than the group in *Dark Woods*, probably as a result of Uthaug's very genre-conscious plot design: these characters are mostly not going to survive, so they are set up to serve as fodder for the shocking spectacle of the killing. They only need one strong characteristic each to mark them as a type in relation to the rest. We see Morten Tobias being the lonely comedy sidekick who can be relied on for laughs, and we see Ingunn being the flirty but reluctant virgin around whom a sense of tension builds. The only character that needs to be more complex is the final girl, Jannicke. With her comes a sense of humanity and relatable reactions that ensure the audience's engagement.

The key characters in a slasher movie are nearly always a group of young people, the ones Dika calls the 'young community', and the main character is often a young woman in this largely homogenous group (1990: 55–8). Jannicke is this main character in *Cold Prey*, and the young community of which she is a part has come to the wild mountains to enjoy their carefree existence, only to end up in mortal danger. *Cold Prey* also takes a leaf from the slashers of the classic American era around 1980 in that it portrays white middle class people exclusively. As Dika pointed out in 1990: 'In essence, these characters embody the America of the print ad, of the television commercial, and are meant to embrace the largest number of members in the film audience (even though this image may be only an ideal rather than an actual representation of that group) and to exclude the fewest. In this way they fall into the category of the "typically American"' (Ibid.: 55–6).

By embracing the often-romanticised Norwegian mountains as its setting, *Cold Prey* creates a Norwegian version of this ideal. Jannicke and her friends are young and white middle class people, speaking a deliberate variety of Norway's dialects, and thus they fall into the category of 'typically Norwegian'. The natural and rustic setting of snow-covered mountains and a romantic mountain lodge, inverted here to slasher horror, gives a touch of national specificity to a tale that is transnationally generic. Ultimately, the slasher movie's generic plot pits the final girl of the young community against the psychopathic killer, and the confrontation plays itself out in a dangerously isolated place. Indeed, decisive to the make-up of the slasher movie, and key to its Norwegian appropriation and particularity, is the isolated place in which the young community comes to a grisly end. The mountain lodge in the bleak, snowy wilderness is the ultimate Norwegian version of this subgenre-defining place.

Uthaug is keenly aware of the engaging potential of the hotel as a filmic space, and he establishes his main location through mood cues that make the setting come alive. When Jannicke and her friends walk towards the forbidding lodge, Uthaug stages their approach in a shot that seems like the hotel's point of view, accentuating our sense of the dreadful unseen with a barely audible sound of breathing. When they break in, the group encounter a dusty reception area replete with cobwebs and a stuffed elk's head, its dead eyes staring darkly and ominously at nothing, but suggesting thoughts of what they might have seen. The howling wind outside completes the mood, and the viewer is put on alert to scan the surroundings for danger.

At intervals, the tense mood is released through the construction of emotion markers. Some of these are false, meaning that our reflexes are triggered without there being cause for concern. One example is when Ingunn spooks Mikal and Eirik during their exploration of the darkened basement: she suddenly lets out a scream and the boys jump. 'Ooooh, an empty room!', Ingunn jokes. Meanwhile, Jannicke goes to close the front door, which has seemingly opened itself. In an angle from outside in the yard we see Jannicke in the door, and suddenly a shadow crosses the frame at close range accompanied by a loud bang on the soundtrack. This marker is real: something moves in the shadows and has become intrusive for the viewer.

The Mountain Man's first victim is Ingunn. This is a character that might better fit the conventional profile of the final girl, because she is sexually innocent. In fact, Ingunn is said to be a virgin. *Cold Prey* plays against the received wisdom of slasher archetypes by letting Ingunn be the first character to die. Mikal gets immaturely upset when Ingunn refuses to have sex with him, in spite of their flirting at the start of the movie. She draws the line at making out, she goes no further, and Mikal leaves her alone in the hotel room they were meant to share for the night. The Mountain Man finds her and kills her with a pick-axe, in an audio-visual orgy of overwhelming violence, naked skin and gushing blood, which culminates at the movie's midpoint. This is a key scene in *Cold Prey*, as it establishes the film's subgenre affiliation and highlights the importance of the place in which the slasher plot unfolds.

Cold Prey has three levels of what Clover calls 'The Terrible Place' (1992: 30), the site of stalking and killing. The first level is the massive Norwegian mountain landscape, the desolate surroundings that hide a deadly threat to the young community. The second level is the abandoned mountain lodge, the seemingly empty hotel where they seek shelter and safety only to find terror and death. Finally, the hotel basement where the Mountain Man resides is the third level, and the deepest and darkest place of all. When Mikal leaves Ingunn, she is left all alone in the most terrible place.

The hotel basement is brown, dark green and dirty. Ingunn is blonde, pale and a virgin. When she attempts to use the shower in her room, only a dark

THE SLASHERS OF NORWAY

Figure 3.2 Ingunn in the terrible place, wounded, doomed and desperate. (Screenshot from *Cold Prey*)

red liquid gurgles through the rusty pipes: stale water, the colour of blood. Ingunn becomes aware of another presence, but when she calls for Mikal, there is no answer. Suddenly the Mountain Man is there, slamming a pick-axe into Ingunn's back. Composer Magnus Beite serves up stinging cues reminiscent of the *Psycho* shower scene as Ingunn begins the fight for her life. Desperately seeking her friends, but unable to call out because of her injuries, she limps through the dark hotel corridors with the Mountain Man in sadistic pursuit. She has just one flight of stairs to climb to safety, so close. Then, out of the darkness he comes, the personification of the terrible place. He is merely a shadow and an axe, and he slams Ingunn to the floor.

In the hotel bar Mikal is blasting music through an old boombox, unable to hear Ingunn's death throes just a few metres away. She sees him, but he neither sees nor hears her crawling slowly up the steps towards him. By now, her pale skin is smeared in sweat and blood and the grime of the hotel floor. A final blow of the pick-axe ends it. Ingunn has lost. The Mountain Man drags her back down the stairs, down into hell. Only an empty flight of stairs is left, steps covered in blood, the descent into the most terrible place. Uthaug dwells on the staircase, pulling his camera back slowly into the dark corridor, as a demonic voice whispers something barely audible on the soundtrack. The scene's coda is a brief heart-to-heart between Mikal and Jannicke, and then the film cuts to flickering lights in the basement corridor and Ingunn's heart-shaped necklace in a pool of blood.

This scene is not only the pay-off to the set-ups that Uthaug has carefully constructed through his earlier mood-cues and emotion markers, it is also the scene that locks *Cold Prey* into its subgenre of slasher movies. Uthaug's use of particular places and spaces is key to the convincing brutality of the scene. The viewer senses that it is impossible for the young community to

43

escape, because the Mountain Man is ingrained in the setting where the action unfolds: the hotel literally breathes in the start of the film, and the Mountain Man breathes with it as the story continues.

From this point on, *Cold Prey* is a generic fight between the two most important characters of the subgenre, while still anchoring their slasher action duel to the specificity of the Norwegian setting. The Mountain Man is Norway's version of Michael Myers or Jason Voorhees, the masked and monstrous killers in the *Halloween* and *Friday the 13th* franchises, and the only example of this serial murdering psychopath in Norwegian horror. There have been other killers in the vein of the classic American slasher movies, for example in Reinert Kiil's low-budget *Christmas Blood* (*Juleblod*, 2017), but the Mountain Man is the only one that returns, a character archetype bordering on the supernatural. This character is essential to the slasher franchise, the final girl being second only to him.

There are mainly two types of slasher killers. One is the Norman Bates type, the psychopathic everyman who can potentially lurk behind any door in a peaceful and urban neighbourhood. The monstrosity of this character lies in their warped psyche. Their exterior betrays little or nothing of this, and they have the ability to appear 'articulate and agile, and usually engage in conversation at some point' (Harper 1993: 42). The other type is the explicitly monstrous killers, characters who are both mentally and physically 'somehow "incomplete" human beings' (Ibid.). They are clearly apart from civilised community and often 'banished to the wilderness, living in forests and deserted houses' (Ibid.). This archetype lives on in *Cold Prey*. The Mountain Man is initially shown only in quick glimpses, becoming more prominent towards the end, and he is tall and broad, hiding his face behind a scarf and goggles. Even in the dark basement of the hotel he makes a point of wearing the ski goggles. He exists at a distance from civilisation and only meets his match when he encounters Jannicke.

The damsel in distress, or the virgin in peril, is nothing new to the horror genre, being a staple of gothic literature. Cynthia Griffin Wolff has written about the heroines of author Ann Radcliffe that '[their] business is to experience difficulty, not to get out of it [. . .]' (1983: 211). The final girl of the slasher represents something else: the virgin in peril who strikes back and ultimately saves herself. This character is not fully developed in *Halloween*. After all, Laurie is saved by Dr Loomis, who represents patriarchy in the story. However, unlike *The Texas Chain Saw Massacre*, *Halloween*'s final girl does not merely flee but also fights back, stabbing Myers in the eye with a coat hanger. With the success of *Halloween*, this type of defiance and self-defence becomes common in the slasher movie, leading Clover to define this character archetype as an emerging hero who bridges the gap between fiction and audience in a way that is essential to the genre: 'She is intelligent, watchful, level-headed; the first character

Figure 3.3 The Mountain Man, Jannicke's slasher film nemesis and a transnational icon of horror. (Screenshot from *Cold Prey*)

to sense something amiss and the only one to deduce from the accumulating evidence the pattern and extent of the threat; the only one [. . .] whose perspective approaches our own privileged understanding of the situation. When she downs the killer, we are triumphant' (1992: 44–5).

In *Cold Prey* there are three characters who survive long enough to realise their predicament over a significant period of time: Mikal, Morten Tobias and Jannicke. In the end, Jannicke is the only one left alive. She tries to escape, like Sally in *The Texas Chain Saw Massacre*, but she is quickly intercepted and forced into a fight to the death, like Laurie in *Halloween*. When Jannicke drives the pick-axe into the chest of the Mountain Man the fight is over. She has defeated the killer with violent force, like Alice in *Friday the 13th*. On her way to becoming the final girl, Jannicke has moved through the three established phases of her character's arc: first she is a leader figure, then she is a terrified victim, and finally she is 'the image of an angry woman' (Ibid.: 17).

Jannicke is first shown as a leader, a kind of mother figure to the others, calm but firm. She takes charge of setting Morten Tobias' broken leg and takes care of him through the raging fever that follows. She also tries to reconcile Ingunn and Mikal, while privately struggling with the notion of moving in with Eirik. Uthaug has been open about Sigourney Weaver's Ripley in *Alien* (Ridley Scott, 1979) and *Aliens* (James Cameron, 1986) being an inspiration for the characterisation of Jannicke, and this is evident in her arc. When Jannicke finds the pool of blood after Ingunn's death, she reaches the first turning point: she becomes the terrified victim who can do nothing but attempt futile escapes from the killer, shock and disbelief transforming her firmness into panic. Uthaug's direction and Berdal's acting makes Jannicke the viewer's point of attachment, as her perspective aligns with our own.

When the situation becomes clear to Jannicke and death seems inevitable, her second turning point appears: she takes command of the situation and makes a plan to trap the Mountain Man and escape with Morten Tobias. The plan fails, the Mountain Man hides in his basement lair, but Jannicke does what Ripley would have done: 'We lure the bastard out of there, and then we shoot him.' The angry woman has emerged, but this plan also fails, and Jannicke must face the Mountain Man alone in the snow in hand-to-hand combat.

Who is the Mountain Man? Is he an unknown person who killed the young boy and his hotel manager parents in the 1970s, the one who chases the young boy in the opening flashback of the movie? This narrative question is answered in the final scene. Uthaug stages several flashbacks throughout the film, scenes that show what Dika calls the past event of the story, and this is how we finally realise that the young boy was chased through the freezing snowscapes by his own father. His parents tried to kill him, in fact they thought they had succeeded, faking a tragic disappearance for the TV cameras: 'He went outside to play . . .', his mother chokes on the news, in the film's very first line of dialogue.

In a way typical for the slasher, the killer comes into being in the past event. The Mountain Man was once a boy who survived attempted murder at the hands of his own parents. Since then, he has presumably resided in secret in the abandoned lodge. Now his murderous instinct, his method of survival, is triggered by the young community invading his space. The Mountain Man enacts his revenge on anyone, without rhyme or reason. Jannicke and her friends have simply made the great mistake of the slasher movie by seeking out the terrible place, the territory of the killer in which they are strangers and he is master. The only one who can stop him is Jannicke, the final girl and the character who the audience has been most clearly aligned with from the beginning of the story. She plays dead while the Mountain Man throws her friends into a deep crevasse in the ice, one by one. When her turn comes, she springs to life and engages the killer in mortal combat, ultimately lodging the pick-axe in his chest and sending him to his death in the crevasse.

Cold Prey features a few amusing nods to a horror classic of a different subgenre – Stanley Kubrick's psychological horror film *The Shining* (1980). The action of both films takes place in an abandoned hotel in winter (the American Rockies in *The Shining* and the Norwegian Jotunheimen in *Cold Prey*). The snowy isolation is complete in both cases. In the newspaper clippings that Jannicke finds in the Mountain Man's hiding place, the closed lodge is labelled a 'Hotel of evil', which is the literal but not very elegant Norwegian title for *The Shining*. A spooky room in the basement, that seems to have burned previously, is numbered 237, the room of the naked ghost in Kubrick's classic. Uthaug's use of the camera also recalls the way that the hotel in *The Shining* is imbued with an uncanny presence of its own, Kubrick and Uthaug both implying the hotel's point of view in select shots. In this way the hotel and the Mountain Man are merged into a greater threat. In staging uncanny and graphic horror at the same time, the Norwegian slasher often invokes the sublime force of nature as setting and source of its generic slasher drama. Taking this cue from *Dark Woods*, *Cold Prey* is a prime example of this particularity of Norwegian horror aesthetics, building its setting into much more than background for the action.

However, the importance of the Norwegian landscapes and settings decreases from the point of the Ingunn murder midway through the film, being eclipsed by a generic slasher hunt where the killer threatens deadly violence upon the young community. This battle could have happened anywhere, as long as there is no chance of help arriving. It could be argued that *Cold Prey* signals a national identity through the use of Norwegian settings, but that it stops short of *thematising* anything specifically Norwegian in its narrative (Hjort 2000: 107–10). Even so, the film is representative of a shift in Norwegian film history because the previously positive connotations of Norwegian nature and culture are twisted into what Gunnar Iversen has called a dissolving field of death and evil: the scene of the crime, the mountain lodge, enables the film to repaint not only the positive image of Norwegian nature but also the romantic symbolism of the nation's culture (Iversen 2011: 304–5). The horrifying action of Norway's slashers is set almost exclusively in rural areas and the wilderness, while urban misery is the domain of the psychological horror movies that I discuss in Chapters 5 and 6.

Legacy of the final girl

It is not Ingrid Bolsø Berdal's Jannicke that gives *Cold Prey* a national specificity or uniqueness in terms of the subgenre. She is a memorable character, but she does not break with slasher tradition. The common perception of the killer and the final girl in the slasher owes a lot to the seminal work of Clover from 1992 and director Wes Craven's postmodern blockbuster *Scream* from 1996. Here, convention says that the killer is a man, that sex leads to death and that the final girl is a virgin. However, it is certainly not always so.

In outlining the development of the subgenre in his 2014 article 'A Historical Approach to the Slasher Film', Sotiris Petridis gives a quite conventional but somewhat problematic overview, which is useful as a framework for review of the slasher's history. His discussion highlights common misconceptions about the subgenre, what I will call the misleading convenience of the *Scream* retelling. The slasher has always been more diverse than convention allows, even in its classic period. As early as *Friday the 13th* in 1980 the final girl was frivolous enough to drink beer and smoke pot. The final girl of the 1981 sequel, *Friday the 13th Part II*, had a boyfriend and was sexually active. Throughout the 1980s there were examples of male or female virgins dying first or early in the plot, survivors being less inhibited or conservative, and also final boys and female killers (Andresen 2016: 97–105).

Clover and Dika both write about the earliest period of the slasher, from the ground-breaker *Halloween* in 1978 to the mid-1980s, but the subgenre has seen many twists and turns after that. Petridis suggests three stages of development: the classic period from 1974 to the late 1980s, the postmodern period in the 1990s, and the neoslasher period after 2000 (2014: 76). He rightly points out that a critical look at the slasher's development after 1990 is crucial to understanding its place in contemporary cinema and horror culture. However, his own linear slasher periodisation is at odds with the cyclical nature of genres.

Petridis' classic period is marked by the consolidation of the slasher movie's basic structure: '[A] killer terrorises a young community in an isolated place and in the end, a person, usually female, survives' (Ibid.: 77). This period sees the shaping of the killer and the final girl according to the conventions established in *Halloween*, and Petridis argues that the normality of the American slasher movie in this first period is a conservative middle-class society in which the young people break with norms by drinking alcohol, using drugs, and having sex. The historical background to this period around 1980 was the conservative presidency of Ronald Reagan, right-wing religious activism and fear of epidemic diseases like AIDS. According to Petridis, this was ingrained in the classic slasher as a moral code: the killer punishes the young people for transgressions, but himself is so threatening to order that he must be defeated and removed (Ibid.: 79–80).

This account is too simplistic. First, the films of the classic period are more diverse in their stories and characterisations: both the killer and the final survivor can be male or female, as previously mentioned. Second, this take on the moral message of the classic period, in line with the misleadingly convenient *Scream* retelling, stops short of the point. Petridis writes that '[the] interplay between the conservative ideas of Reagan's era and the AIDS epidemic provides the basis for the punishment of the sexual act in slasher films of the classical period. The narratives of these films are about young people who have unprotected sex and then die' (Ibid.: 80). This begs the question, how do we know if these young people have unprotected sex or not? Protection is never an issue in any slasher film of the classic period. Third, the assertion of relation between the films and society overlooks the fact that most of the slasher's classic conventions were established in the 1960s and 1970s. Even the breakthrough films of the subgenre, *Halloween* and *Friday the 13th*, were released prior to Reagan winning the November 1980 presidential election. The classic slashers are evidently not responses to the Reagan era.

The representation of genders in the classic slasher, the core of killers and victims and final girls, is not as straightforward as Clover and Petridis suggest (Staiger 2005: 174). There is also reason to be critical of the common perception that such movies revel in a glorification of the male killer's punishment of promiscuous young women who fail to adhere to conservative values. What does the plot and action of such films say about patriarchy and ideology? What does it say about gender issues in modern society when women are hunted and killed in the way that we see in classic slashers? Several film scholars have pointed out that slashers like *Halloween* do not at all condemn their young characters' behaviour, and they do not portray the murdered young women as unlikeable or unsympathetic (Wood [1986] 2003: 174; Tudor 1989: 202; Hutchings 2004: 200–1). Peter Hutchings has written that there is a deeper satire at work in the slasher film which often goes unrecognised by critics, stating that 'if young people are being punished in these films, they are being punished not for their pleasure-seeking ways but for their complacency' (2004: 201). The Norwegian slasher *Cold Prey* falls in line with this, and the slasher is in fact most often on the side of the young in its core message: 'Watch out because the world in which you live has secrets that can and will harm you' (Ibid.). Death can come to all, be they virtuous or not, as in the case of *Cold Prey*.

In the slasher we root for the final girl. It should follow logically that the storytelling we appreciate in these films, crude as it is, has a clear bias against the oppressor. The slasher's structural tension and release would certainly not exist without the masked killer, and there is a lot of excitement and humour to be gleaned from these characters being both mysterious and dangerously attractive, yet it is impossible to argue that the audience's allegiance lies with anyone but the heroine. The killer of the classic slasher can be regarded as a fundamentalist oppressor. The movies can be read as critical of structural patriarchy in modern society, with the killer as a violently conservative antithesis to progressive individualism and personal liberty. Rather than asking why the young community is punished, we could ask what forces the punisher-caricature represents. The answer will often be the reactionary, that which has suffered a real or imaginary loss and seeks revenge.

The final girl does not survive by adhering to conservative values. Even the archetype Laurie Strode in *Halloween* indulges in a little bit of marijuana. Indeed, if the violence of the slasher is construed as punishing women for their sexuality, it makes no sense in the first place for the killer to go after the white virgin that Strode is perceived to represent, yet so he does. This is the insoluble logical fallacy in the misleadingly convenient *Scream* retelling of the slasher's conventions: the killer does not do what convention says he does, and the survivor is not who convention says she is. It is more accurate to say that the final girl survives her ordeal because she is resourceful in the face of danger. Indeed, after the end of the slasher's classic period it was the strong female characters who headlined the subgenre's renaissance.

The 1990s saw a renewal of the slasher format. Pastiche and parody became an important part of the subgenre's expression, with Wes Craven's *Scream* as the leading example. Film critic Jim Harper has described the slasher's artistic and commercial situation at the dawn of the 1990s as critical: 'If the late eighties saw the decline of the slasher movie, the early nineties appeared to drive several nails into its coffin lid. [. . .] To many people it appeared that the slasher movie had finally run its course' (2004: 24). However, the subgenre did not become a mere fad, thanks to a new and entertaining approach to its conventions. Petridis labels this the postmodernist period: 'Slasher films started to mock the conventions of the classical period by self-referential elements in the narrative. [. . .] [The] slasher films of the 1990s played with this predictability and included hyperconscious characters that knew the formula of the subgenre and were trying to alter it' (2014: 80).

Self-referential content was not entirely new to the subgenre at that point. Even the prototype *Halloween* had several nods to its own forebears, like the opening sequence's point-of-view photography lifted from the Italian giallo film, and the use of Dario Argento's clown mask from *Four Flies on Grey Velvet* in 1971. There had even been ironic and parodic takes on the subgenre in the classic period long before Wes Craven's efforts in the 1990s, like Fred Walton's *April Fool's Day* in 1986. Even so, the extent and popularity of *Scream*'s intense self-reflection and irony was new, as well as its narrative familiarity with the subgenre's history. Norwegian genre directors like Roar Uthaug and Tommy Wirkola grew up with the classic slasher, but also came of age in the era of the subgenre's 1990s development, and they would bring that stylistic sensibility to their own work in different ways.

Equally importantly, Kathleen Rowe Karlyn has asserted that the story of *Scream* and its main character Sydney Prescott (Neve Campbell) not only represented genre filmmaking with a clear ironic distance to its own conventions, but also a renewal of feminist ideals and themes in the horror film of the 1990s: 'Built around themes of female empowerment and narratively driven by the ambivalent but powerful connection between mother and daughter, the trilogy [completed by *Scream 2* in 1997 and *Scream 3* in 2000, yet still ongoing] raises the issue of bonds among women across time [. . .]' (2009: 180). The slasher once again became popular, but this postmodern period would not last for long.

After the turn of the millennium, and in the wake of the September 11 attacks in the USA in 2001, the subgenre would be characterised by what Petridis calls the neoslasher, which in turn splits into two sub-categories: 'the remakes and the originals' (2014: 82). American remakes of Asian horror films started with a new version of the Japanese *Ringu* (Hideo Nakata, 1998): *The*

Ring by Gore Verbinski in 2002. Filmmakers soon turned their attention to American classics as well. In a sequence identical to the order of the originals came *The Texas Chainsaw Massacre* (Marcus Nispel, 2003), *Black Christmas* (Glen Morgan, 2006), *Halloween* (Rob Zombie, 2007), *Friday the 13th* (Marcus Nispel, 2009) and *A Nightmare on Elm Street* (Samuel Bayer, 2010). At the same time there were also original films, like the self-proclaimed old-fashioned *Hatchet* (Adam Green, 2006) and the satirical horror comedy *The Cabin in the Woods* (Drew Goddard, 2012).

A hallmark of the neoslasher is the probing of the killer's mind and motivation, something that was not common in the classic period and only given a cursory glance in the postmodern slasher films. In the neoslasher, however, the inexplicable violence and aggression of the classic slasher is now replaced with a focus on the background and origin of evil. For instance, Rob Zombie's *Halloween* remake spends nearly half its running time showing the miserable childhood of Michael Myers. There was no hint of this at all in John Carpenter's original, where Myers was explicitly stated to be the embodiment of evil unexplained. This is a significant difference between early and later American slasher films, and Petridis claims that victims are also chosen in a different way in the later films: 'In the classic period, because of the AIDS epidemic, everyone who had sex ended up dead and only the girl who had virginal characteristics survived. [. . .] In neoslashers, [some of the victims] are connected to the killer, [. . .] while others are killed because they were in the wrong place at the wrong time' (Ibid.: 83).

It is indeed common to describe the classic slashers the way Petridis does, as a story in which sex equals death. This is demonstrably mistaken, however, even when looking at the well-known classic entries. For example, the final girl of *Friday the 13th Part II*, the first film of the franchise where Jason Voorhees and not his mum is actually the killer, is a sexually active young woman in a steady relationship. It is also mistaken to state that the neoslashers lack the alleged conservative moral code of the classics. In the first neoslasher remake, *The Texas Chainsaw Massacre* from 2003, the sole survivor is Erin (Jessica Biel), a virginal and handy young woman. In the very first dialogue scene of the movie the young community talk about 'sexually transmitted disease' while two of them are making out in the backseat of a car. Those two are later killed in horrible ways. Everyone except Erin smokes marijuana, and one of the men of the degenerate killer family exclaims, 'you kids taking drugs?', with a disgusted look on his face. It could easily be argued that the remake adheres more overtly to the conventional moral code than the original does, and it is highly questionable whether the neoslasher's final girl is significantly different from the final girl of the classic period.

The neoslasher remake of *Halloween* from 2007 is first and foremost different in story terms by painting the killer's background in detail, explaining the reason for his madness and evil: a bad childhood. The neoslasher *Halloween* is reminiscent of later Hollywood movies like *Joker* (Todd Phillips, 2019), in the way that individual responsibility for one's actions seems to recede in the face of societal and parental failures. In 2007's *Halloween*, the killer's alcoholic father is abusive to the point of caricature, and Michael Myers (Daeg Faerch) kills him, as well as his own big sister and her boyfriend, as revenge for the abuse. His little sister is the only one who is spared, and she grows up in a foster home as Laurie Strode (Scout Taylor-Compton). Laurie becomes the movie's final girl, like she was in the original, doing well in school and earning pocket money by babysitting. In the 2007 version she does say 'I need a boyfriend', but that is as far as the film goes in distancing its Laurie from the virginal 1978 template. Language and violence are overwhelmingly more brutal in the remakes of the 2000s, but there is no discernible difference in moral codes between the originals and the remakes of *Halloween* and *Friday the 13th*. The killer can still be seen as representing reactionary and oppressively conservative fundamentalism, even if he is now given a clear psychological motivation, a kind of excuse, for his horrific actions.

To be sure, *Cold Prey* has much more in common with the American remake cycle than the original slashers in terms of photography, sound, editing, acting and graphic depictions of violence. Uthaug pointed this out to the author, saying that part of his pitch to investors involved showing them the trailer for the 2003 *The Texas Chainsaw Massacre* remake and telling them to imagine it as 'cold and blue' instead of 'hot and brown' (Uthaug 2015). His slasher film can hardly be described as a postmodern take on the subgenre, having little in the way of heavily ironic self-reflexivity in either its narrative or its style. Indeed, few Norwegian horror films have the postmodern hallmarks of hyperconscious characters and overtly self-referential elements.

Dark Woods and *Cold Prey* are not ironic, but serious slashers, and it is interesting to note that they appeared in cinemas at the same time as the wave of American neoslasher remakes. *Cold Prey* in particular shares its brutal on-screen violence with the neoslashers and sets a high bar for its successors. However, the early killing of a virgin and a sexually active final girl is nothing new. Contrary to conventional wisdom, this was regularly seen in classic slashers. Jannicke has a classic era precursor in Ginny (Amy Steel) in *Friday the 13th Part II*, and refusing sexual intercourse leads to death for Ingunn in *Cold Prey* just like it did for Karen (Carolyn Houlihan) in *The Burning* (Tony Maylam, 1981). Even so, the convention of the final girl not having sex on camera is still strictly adhered to, in both the American neoslasher remakes and the first proper Norwegian slasher, *Cold Prey*.

4. OPEN BODIES IN RURAL NIGHTMARES

Dark Woods (*Villmark*) aligned the past of the Norwegian horror classic *Lake of the Dead* (*De dødes tjern*) with a modern genre expression, and *Cold Prey* (*Fritt vilt*) embraced a specific subgenre to become the first diecast Norwegian slasher film. Of great importance to this kind of horror film is the opening of the body, the suspenseful stabbing and slashing that constitutes the arguably greatest attraction of the subgenre. After a relatively subdued launch with *Dark Woods*, the more self-consciously generic *Cold Prey* revelled in this hallmark, guiding the Norwegian slasher into a much more graphically intense landscape.

The horror genre is by nature transnational, but the slasher film found its form in American independent cinema. Roar Uthaug's *Cold Prey* is essentially a Norwegian take on the classic American slasher that came into being in the late 1970s and early 1980s, and its commercial success prepared the ground for other slashers to follow. What they all have in common is the rural and wild settings that hide threats of death and destruction, a landscape that is mythical in its portraits of degenerate countryside people and at the same time nationally specific enough to set the Norwegian subgenre apart. One motif encompasses most Norwegian slashers: tense anxiety, and sometimes violent conflict, between the urbane and the rural, between townspeople and country folk.

Mutilation and murder in rural Norway

The title sequence of *Cold Prey* presents a montage of real news coverage from papers and television: short bursts of headlines and reports about missing persons in the mountains and desperate search and rescue missions. Time and time again people are feared to have perished, and the montage lingers on the headline 'Lost without trace'. In this way the filmmakers try to connect their slasher movie to the recognisable horror that news coverage imparts on us every day in real life. Their goal is a sense of authenticity and realism, the opening of a dark journey into a somehow credibly Norwegian fictional universe.

Cynthia A. Freeland has pointed out that the attraction of the slasher movie is very similar to the attraction of news coverage: horrific acts, violent attacks on the body, the suffering of innocent victims. Freeland claims that the slasher depicts a horror which is unusually realistic: 'It presents violent spectacles with an uncanny immediacy right before our eyes – reflecting the immediacy that the camera also facilitates on our nightly news' (2000: 188). Since Freeland wrote this, the immediacy of news coverage has increased manifold, the live sensation available at the click of a mouse or swipe of a screen. As she states it, the slasher puts the attraction of tension and violence before any semblance of a sophisticated plot.

In contrast to the fantastic and supernatural horror of classic Universal and Hammer movies, Freeland describes slasher killers in the tradition of Norman Bates as characters of what she calls *realist horror*, where 'the monster is a true-to-life rather than supernatural being', a killer who is 'a realistic or possible monster' (1995: 130). The Mountain Man in *Cold Prey* is such a possible monster, admittedly not one you are likely to meet in real life, but still a fairly realistic murderer. To be sure, he is far removed from the pathetic Bates in terms of brutality, but he is also not a supernatural monster, at least not yet.

Uthaug stages about thirty-five real emotion markers in *Cold Prey*, in addition to quite a few false ones that make the audience both jump and laugh in spite of themselves. This number is a considerable step up from the rather sober *Dark Woods*. From the point of *Cold Prey*, the Norwegian slashers become increasingly disinterested in narrative and ever more focused on the spectacle of random violence and murder in the great outdoors. The subtext, part of the paradoxical appeal of such films, seems to be that the horrible thing can happen to *you*, at *any time*, without an apparent motive or purpose (Ibid.: 138–40). In the Norwegian slashers, however, there is an important amendment to this: it can happen to *you*, at *any time*, but only if you are foolish enough to venture into the Norwegian rural areas or wilderness.

The violent attack on the body in Norwegian slashers, the destruction of flesh, is at its most brutal in Patrik Syversen's *Manhunt* (*Rovdyr*) from 2008.

The slasher in general is a type of horror film where characters are routinely killed in disgusting yet inventive ways, but an important cinematic trend after 2000 has become known as *torture porn*. *Saw* (James Wan, 2004) and *Hostel* (Eli Roth, 2005) paved the way in American cinema, setting up franchises and creating the horror environment in which Syversen's debut feature was made. *Manhunt* certainly shares these series' intense focus on bodily suffering and death, and it is easily the most graphic and unpleasant viewing experience of all films covered in this book.

As always in Norwegian slashers, we meet a group of young people on a trip into the rural or wild areas of the country, but with a twist of period setting: this is a summer day in 1974, and four people are driving on their way to a cabin in the woods: Camilla (Henriette Bruusgaard) and Roger (Lasse Valdal) are dating, Mia (Nini Bull Robsahm) and Jørgen (Jørn-Bjørn Fuller-Gee) are sister and brother. Roger is a whiny and dominating guy who dictates the mood of the group, and who none of the other three seem to get along with. When the group makes a stop at a gas station to refuel and have lunch, it becomes clear that they have arrived in a place extremely hostile to people from the city. They barely avoid a violent confrontation with some of the locals, partly contrived by Roger's bad temper, and they reluctantly pick up the obviously frightened hitchhiker Renate (Janne Starup Bønes). As they drive on, they are followed and intercepted by three hunters who proceed to shoot Renate dead, maim and kill Mia, and abduct the rest of the group.

Camilla, Roger and Jørgen wake up somewhere in the woods, bound and gagged. They are able to break free of the ropes, but they have no idea where they are. Suddenly the sound of a horn echoes through the forest: the woodsmen are ready for the hunt. The city people, basically foreigners in these parts, are the prey. In store for them is sadistic mutilation and death in the gloomy forest. In the end, only Camilla is left standing, having killed three of the hunters using a knife, a shotgun and a bow and arrow respectively. Camilla finds her way to a road and gets picked up by the café lady (Jorunn Kjellsby) who was in charge of the gas station that the group visited earlier. The car drives off, but Camilla's panic reignites when she discovers that the car doors are locked from the outside. Fade to red.

With *Manhunt*, Patrik Syversen (born 1982) draws inspiration from movies like *The Last House on the Left* (Wes Craven, 1972), and in particular *I Spit on Your Grave* (Meir Zarchi, 1978). This is the type of horror story that Carol J. Clover calls 'the revenge of the woman on her rapist, and the revenge of the city on the country' (1992: 115), although one could also reasonably suggest that the countryside folk enact their own perceived revenge on the city folk to begin with in a film like *Manhunt*. The contrast and conflict between city dwellers and country folk is not just a defining trait of Norwegian slashers, it is one of the most common points of departure for horror tales in general, setting the stage for a mythical confrontation where 'people like us', the city dwellers, are endangered by people who are not like us, 'the threatening rural Other' (Ibid.: 124).

The Others in *Manhunt* are painted as primitive and violent men. The only woman among them is the café lady, and she seems to know all about the deadly game. This cast of characters is typical of the horror film: adult men with no apparent family connections are overrepresented among villagers and rural inhabitants. These men do not seem to have paid jobs, and they can be encountered either alone or in groups. In the rural village of horror, the family unit is often a terrible and unhinged thing. This kind of horror family is the opposite of the healthy and positive nuclear family, a kind of incomplete and perverted household.

The faces of the hunters in *Manhunt* (the film's Norwegian title *Rovdyr* literally translates as *Predators*) are rarely shown. Syversen leaves their faces, and their eyes in particular, mostly out of frame. This is not because their identities matter in terms of the plot, nor in preparation for some big reveal. It is purely because these characters' identities are secondary to their function as representatives of the faceless *Texas, Norway* as Gunnar Iversen (2009) has labelled such generic and mythic constructs. The hunters personify the inbred evil of rural Norway, or more precisely: they represent the inbred evil of a Norwegian version of the mythical rural America from movies like *Deliverance* (John Boorman, 1972).

Setting the plot in 1974 is an obvious nod to one of its chief inspirations, *The Texas Chain Saw Massacre*. In both cases the killers are nameless men with questionable personal hygiene, and the rural landscape is forbidding rather than inviting. The Norwegian woods in *Manhunt* is a dark place, the sunlight never makes its way to the undergrowth. The hunters, representing the Others, thrive in this gloomy landscape. Indeed, they are as one with it, barely discernible among the grey trunks. The visiting city people, on the other hand, are lost in a landscape with which they are utterly unfamiliar. Like its models in American cinema, *Manhunt* can be described as 'the rural gothic' (Wells 2000: 87), a horror story from the countryside world of the Others, where those like us do not belong.

While the *young community* is the focus of the slasher plot, there is traditionally also a very important *old community* in such films. This old community is often a group of middle-aged to elderly people who mean well but ultimately fail to aid or save the young community from death and destruction. They can be police officers and doctors, parents and teachers, all invested in the well-being of the young protagonists but unable to stem the tide of the killer's violent actions. In the classic horror prior to the innovations of the 1960s and 70s, experts and authorities were usually able to neutralise and defeat evil, but there is no such help in the world of the slasher. Sometimes one of the old will try to warn the young of their danger, like Crazy Ralph (Walt Gorney) in *Friday the 13th*: 'I am a messenger from God. You're doomed if you stay here.' Naturally there would be no movie if the young protagonists heeded the warning, turned around and went home. In the sequel, Crazy Ralph gives another group of young people another unheeded warning: 'I told the others. They didn't believe me.'

This character, a kind of soothsayer, does not exist in the Norwegian slasher. There is no one of the old who tries to explain to the young how to avoid becoming victims. Indeed, the old in *Manhunt* are not merely unable to save the young people – the killers are themselves an accepted part of the old community. City and countryside are in open conflict here, but there is also an added generational divide between the young good and the older evil. The battle rages between two communities, the Urbane and the Others.

However, how *good* is this young and urbane community? There is obviously no excuse for the slaughter, but Syversen's movie is characterised by a numbing coldness in its depiction of the young main characters, a lack of sympathetic engagement that marks *Manhunt* as a very different viewing experience from *Cold Prey*. Granted, the Others, the country people, are clearly identified in slasher terms as the villains, the people who Clover says 'live beyond the reaches of social law' (1992: 125). They have worn and dirty clothes and do not seem interested in dental care, unlike the better dressed and obviously more affluent city people who are invading their space. All the same, they are not the only ones being portrayed in a negative light. Where the classic slasher clearly aims to make the audience root for the victims, the final girl in particular, *Manhunt* does not.

The young community that we meet in this film are selfish, bickering and generally unsympathetic. This makes the movie particularly uncomfortable to watch. The violence is graphically intense beyond anything previously seen in Norwegian cinema, but the viewer is also deprived of any sympathetic anchoring point among the characters. Camilla would be the most likely candidate, but she is much less self-assured and resourceful than Jannicke in *Cold Prey*. Where Jannicke confronts the Mountain Man in an attempt to save her boyfriend's life, Camilla leaves her boyfriend tied to a tree, which leads to his death. It might be more realistic, but it also leaves the viewer cold. After all, a major attraction of the horror genre in general is the experience of rooting for characters who ultimately overcome evil. In *Manhunt* there is simply no one to root for.

Two more things set *Manhunt* apart from the rest of the Norwegian slashers in terms of plot and action. First, there is no traumatic past event providing a background to the present events of the film. Second, this is the only instance in the Norwegian slasher of killers hunting in packs. When combined with the intensely graphic bodily destruction, in nauseatingly gory detail, and the lack of sympathetic engagement with the characters, this makes *Manhunt* the bleakest and most disturbing of the lot. Syversen does not structure the action around the final girl's dawning realisation of her plight, the killers' intentions are revealed very early in the film, and most of the running time is a drawn-out fight in the tradition of the last half hour of *The Texas Chain Saw Massacre*. Whether Camilla will ultimately survive at all is called into question, as it seems more likely that she will end up like the hitcher Renate. Camilla is, in the end, the character who has seen the horror, but she cannot escape it. She survives to this point, but she is apparently still in the clutches of the rural Others.

'I HAVE KILLED HIM BEFORE': *COLD PREY II* AND *COLD PREY III*

Halloween II followed the on-going misdeeds of Michael Myers on the same All Hallow's Eve as its precursor, literally no time passing from one film to the next. The first Norwegian horror sequel, 2008's *Cold Prey II* (*Fritt vilt II*) by Mats Stenberg, stuck to this concept by continuing the story of Jannicke on the same day that the original *Cold Prey* ended. In order to make such a sequel possible, the Mountain Man had to come back from the dead.

Jannicke (Ingrid Bolsø Berdal) is found wandering along a road in the Jotunheimen mountains, having survived the massacre of the previous film. She is admitted to a small hospital in Otta and tells her story to the local sheriff Einar (Per Schaaning). He decides to investigate the crevasse described by Jannicke, and the police find the bodies of her friends as well as their dead killer, the Mountain Man. When a nurse examines the corpse of the killer, the body moves. Resuscitation is ordered, and a desperate Jannicke is unable to stop the resurrection of her friends' bane: the Mountain Man is breathing again, chained to a stretcher. The doctors put Jannicke on a regimen of potent drugs, while also chaining her to the hospital bed. Meanwhile the sheriff reopens several missing person files. Numerous frozen bodies are discovered deep in the ice where the Mountain Man dumped Jannicke's friends. Now the police can officially close some old cases, but at the hospital a deadly threat is about to break free.

A hallmark of the slasher subgenre is the production of sequels and remakes. The massive popularity of *Cold Prey* carried over to *Cold Prey II*, thus making *Cold Prey III* all but inevitable. Mats Stenberg, a Swedish commercials director making his first feature film, imbues *Cold Prey II* with a somewhat more sophisticated and elegant visual style than Uthaug's raw and direct approach. One of Stenberg's several flourishes is a title sequence that tracks along the frozen remains of people in the crevasse, presumably Jannicke's murdered friends, and ends up pulling out of the crevasse and onto the desolate icy plain where the previous film ended in the showdown between Jannicke and the Mountain Man.

However, despite the noticeable change of directorial touch, including eye-catching edits like a cut from Jannicke framed in the rear-view mirror of a car to a video game car framed on a gaming device, there is no doubt that *Cold Prey II* essentially feels like an unapologetic continuation of the original. Jannicke and the Mountain Man had by then become iconic characters of Norwegian horror cinema, the way that Laurie Strode and Michael Myers had in American horror before them, and the commercial success of the sequel would effectively create Norway's only horror cinema trilogy to date.

The iconic killer is often the constant in a slasher movie series, while victims come and go. This is also true for the only such series in Norwegian cinema. Jannicke anchors the first two *Cold Prey* movies, but she is ultimately left out of the third entry when the filmmakers decide to make it a prequel. The Mountain Man is the only character who appears in all three plots. In *Cold Prey II* he breaks free from the stretcher and goes on another murderous rampage that threatens the only three patients of the soon to be defunct hospital: Jannicke, the old lady Marie (Inger Johanne Ravn) and the young boy Daniel (Vetle Qvenild Werring). With the aid of the doctor Camilla (Marthe Snorresdotter Rovik), Jannicke must try to save those she can by getting them out of the hospital before the Mountain Man kills them.

When her nemesis wakes up on the autopsy table, the film draws a clear line of demarcation to its predecessor. This is no longer Norway's version of the realistic killer. His reanimation is a decisive step into the supernatural. Even if Michael Myers proved impossible to kill in *Halloween*, he did not return from the dead in *Halloween II* the way the Mountain Man does in *Cold Prey II*. This type of return is the domain of supernatural slasher killers like Jason and Freddy. Stenberg dwells on this development in a scene that follows the killer's return to life. The senior physician Hermann (Fridtjov Såheim) tries to comfort his staff by telling them of known cases of extreme hypothermia, and the distraught nurse Audhild (Johanna Mørck) is having none of it: 'But he was dead.'

For the constant to be possible in a franchise, a line must sometimes be crossed. The killer cannot remain the realistic psychopath of Freeland's description; he or she must become supernatural. The Mountain Man becomes this mythical figure in *Cold Prey II*. Not only does he awake from death, but he also shows an uncanny ability to negotiate his way around the dark corridors of a place he supposedly has never seen, cutting phone lines and disabling the power grid. He seems more cunning, he kills more people and he lures the police officers into an artfully elaborate trap in the hospital, before escaping back to his own fortress of solitude in the mountains. He used to be merely a brutal loner, but he has now become an agile killing machine. The terrible place of the story is no longer strictly his own domain; it has been extended to a hospital he does not know in a village he has supposedly never been to before. The staging of the plot in *Cold Prey II*, along with the altered characterisation of the killer, expands the mythology of the series. I noted earlier that the slasher killers of Norwegian horror have been principally static in terms of geography, only killing those who venture into their habitat, but it could be argued that *Cold Prey II* represents an exception: the Mountain Man can come to *where you are*, if someone is careless enough to bring his corpse there.

The sheriff's investigation into the missing family from the original film's mountain lodge leads him to doctor Haldor (Bernhard Ramstad). His story is one of awe and horror. The family's baby, now grown into the murderous Mountain Man, was stillborn. The doctor filed the death certificate after about four hours, but then the child woke up. 'He was just lying there,' says the doctor, 'quiet as a mouse.' The group including the doctor, the sheriff and the senior hospital physician makes up what Andrew Tudor would call the ineffective expertise of the story: neither medicine nor police force will suffice in battling the Mountain Man, the old authorities are powerless, and deciding the outcome is all up to Jannicke, the film's most important *everyperson* (Tudor 1989: 22, 108).

Jannicke is still the final girl in *Cold Prey II*, but not alone. This time she also saves young Daniel's life, while receiving invaluable help from Camilla, the doctor, in her final showdown with the Mountain Man. Camilla actually fits the description of a final girl herself: she and her situation are at the centre of events, she is the one who discovers the murders, she sees the killer, but ultimately she cannot take charge of the situation since Jannicke already occupies the spot of the main character. However, Jannicke would not have survived *Cold Prey II* if Camilla had not intervened at the final moment. Only together can they defeat the reactionary and oppressive force that the Mountain Man personifies.

In the previous chapter I noted the deliberate parallels between Jannicke and the tormented Ellen Ripley of the *Alien* series, and this connection is still apparent in *Cold Prey II*. A chief example is the dream sequence at the film's mid-point that strongly resembles the dream sequence in James Cameron's *Aliens* from 1986. Another similarity is the relationship between Jannicke and Daniel, which seems modelled on Ripley's care and attention for the young girl Newt in *Aliens*. Director Stenberg and actor Berdal take some deep dives into the post-traumatic condition of Jannicke as the film progresses, and they orchestrate a decisive turning point towards the end of the film. When the Mountain Man escapes from the hospital and heads back into the mountains, with Daniel safely in the care of his mother, the camera dwells extensively on Jannicke's face as her anger dissolves into an expression of finality and determination. Jannicke comes to terms with her fate and resolves to hunt down and kill the Mountain Man, or die trying.

Returning to the abandoned mountain lodge of the first film, Jannicke enters her dead friends' names in the guestbook before signing her own. The cold and

OPEN BODIES IN RURAL NIGHTMARES

Figure 4.1 Jannicke fixes her eyes on the mountains in the distance, resolving to end the terror of the Mountain Man at whatever cost to herself. (Screenshot from *Cold Prey II*)

gloomy desolation of Jotunheimen is where the nightmare begins and ends. Jannicke soon finds herself in another mortal combat with the Mountain Man, and she is about to lose when Camilla turns up and shoots the man's fingers off. He turns from Jannicke to the other woman in a rage. In the end, Jannicke goes for the pick-axe again. She throws it at the Mountain Man's back as he is trying to crush Camilla's skull. The axe pierces him, protruding from his chest, and he falls to the ground. Jannicke and Camilla stare at the Mountain Man in the snow before them, but Jannicke has learned her lesson: she grabs a shotgun. Camilla says, 'He is dead now', but Jannicke replies, 'I have killed him before', and shoots.

The specific space of the Norwegian horror film is the frame for the story of Jannicke, the final girl. Uthaug's and Stenberg's *Cold Prey* movies are easily recognisable as slasher movies, cut from the same cloth as both classic and later iterations of the American subgenre, but they also add places and landscapes that set them apart in a transnational tradition of generically over-familiar storytelling. The melancholy landscapes often associated with the Nordic region are very much a dominating presence in the Norwegian slashers.

Moreover, the bleak countryside and the nearly defunct hospital of *Cold Prey II* trade on a very real worry among people in modern Norway: the centralisation of resources and services that increasingly leaves the periphery of the country fighting to maintain a traditional, if somewhat idealised, way of life. People move to the cities, the countryside crumbles, and the national-romantic image of a thriving social democracy does not ring so true anymore. In fact, the equity of the country's people has eroded significantly since the 1980s, the rich getting richer while the lower income classes lag behind (Statistics Norway 2020). Against this backdrop, the decay of the countryside that proliferates in Norwegian horror cinema has a definite contemporary sting. The psychological horror films of the next two chapters might be more sophisticated treatments of the decline of social democracy, but the slasher films exploit both the myth of the countryside and the modern-day challenges of its citizens.

Between the two *Cold Prey* sequels director Severin Eskeland released his debut feature *Detour* (*Snarveien*, 2009). This film is not a slasher, although it does have elements of stalking in its story about two young people who cross the border into Sweden to buy a carload of cheap booze for a friend's wedding. Lina (Marte Germaine Christensen) and Martin (Sondre Krogtoft Larsen) are forced to take a detour through the woods on their way back to Norway, and they get trapped in a potentially deadly game of cat and mouse with a deranged family that films and streams a live snuff movie. *Detour* hints at the psychologically driven horror that Eskeland would later pursue with *Lust* (*Lyst*, 2017), eschewing the more popular slasher aesthetic of the period. Yet the desolate setting, the rural backwater border region of Norway and Sweden, is in line with the diecast Norwegian slashers. As is the premise of alcohol being expensive in prosperous Norway, or at least the notion that money can be saved by buying it cheaper in Sweden. Unlike the proper slashers, though, *Detour* sees all the bad guys die while the young people survive, neutering the horror. Possibly for this reason, or perhaps because the film was released in the summer season (very unusual for Norwegian films at the time), *Detour* was much less popular with audiences than other Norwegian horror movies of the period. In retrospect, however, it is a unique movie in Norway's horror cinema tradition, because of its core story of live snuff.

To this day, *Cold Prey II* remains the most commercially successful of all Norwegian slasher movies with 268,427 tickets sold (*Film & Kino* 2014: 59), and a continuation made sense for the producers. Mikkel Brænne Sandemose, another first-time feature director, was tasked with making *Cold Prey III* (*Fritt vilt III*, 2010). This story would go back in time, the nature of the so-called *prequel* type of franchise entry, to chart the origin and coming of age of the Mountain Man. *Cold Prey III* starts by elaborating on the tragic family events of 1976 that we already saw glimpses of in the original film. A young boy of 11 is severely abused at the mountain lodge, both emotionally and physically, by his hotel manager parents (although the man might not be the boy's biological father). He is ultimately chased to his apparent death in the snow, but as we already know, he survives. The boy's first act of revenge on the world is killing his parents.

Twelve years later, in 1988, a group of friends are heading for a night of camping in the wilderness. The time period is marked by Kim Wilde's version of The Supremes' 'You Keep Me Hangin' On', which was a number one hit in Norway in early 1987. A discussion about the new and ground-breaking portable car telephone also helps to turn back time, with Hedda (Ida Marie

Bakkerud) asking excitedly, 'Can I phone home?' There would clearly be no need to neutralise mobile phones in this film.

One reason why Norwegian slashers tend to set the action in the countryside and wilderness is probably the ease with which isolation can be achieved in such places, an isolation that is intrinsically important to the generic slasher plot. The technology of the mobile phone has created a new challenge for horror filmmakers, and films like *Dark Woods* and *Cold Prey* find it necessary to show and tell the audience that the characters have come to areas with no mobile phone signals. The village setting of *Cold Prey II* makes this impossible, and so the filmmakers contrive a scene in which Jannicke ambushes Camilla and Camilla's mobile phone breaks apart upon hitting the floor. There is indeed a long tradition for technology-fuelled horror in film, or more precisely, of technology's failure to help. Tom Gunning has written that, 'To talk by telephone, [...] is to risk being cut off' (1991: 195), highlighting the fear of communications technology not working when you need it. Clover elaborates on this role of malfunctioning technology in the slasher: 'Victims sometimes avail themselves of firearms, but like telephones, fire alarms, elevators, doorbells, and car engines, guns fail in a pinch. In some basic sense, the emotional terrain of the slasher is pretechnological' (1992: 32). When the young community of the original *Cold Prey* arrive at the mountain lodge in 2006, they have already ascertained that their mobile phones have no signal, and in the hotel reception they also find the landline dead. The impossibility of making that one decisive call for help makes the suffering of isolation all the more intense. So near, and yet so far.

The 1988 group of young friends in *Cold Prey III* intends to visit the abandoned mountain lodge, out of some morbid fascination with the mystery of the missing family. Upon arrival, Siri (Julie Rusti) makes it clear that she doesn't want to spend the night in the spooky hotel after all. They settle for a quiet lake in the forest, in a start-stop situation which illustrates a common challenge in horror movie sequels: the filmmakers want their characters to seek out the same dangerous place that we already know, but the location must still be avoided so as to not repeat the setting completely in a generic retelling of the already generic tale. This leads to the group negotiating landscapes that change considerably in a very short space of story time. Naked mountain peaks and deep forests are combined in a way that seems inauthentic, but this is probably contrived for a sense of Norwegian nature nostalgia much more than realism. In this unreal place, a mythical Norwegian landscape, the young will suffer and die.

Siri flirts with Knut (Sturla Valldal Rui) and the two of them sneak off on their own during the night. When they fall into a trapping pit, Knut is gravely wounded, and Siri runs away in a state of shock. The trap has been set by the Mountain Man, who is hunting game illegally, and when he finds Knut in the trap his thirst for maiming and killing humans is engaged anew. Not living at the mountain lodge at this time, the Mountain Man is hiding from authorities in the home of the woodsman Jon (Nils Johnson). Knut and all his friends will now have to be killed in order to preserve the secret of the Mountain Man's existence. In fact, even Jon dies at the end of the film, and the Mountain Man remains unknown as he wanders into the snows of Jotunheimen to set up base at his parents' defunct hotel. The mythical approach to the landscapes of *Cold Prey III* is highlighted by how the Mountain Man leaves Jon's house in the woods in the summer but arrives at the mountain lodge in the winter, just a few shots later. Iconic images have precedence over spatial and temporal precision or logic in Sandemose's less substantial and more superficial take on the *Cold Prey* mythos.

An inherent risk of making prequels is the removal of mystique. The opening sequence of *Cold Prey III* shows us many details of the disturbing treatment the Mountain Man went through at the hands of his parents as a child, and this leads to a certain humanisation of the killer reminiscent of Rob Zombie's recreated Michael Myers in 2007's *Halloween*. Through the Mountain Man's relationship with Jon, we see how the *Cold Prey* killer learns his deadly arts. With the loss of mystery, the only attraction left is the brutality of the killings. Also, Jannicke's absence is keenly felt: *Cold Prey III* provides less engagement between characters and audience than its two predecessors. The film relies almost exclusively on manipulation of audience reactions through emotion markers, where loud sounds and intense visuals combine in jump-scares, rather than narrative tension and character development.

Cold Prey III employs what Iversen calls the mythical notion of a rustic *Texas, Norway* in a much more direct way than its predecessors. In the first film the Mountain Man was the only representative of the rural Others, while *Cold Prey II* gave a sympathetic depiction of all the country folk except the killer. In the last film of the series the mythical Texas countryside is truly lifted from American horror movies into the Norwegian woods in a way that is strongly reminiscent of *Manhunt* two years prior. This is personified in the character of Jon, the man of the woods, the loner who rejects interaction with a civilisation he despises. His home is generically recognisable from classics like *The Texas Chain Saw Massacre*: rusted machines, a worn-down house, and the absence of paid work. In this terrible place, Jon hides the Mountain Man and acts as a father figure only marginally less evil than the one who was killed in the film's early scenes.

To give weight to Jon's evil, the film shows his racist attitude toward Anders (Kim S. Falck-Jørgensen), and it features a scene in which he rapes Siri. Both of these are firsts for Norwegian horror cinema. The latter action is particularly noteworthy, since film critic Jim Harper claimed in his excellent 2004 slasher catalogue, *Legacy of Blood*, that 'no rape is ever portrayed in a slasher movie'

(2004: 48). Sandemose builds up to this assault from the very first time that Siri and Jon meet. Their eyes lock for an uncomfortable interval and it is plainly foreshadowed that they will meet again. When Jon later picks up a distraught Siri after the fall into the animal trap, the camera takes Jon's point of view as he gazes at her breasts. The killers' sadistic games were certainly sexualised in *Manhunt*, but *Cold Prey III* builds to the realisation of a rape scene.

The basement is the most terrible place in Jon's house. Siri is locked in a dark room where she catches only glimpses of what the Mountain Man has done to her friends. Her own role seems intended to be that of Jon's sex slave. 'She is mine', he tells the Mountain Man. Siri fights off Jon's assault for a while but in the end, she is pressed to the floor. *Cold Prey III* thus violates one of the perceived slasher movie conventions: Siri is not killed early on as apparent punishment for being promiscuous, but she is sexually assaulted and raped by an older man who is not even the killer of the story. The fact that a dying Jon later helps Hedda in fighting the Mountain Man does not ameliorate our impression of him, and at any rate his efforts do not affect the outcome of the story. *Cold Prey III* seems to lack any of the moral codes that have been suggested for different eras of the slasher's history. In fact, the film's plot seems lost in the darkness of its landscapes with no point to make, existing purely to get the Mountain Man from the opening sequence to the ending without being discovered, and effectively dissolving any potential moral concerns of the subgenre as it goes along.

The hopeless darkness of the young community's nightmare does have a contrast in the scenic idyll of the lake where they spend the first night. Most of them wake up there to beautiful sunshine and a deer grazing by the water, truly an image right out of the national-romantic idealisation of Norway and its wilderness. When they decide to go looking for the missing Siri and Knut, however, all hell breaks loose. For the remainder of the film, more than half its running time, they are hunted and slaughtered by the Mountain Man. In the shadows under the trees of the Norwegian wilderness paradise, death itself awaits.

By the third *Cold Prey* movie the Norwegian slasher has been utterly standardised. Not only do the generic stories take place exclusively in rural areas or wilderness, in the woods and mountains of Norway, but the frequency and precision with which the films seek to elicit particular audience responses has also stabilised at a relatively high level, comparable to their American neo-slasher counterparts of the era. For the final twenty minutes of *Cold Prey III* the density of jump-scares overwhelms the viewer with a continuous burst of elicitation.

After a gentle start with Pål Øie's *Dark Woods* and the intensification of Roar Uthaug's original *Cold Prey*, the number of emotion markers in Norwegian slashers would remain high. Nevertheless, audiences did not respond predictably, as no slasher has come close to the ticket sales of *Cold Prey* and its sequel *Cold Prey II*. This would surely mean that the original *Cold Prey* had considerable novelty value: the audience had been primed by the ground-breaking *Dark Woods* in 2003 and got its first proper Norwegian slasher in 2006. *Cold Prey* met expectations to such a degree that its sequel became as hyped and pre-sold as a horror film can get in Norway. *Cold Prey III*, however, saw a steep decline in attendance despite its marketing campaign. More than 100,000 tickets down from the high-water mark of its predecessor, *Cold Prey III* sold 152,308 tickets, clearly the weakest showing in the series (*Film & Kino* 2013: 62). In retrospect, this was a healthy number in a country with no more than about 4,860,000 inhabitants at the time, by any other bar than the one set by the *Cold Prey* series itself. Only in the context of the series' own success can the third film be considered a commercial disappointment.

The real-life horror of the 22 July terrorist attacks in 2011 would conceivably alter the climate for production and reception of these kinds of slasher stories in Norwegian cinema. However, the trend of mainstream slasher horror was already waning in Norway at the time, exemplified by the downturn in ticket sales for *Cold Prey III* in 2010. Norwegian horror films would continue to appear, both independently produced and publicly funded, even in the guise of slasher-related movies like *Dark Woods 2* (*Villmark 2*, Pål Øie, 2015). Any potential effect of the terror attacks on horror cinema production would be speculation, and it should be noted that Norwegian cinema and television were controversially quick to treat the traumatic national events of 22 July, for example in Erik Poppe's film *Utøya: July 22* (*Utøya 22. juli*, 2018) and in the *22 July* (2020) series made for *NRK* by Sara Johnsen and Pål Sletaune. The trend of rather prestigious Norwegian slasher cinema had come and gone in the period from *Dark Woods* in 2003 to the conclusion of the *Cold Prey* trilogy in 2010.

Cold Prey III marks the end of the series and the death of the final girl. As the local sheriff Einar (Terje Ranes) fails to comprehend the true criminal events that have transpired under his well-meaning but flawed jurisdiction, never realising that the boy who disappeared in 1976 actually survived, the Mountain Man slips off to hide at the mountain lodge in 1988 where Jannicke and her friends will meet him eighteen years later. A symbolic end to the tale is the fact that there is no final girl in *Cold Prey III*. Indeed, there cannot be. Hedda comes close to surviving, but that would have made the previous two movies impossible. Had this been the first of the series there would have been no reason for her to die, but the fictional world of the franchise demands that she dies so that the secret can live on.

Hedda is the leader who takes charge once she understands that something is terribly wrong in these woods. She is the only character left standing to confront the Mountain Man at the end of the film, as Jannicke does in the first film. This time the killer handles a knife, a shotgun, and a bow and arrow, so he has changed from the pre-technological murderer of the previous films, a strange fact considering the chronology of story events: in *Cold Prey II*, subsequent to *Cold Prey III* in the chronology, he throws a shotgun aside in favour of the pick-axe. At any rate, this retroactive upgrade in weaponry makes him even harder to defeat in the prequel, and Hedda fails to do so. The sheriff intervenes at Jon's house when only Hedda is left alive, thinking that his brother Jon has killed everyone but her of the young community. Hedda points her shotgun at the Mountain Man over the sheriff's shoulder, getting shot to death by the sheriff in a fateful misunderstanding of self-defence. Einar the sheriff carries the dead body of the would-be final girl out of Jon's burning house, the fiery terrible place of the final confrontation, at the end of the series. Only the sheriff survives the plot of *Cold Prey III*, and all the killings can be attributed to his brother Jon.

The final girl as Clover defined her is more the exception than the rule in the American slashers of the late 1970s and early 1980s, with Laurie Strode in *Halloween* and Nancy Thompson in *A Nightmare on Elm Street* being the chief examples. That period also saw variations on the characters of victims and survivors that have continued through later eras of the slasher film, but these are often overlooked in histories of the subgenre. The final girl of *Friday the 13th* was Alice, who smoked and drank. The first two victims of that film's present events were Annie (Robbie Morgan), who never had the chance to indulge in anything relating to sex or drugs, and Ned (Mark Nelson), who was not sexually active. There is simply no clear evidence of the perceived convention that in slashers, sex equals death. The slasher movie has never had an unambiguous moral code or a clearly conventional final girl across a considerable length of time. There had been a final girl in the independent underground slasher *22* (Pål Aam and Eystein Hanssen, 2001), but in the mainstream of the Norwegian subgenre this archetype is missing from all films except *Cold Prey*, and to some extent *Cold Prey II* and the more recent independent low-budget slasher *Bloody Water* (*Skjærgården*, 2016) by Frode Nordås. An example of severe variation is found in *All Must Die* (*Alle må dø*, 2020) by Geir Greni, which is noteworthy for featuring women from ground-breaking previous Norwegian horror films, Viktoria Winge (*Cold Prey*) and Julia Schacht (*Next Door*). Their characters are part of a hen night trip into the forest that goes predictably wrong. Winge's character Gina initially has many hallmarks of a final girl, but a narrative twist concerning her psychiatric issues (Gina is suffering from a kind of suicidal schizophrenic disorder) turns the film into as much of a psychological horror movie as a slasher, and effectively rules Gina out as a subgeneric final girl. She is much more complicated than this archetype, in fact she is a mass murderer, and her story is arguably not so well served by the conventional slasher format.

Jannicke of the original *Cold Prey* remains the only true final girl of Norwegian horror cinema, adhering as strictly to convention as necessary to be thus described. Norway's slasher films in general are as varied in their character portrayals as the subgenre's transnational history would suggest. At the end of the slasher's dark night, it is not in the portrayal of characters, but in the use of settings and landscapes, that the Norwegian brand of the subgenre stands out.

The terrible places of Norwegian slashers

Vera Dika once described the slasher as a type of horror film where setting is of paramount importance, a story where 'either the killer returns to a setting or the members of the young community travel to the setting where the killer lives' (1990: 58). The slashers of Norway nearly always opt for the latter, depicting groups of young people who travel to places where they do not belong, out there where evil resides: Norway's wilderness.

Isolation remains decisive for the generic plots of slasher movies to unfold, and the films are mostly set in one single distinctive place from which the young community have little chance of escape. This place needs to strike a balance between being believable and not too specific, allowing the setting of stalk and slash to feel interestingly authentic for a global core audience without necessarily pinpointing a real-world location. In this way the slasher subgenre travels easily, a highly generic story set in a fairly realistic and familiar place, and its conventions can successfully be removed from America to Norway. When the Norwegian slashers accomplish the telling of this generic type of story while creating new and authentic settings, they communicate with a global audience while also bringing their own hallmark to the subgenre.

Among the slashers of Norwegian cinema, only the first two *Cold Prey* movies and Reinert Kiil's more recent low-budget slasher *Christmas Blood* (*Juleblod*, 2017) specify settings as real places. The original *Cold Prey* story takes place in the Jotunheimen national park, a real-world Norwegian location, and is partially filmed at the Leirvassbu tourist lodge in Lom. The sequel takes place in the town of Otta in the Gudbrandsdalen valley, north of Oslo and south of Trondheim, which will be very recognisable for many Norwegian viewers. The third film of the franchise specifies its locations to a much lesser degree. In a similar way to *Dark Woods* and *Manhunt* before it, the story and action of *Cold Prey III* are set in geographically approximate Norwegian woodlands. For international viewers, it is very unlikely that pinpointing real-world locations has any meaningful impact. It seems, however, that a mythical yet authentic Norwegian space does enhance the generic stories in a way that engages both domestic, regional and overseas audiences.

The cinematic space in which most of the slasher's action unfolds is often limited, like the haunted house in *The Amityville Horror* (Stuart Rosenberg, 1979). 'Into such houses unwitting victims wander in film after film', Clover writes, 'and it is the conventional task of the genre to register in close detail the victims' dawning understanding, as they survey the visible evidence, of the human crimes and perversions that have transpired here' (1992: 31). The abandoned lodge in *Cold Prey* is this very house of dread, a solid slasher setting with locked doors and boarded-up windows, where the darkest parts of the story play out.

The terrible place was a different thing in horror cinema before 1960. Authorities and experts could be trusted back then, and the monster was defeated. This type of horror story took place in what Andrew Tudor describes as 'the Gothic *elsewhen* of an imaginary Transylvania or among the exotic equipment of a fanciful laboratory' (2002: 109). Both time and place were alien to the viewer, not the here and now of contemporary recognition. The monsters of slasher movies, on the other hand, often survive and ridicule the incompetence of authorities. Experts cannot be trusted, and the cinematic space is not the gloomy castles of vaguely foreign lands but an authentic here and now, 'contemporary and prosaic everyday settings such as small towns, suburbs, ordinary houses, family groups, and the like' (Ibid.).

The typical cinematic space of the classic American slasher is the suburb, the South, summer camps and colleges. In the Norwegian branch of the subgenre, one that only came into existence after 2000, the typical cinematic space is the North, a rural and mythical landscape, the village and the wilderness of a Norway only found in horror movies. The young community of these slashers always travel to where the killer lives, never the other way around. He, for it is always a male killer in Norway's slashers, never breaks boundaries by going where the young community is at home. The young go where they should not, and this place is a national-romantic Norway that has been perverted into a deadly nightmare. There is irony in this treatment of national landscapes, but the stories seem decidedly old-fashioned.

Indeed, Norwegian slashers have little of the self-reflection and pastiche that marked the American subgenre in the 1990s. They also have very little of the fantastic that marked its 1980s. The Norwegian slashers are serious in a realistic fashion, closer to the American classic period's *Halloween* and *Friday the 13th*. In terms of film style, however, they are closer to the remakes of those films in the 2000s. When director Wes Craven talked about the experience of making *A Nightmare on Elm Street*, he stated how he felt that Hollywood wanted horror movies to be less threatening than in the 1970s, that a scary movie 'was one that wouldn't disturb you but one that would make you jump' (Wells 2000: 93). This ideal is mostly true for the Norwegian slashers: they make you jump without disturbing you profoundly, with a qualified exception for the creepy and borderline supernatural backstory of the Mountain Man, as told by the doctor who filed his death certificate prematurely. The *Cold Prey* films take effective advantage of a certain national-romantic backdrop to stage emotion markers that make you jump. They have certainly been successful in doing so, gaining a considerable national audience as well as attention abroad. Danish film scholar Rikke Schubart once expressed disappointment that Denmark had not produced this type of horror entertainment, calling *Cold Prey* 'a serious horror franchise, which is not a teenage comedy but a terrifyingly serious bid for entertainment across age groups' (2010).

The Norwegian slashers might perhaps be as typically American as they are specifically Norwegian, but they are still a Nordic rarity. Norway stands out among the Nordic countries with its consistent output of horror movies since 2003, and the Norwegian slashers have obtained a style of their own through the Norwegian mythical places that are used as settings for their generic stories. They may not differ much from their American counterparts in terms of plot, but they definitely differ in terms of spaces. Interestingly, this use of landscapes is also important in most of the Norwegian psychological horror films.

5. NORWEGIAN PSYCHOLOGICAL HORROR

Norway is correctly perceived as a peaceful and prosperous country. Yet the dark side of this social-democratic nation has reared its head not only in the dystopian slasher fantasies that were discussed in the previous two chapters, films that bask in the perversion of national romantic landscapes to create highly generic horror entertainment. The darkness has also surfaced in films that are arguably more disturbing: psychological horror movies. This is a different type of horror, in which the violent threat to the body is eclipsed by the disorientation in space and time that threatens the sanity of the mind.

In the spiritual realm of the psychological horror movie, defeating evil is harder than what is the case in the material world of the slasher. The killer of the *Cold Prey* (*Fritt vilt*) series can ultimately be overcome through the use of physical force, but the main characters of the psychological horror film in Norway are stricken by a debilitating spatial and temporal disorientation. A kind of mental and emotional isolation is the fundamental premise that gives rise to very different types of subgenre films. Pål Sletaune's *The Monitor* (*Babycall*, 2011) is a ghost story, Pål Øie's *Hidden* (*Skjult*, 2009) is a slasher-related tale of possession, and Joachim Trier's *Thelma* (2017) is a coming-of-age story centred on a young woman with supernatural powers. Eskil Vogt's *The Innocents* (*De uskyldige*, 2021) is a further exploration of supernatural themes in current Norwegian cinema, putting children front and centre unlike any other psychological horror film in the country's film history.

The film that started this type of horror in post-2000 Norwegian cinema, Sletaune's *Next Door* (*Naboer*, 2005), is the most intense and modernist example of the subgenre. Where the slasher movie is a surface-oriented thrill ride with a heavy focus on physical stalking and the opening of the body, the psychological horror film in Norwegian cinema deals with the inward escape, with closed doors and hidden rooms, and with the rational and logical impossibility of the main characters' experiences of the world they inhabit.

The impossible tale: psychological horror

John rounds the corner in the hallway, but all that he sees is a blank wall. Where once there was a door, there is now simply a concrete surface. The entrance to the apartment next door is gone, leaving no sign of the two young women who lived there, the neighbours that John has had dramatic and traumatic interactions with over the past few weeks. John then attempts to hack his way through to the apartment he is convinced exists on the other side, but the concrete merely hides a solid brick wall. His experiences next door cannot be trusted, his grasp of past and present events is unreliable. Spatial and temporal disorientation is at the heart of John's distress, the clues and keys to a repressed criminal act that threatens to break its way back to the surface.

In this way Pål Sletaune's *Next Door* from 2005 nails an important hallmark of the psychological horror movie: the disorientation of the unreliable narrator. As viewers we cannot trust the objective truth of the plot that we experience through John's eyes and ears. Indeed, films in this subgenre of horror will often strive to deliver a tale that doesn't make objective sense as plot and story. The uneasy mood of these films is not derived from the fear of monsters or psychopathic killers lurking in the shadows, but rather from the psychological and emotional isolation of their main characters, the unreliable narrators of the story. Among the filmmakers that have obviously influenced the psychological horror of Norway are Roman Polanski, David Lynch and Stanley Kubrick, masters of the impossible tale.

To a certain extent psychological horror can be defined by its contrast to the slasher. James Kendrick has written that the development of the horror genre has always oscillated between 'the visceral and the suggestive, the graphic and the contemplative, the material and the spiritual' (2010: 144). The slashers revel in external threats: physical violence, bodily harm, cruel death and destruction. Psychological horror, on the other hand, is concerned with internal issues: subjective psychological states, a fumbling relationship with the real world and the people in it, experiences of the spiritual and supernatural. Where the slasher emphasises what Kendrick calls 'abject physical horror' (Ibid.: 155), the psychological horror film has an entirely different purpose. This subgenre intends to explore the labyrinth of the mind, and this maze is often cut off from objective material reality.

Psychological horror exchanges the slasher's deadly here and now, in which the killer hunts innocent victims, for a misty mental landscape where the borders between reality and fantasy are obscured. There might be physical threats, but the most important aspect of films in this subgenre will often be the subjective experience of emotional collapse and isolation. Another common motif in this type of horror is the crossing of borders between different worlds, and sometimes the experience of a spiritual realm or life beyond death.

Some of director Roman Polanski's classics are among the most frequently cited ground-breaking films in the subgenre, including *Repulsion* (1965), *Rosemary's Baby* (1968) and *The Tenant* (1976). Another milestone is Stanley Kubrick's *The Shining* (1980), an adaptation of the Stephen King novel. To be sure, there can be psychopathic killers in movies of this kind, like Jack Nicholson's unhinged main character in *The Shining*. Still, it is truly the mind that constitutes the landscape of the plot and story in the psychological horror subgenre. In Kubrick's movie, this hallmark is visualised through the garden maze outside the equally maze-like hotel, and such tales of psychological horror are likely to offer conceptual treatments of evil, violence and death in very different ways than the slasher.

As a concept and genre label the psychological horror film frequently overlaps with the thriller, and the crime thriller in particular. Norwegian cinema saw a wave of crime movies in the 1990s that were related to the subsequent horror movies. Among them was the internationally acclaimed Erik Skjoldbjærg film *Insomnia* (1997), an early example of the aesthetic that came to be known as Nordic noir. Other crime films of the era included *Blessed Are Those Who Thirst* (*Salige er de som tørster*, Carl Jørgen Kiøning, 1997) and *Eva's Eye* (*Evas øye*, Berit Nesheim, 1999), which were based on crime novels by Anne Holt and Karin Fossum respectively. There were also two movies that might have aspired to the horror genre but remained essentially crime stories: *Isle of Darkness* (*Mørkets øy*, Trygve Allister Diesen, 1997) and *Bloody Angels* (*1732 Høtten*, Karin Julsrud, 1998).

Crime thrillers, or detective movies, usually focus their stories on police officers and investigators who work to solve crimes while also dealing with challenges in their own and others' private lives. American cinema has given us plenty of crime thrillers that also dip into the horror genre, like *The Silence of the Lambs* (Jonathan Demme, 1991) and *Seven* (David Fincher, 1995). The line between crime thrillers and horror movies can usually be drawn at the point of character subjectivity, although this is not always an altogether neat exercise.

The psychological horror movie focuses heavily on the main character's subjective experience of the world, and often their denial of the reality of events around them. Subjective states of mind feed the plot and story of the psychological horror film, and these narratives are rarely in the realm of classical cinematic storytelling. Screenwriters and directors who work in this subgenre will often aim to challenge the conventions of three-act stories with clear conflicts and resolutions, upsetting classical goal orientation and spatio-temporal causality by muddying the narrative as well as the cinematic space. The purpose of the film will often be to achieve a sense of disorientation that unsettles the viewer, to create a seemingly impossible tale that refuses to adhere to objective story and plot logic.

Although questions of what is really going on, and what has actually happened, will likely account for much of the viewer's engagement with psychological horror movies, it is equally clear that the experience of film style is of paramount importance in creating the mood that compels our interest. While the slasher is plot-oriented, the psychological horror film is a mood film, and proper engagement hinges on conditioning the audience through the creation of subtle moods. Non-narrative elements of the film – settings, camera movements, sound design, music and editing – take centre stage as the goal orientation of a conventional plot recedes, and the impossible tale elicits reactions through depictions of subjective mental and emotional states (Smith 1999: 111–26; Freeland 2000: 222).

The horror cycles of Universal and Hammer have been called a safe type, placing its characters and events in a gothic and mythic *elsewhen*, while the more realistic here and now of the classic slasher constituted a paranoid type of horror that brought the threat home to our own *everyday* world (Tudor 2002: 108–9). However, in both cases the threat was external. The psychological horror subgenre, on the other hand, must surely be called more paranoid still: thrusting the threat deep into the minds of its characters, where the horrific becomes truly inescapable. A hundred years ago this tradition was already being established in silent films like Robert Wiene's German expressionist classic *The Cabinet of Dr. Caligari* (1920), and the mental condition of main characters is often at issue in acclaimed psychological horror movies like Nicolas Roeg's *Don't Look Now* (1973) and M. Night Shyamalan's *The Sixth Sense* (1999). The latter and the low-budget found footage horror *The Blair Witch Project* (Daniel Myrick and Eduardo Sánchez, 1999) initiated a burst of psychological horror at the turn of the millennium, preceding *What Lies Beneath* (Robert Zemeckis, 2000), *The Others* (Alejandro Amenábar, 2001) and *The Exorcism of Emily Rose* (Scott Derrickson, 2005), among others. This cycle also coincided with the launch of the psychological horror subgenre in Norwegian cinema.

Under lock and key: *Next Door*

The liberalisation of Norwegian censorship laws around 2000 not only opened the door for slashers like *Cold Prey* and *Manhunt (Rovdyr)*, but also made possible the sexualised violence of Pål Sletaune's *Next Door*, the first modern Norwegian psychological horror thriller. Pål Sletaune (born 1961) has been one of the most important directors in Norwegian cinema since the 1990s, when he made his mark both domestically and internationally with the feature film debut *Junk Mail (Budbringeren)* in 1997. He was offered the job of directing the Hollywood movie *American Beauty* (Sam Mendes, 1999), but chose to stay in Norway to make his well-received second feature *You Really Got Me (Amatørene*, 2001) instead. After exploring quirky characters and slightly absurd relationship dynamics in gritty tones of comedic realism with his first two films, Sletaune turned to horror. Both *Next Door* and *The Monitor* are fairly traditional psychological horror movies, and Sletaune must be considered a pioneer of the subgenre in Norway. Even so, he has stated to the author that his work is 'involuntarily commercial' (Sletaune 2016), explaining that circumstances led him to genre filmmaking more than any conscious artistic design on his part.

The psychological horror in Norwegian cinema can be traced to the genre forebear *Lake of the Dead (De dødes tjern*, Kåre Bergstrøm) from 1958. Besides Sletaune's two entries we find Pål Øie's *Hidden*, Joachim Trier's *Thelma* and Eskil Vogt's *The Innocents* in the mainstream. In addition, the low-budget independent features *Myling: The Myth Awakens (Utburd*, Astrid Thorvaldsen, 2014), *The House (Huset*, Reinert Kiil, 2016), *Lust (Lyst*, Severin Eskeland, 2017) and *Haunted (Hjemsøkt*, Carl Christian Raabe, 2017) have also had national cinema distribution despite being produced outside of public funding. In late 2019 the subgenre came to a kind of full circle with the release of Nini Bull Robsahm's *Lake of Death (De dødes tjern)*, a new adaptation of the book that inspired the 1958 classic.

This body of work makes up one of the very clear main paths in Norwegian horror cinema, the other being the slasher tradition previously discussed in Chapters 3 and 4. As for the attraction that both the slasher tale and the psychological horror story can hold for audiences, Sletaune was outspoken at the time of *Next Door*'s release:

> We're attracted to the blackest of the black. There is a reason why people are attracted to destruction and death in drama and film. Why? You don't want to watch someone having a picnic in a field for two and a half hours. You are attracted to the possibility that things can go south, that there is something dangerous and deadly out there. (Sletaune 2005)

One might add the possibility of something dangerous and deadly *in here* when it comes to the psychological horror movie. In *Next Door* the viewer is narratively speaking at the mercy of John (Kristoffer Joner). He is abandoned by his partner Ingrid (Anna Bache-Wiig), who accuses him of being dangerously introverted and in need of getting a life. After Ingrid moves out of their apartment John discovers that new neighbours have moved in next door: the young women Anne (Cecilie Mosli) and Kim (Julia Schacht). When John introduces himself, they both reply, 'I know', and they do indeed seem to know a lot more about John and his private life than what is realistically possible.

Anne tells John that Kim is suffering from some kind of post-traumatic disorder after having been attacked and physically abused by a strange man who entered their apartment. John helps them place a large cabinet in front of their door to keep intruders out, seemingly with no thought for how he will get himself out. The apartment next door seems impossibly big and complex to John, and at one point in his growing confusion Anne asks him if he's been there before. John answers that of course he has not, but Anne dismisses him: 'You just don't recognize it.' Soon after, Kim makes overt sexual advances towards him, and the energy between them builds to a point where they attack each other and have sex that crosses the border into explicitly brutal violence. Both Kim and John seem to be experiencing waking nightmares, but they are unable to understand each other's emotional positions.

Inexplicably, Ingrid's new boyfriend Åke (Michael Nyqvist) also shows up in the apartment next door, and John disintegrates in an emotional breakdown. At last, he finds only a concrete wall where he was sure the entrance to Anne's and Kim's apartment had been. Somehow, John's subjective experiences and selective recollections have merged into a state of isolation in an attempt to deny the horrifying truth: he has murdered Ingrid and Åke. Anne and Kim both seem to have been voices from his subconscious, challenging and accusing him, fragments of his mind that threaten to expose the repressed reality of his situation.

Next Door was the first Norwegian horror movie to receive a strict 18-year rating, meaning that no one under that age was allowed to see it in cinemas. Several years later, the slasher *Manhunt* would also get an 18 rating, potentially blocking a considerable part of its core adolescent audience from admission. However, unlike what appears to have been the case with *Manhunt*, the filmmakers behind *Next Door* were completely aware of what rating the graphic and sexualised violence of the film would lead to.

Sletaune has stated that his movie features 'scenes that transgress many boundaries, but that's also what the film is about' (Ibid.). *Next Door* thematises and visualises the mental and emotional condition of a man who gets sexually aroused by mistreating women, and who at the same time is ashamed of what he feels and does. The endless number of doors, rooms and corridors in the apartment next door is a visualisation of John's twisted and sequestered mind. He is trying to keep the horrible truth under lock and key, but his subconscious is fighting him, slowly willing the repressed back to the surface of reality. The disturbing sex scene with John and Kim that degenerates into violence is over ten minutes long, and it is made even more uncomfortable by the fact that Kim is the one who initiates both the sex and the violence. The viewer will later come to realise that Kim does not really exist, that she is one of many characters in John's processing of the world and his situation, but repeat viewings are no less uncomfortable. The scene can scarcely become any easier to watch once we learn that John has seemingly done something even more horrific in what might be the objective real world of the film's narrative.

Anne and Kim live in an endless maze of rooms with impossible angles and unrealistically narrow corridors. The apartment is also filled with objects that have no apparent connection to the women who live there, things that instead are repeatedly tied to John. When John calls the operator to get his new neighbours' telephone number, he is given his own number in return. The scraps on John's dinner table are also identical to scraps that he sees on the young women's table, one of many signs that their apartment represents John's subconscious and his life experiences. However, it might be too simplistic to interpret the spaces of *Next Door* as only existing in John's mind.

The urban setting of the story in *Next Door*, as well as the complex and hazy lay-out of the film's interiors, makes this a very special entry in the Norwegian horror genre. Spaces play a different part in this film than they do in the slasher movies previously discussed. In the latter subgenre, we are given over to the sublime and awesome isolation of nature, the exterior woods and mountains of the Norwegian wilderness. *Next Door* presents a different kind of isolation, that which connotes the repressed and frames the subjectivity of the main character in oppressive interiors of rooms and corridors. This is akin to the terrible hotel in *Cold Prey*, but something else entirely in terms of subjective experiences communicated through the filmmaker's manipulation of unrealistic spaces. This challenge appealed to Sletaune: 'My earlier movies were told as third-person narratives, and now I wanted to make a subjective movie in the first person, a me-film. [. . .] When you enter a nightmare, there is a whole spectrum of emotions and possibilities for expressions that you can take advantage of' (Ibid.).

The director's intention is to align the viewer with John, to achieve the experience that film critic Bill Thompson had when watching the movie: 'His reality is our reality, his shame is our shame, his pain is our pain' (2013). The viewer is closely aligned with John throughout the film, our access to information mirrors his: we see what he sees, and we know what he knows (Smith 1995: 142–86). The reality of events is suppressed to the point of psychosis, and the viewer has to piece the story information together from clues in the set design and dialogue to glimpse the truth, or at least what in the end seems the most likely truth.

Some viewers might guess the twist at the end well before it arrives, in fact the curve leading to the girls' front door means that the door opens into the same space as John's own front door ahead of the curve, but Sletaune makes sure that this revelation does not provide an unambiguous resolution to the story. The film is not structured like a conventional narrative, rather applying a kind of dream logic to the way scenes are strung together. The mistreatment of Kim is given an extraordinarily large spot in *Next Door*'s relatively modest running time of seventy-five minutes, indeed emerging as the magnetic point of the story from which other recollections and notions seem to flow backwards and forwards in time. Sletaune supports an interpretation like this by placing a door on either side of the room in which the scene takes place. John is on a dark and painful journey through his own mind and existence. The terrible truth is revealed at the end, when John lies down to sleep next to Ingrid's dead body.

Ahead of the film's opening image we hear the sound of traffic. All of Sletaune's movies are decidedly urban, including when he enters the horror genre. The first image in *Next Door* is of a non-descript backyard with empty windows staring into the street, a motif that would be amplified significantly in *The Monitor* some years later. Ingrid arrives by car and enters the building where John lives. His tortured mind is not open to its surroundings, it has shut itself off from the world in a desperate defensive manoeuvre. One has to visit an apartment building, enter an elevator, and ride it all the way up to the fifth floor where there seems to be only one flat, in order to get in contact with John's world. Ingrid rings the doorbell and is admitted. 'Is there anyone here?' she asks. 'No no no, I'm alone', answers John. Ingrid has splintered into different aspects in his mind, different parts of his imagination of her. This first voice in his head is Ingrid herself, the accuser, the speaker of terrible truth, but also a memory of happier times. Very soon, different aspects will present themselves, other characters that represent parts of his imagined Ingrid: Anne and Kim.

Sletaune's starting point for the story was the scene where John meets Anne for the first time, in the elevator: a young man meets a young woman with a torn skirt and wonders what has happened to her (Sletaune 2016). He discovers her apartment, where Anne is living with a woman who she claims to be her sister Kim. Exaggerated amounts of personal objects are collected there, memories and impressions from lives that have already been lived, as well as massive amounts of foodstuffs. Anne says it's all about being prepared, in case they have to shut themselves in. John has already shut himself in, emotionally and psychologically, and his meeting with Anne and Kim is Sletaune's depiction of his journey inward. John escapes further and further into the apartment next door, which is getting narrower and darker.

The central scene of sex and abuse takes place in what looks like a hotel room. It resembles a room from the social-democratic 1970s in Scandinavia: brown furniture and wallpaper, and a busily patterned carpet that is also seen in John's own apartment. What does the 1970s represent in terms of

NORWEGIAN PSYCHOLOGICAL HORROR

the perception of the history of Norway? Probably a sense of nostalgia, an image of a time in the country's history when social-democratic ideals were paramount to the post-war rebuilding of society and industry, the creation of the welfare state, a time when the notion that the haves were obligated to help elevate the have-nots in the pursuit of national equity was a strong and unifying political force. In the sordid universe of *Next Door*, the 1970s setting of the scene represents a time and place of lost innocence, or more precisely the yearning for an innocent time before the fall.

The rest of the movie is set in a contemporary time and place, arguably excepting the admittedly confused interior of the apartment next door, but this particular scene is certainly detached. It is dated to the 1970s, or quite possibly even a decade earlier, but beyond that it is devoid of distinctions or personal objects. In contrast to every other room in the apartment next door, this room is almost empty. The consequence of the frugal mise-en-scène that Sletaune orchestrates in this scene is a sharp focus on bodily lust and harm that becomes particularly uncompromising and ruthless. The space is a mental stage floor where John's darkest desires are performed.

Kim is the aggressor at the start of the scene. She seems to be trying to seduce John, but we will soon come to learn that she is merely a part of John's inner battle, an aspect of his defence against terrible accusations. Kim is John's fetishist fantasy. She asks John to close his eyes while she tells him of a sexual encounter with three men. 'You have to picture it', she says, effectively urging John to travel inward. She starts touching herself while recounting a sexual fantasy that we later realise is one that John forced Ingrid to tell him. Kim starts simulating loud sex and John seems to get both excited and embarrassed. 'Come here and sit down', Kim says to him. John hesitantly sits down next

Figure 5.1 John sits down opposite Kim, on the surreal stage where Norway's first modern psychological horror film reaches its terrible climax. (Screenshot from *Next Door*)

79

to her, whereupon she hits him in the face three times. The sudden shift from sex to violence is shocking. Kim is another voice in John's head: alluring but dangerous, revealing John's darkest impulses on the stage of the non-descript social-democratic room. This place has no visible connections to other places or other people, letting John's destructive fantasies take centre stage as they ruin the image and memory of an innocent time. He hits back at Kim, as if he has somehow gotten permission to do so. John the abuser and Kim the fantasy victim fist-punch each other until they start bleeding from lips and noses, and the bright red makes a strong impression among the otherwise muted colours of the scene. Kim undresses and the two engage in sexual intercourse while continuing to hit each other. The music score underlines the horrific development with dramatic orchestra stabs to every punch.

Sletaune then cuts abruptly to a shocked and bloodied John breaking down in front of the mirror in his own bathroom. The dream logic of the story has yielded a nightmare. The voices in the head are all part of the puzzle that is John. Ingrid is there, both a warm memory and a mature voice that confronts and reprimands him. Kim is there, seductive and childish. When John attempts to withdraw from the situation before it escalates, she reacts sourly: 'I can't be bothered talking to you when you're mad. [. . .] I can't be bothered to let you out when you're cranky.' John is trapped in the apartment next door. It can only be opened from the inside, but you need a key to do so.

Åke is also there, a threatening male character who John has no chance of physically defeating. However, Åke soon becomes as childish in his dialogue as Kim, asking John why he is so cranky. As John desperately tries to escape the apartment, Åke hands him a set of keys. None of them work, John remains trapped, and the apartment becomes ever more surreal and nightmarish, resembling the dungeon of a gothic castle in some classic horror film. Sletaune's audio-visual horror orientation intensifies as sound and music underline the increasingly graphic focus on bodily illness and harm. This viewer experience of horror is doubly strong in *Next Door* because of Sletaune's deliberately unpleasant staging of sex and violence. The movie's space is filled with dread as a result of perverse desires. This is truly a psychological horror movie's version of the slasher's terrible place. However, there is a flicker of light in the darkness: the redemptive voice in John's head is Anne. 'Why are you so mad at Ingrid?' she asks. John returns a question to her, probing the voice in his head, one of the creatures of his subconscious: 'Why do you keep me locked inside?' Anne finally tells him that it is too late to escape, that he has already killed someone. At that moment the apartment next door disappears.

In the same way that the classic slasher is pre-occupied with the return of the dead, a motif that has always been present in horror, many psychological horror films are thematically and stylistically focused on what lies hidden in the mind. Both the return of the dead to the land of the living, and the rediscovery of the lost or forgotten, can be denoted by the term *the return of the repressed*, which was established for film analysis by film critic Robin Wood in his milestone essay 'The American Nightmare. Horror in the 70s' (1986). John's knowledge and recollection of having murdered his partner Ingrid have been repressed in his mind, but they are slowly forcing their way back to the surface through his subjective experience of interacting with the two women next door. Such motives are also familiar to us from gothic literature. William Patrick Day has written that '[the] Gothic fantasy is a fable about the collapse of identity [. . .]' (1985: 75). Sletaune's *Next Door* is a gothic tale of emotional decay and a protective double identity, a kind of modern version of the duality in *Strange Case of Dr. Jekyll and Mr. Hyde* (Robert Louis Stevenson, 1886). John represses the knowledge of his own destructive desires, obviously of a sexual sort, and consequently he becomes a disturbed and split personality. As Day writes, 'by definition, the Gothic protagonist can never become a single self' (Ibid.: 77).

John's painful disorientation is shared by the viewer. The apartment next door becomes ever more mysterious and immense, and the confusion about what is actually occurring becomes greater every time John meets Kim. John gets more entangled in his own mind, struggling under self-imposed lock and key, but at the same time the viewer gets closer and closer to the horrific reality of his situation. The end comes when John gets into bed next to Ingrid's dead body, while the janitor is trying to force open his front door. The apartment next door is gone, and there is no other way for him to escape but inwards. 'You know that I could never hurt you?' he asks the dead Ingrid. He gets under the covers, next to her cold body, and shuts himself inside.

THE UNHOMELY SPACES OF NORWEGIAN HORROR

The disorientation of *Next Door*, the dissipation of space and time, is one of the hallmarks of the psychological horror film. An obvious precursor to Sletaune's movie is Roman Polanski's *Repulsion* from 1965, where the rooms of the main character's apartment are audio-visual expressions of subjective experiences. Sletaune himself states that Polanski's early films have been major influences for him, along with the works of David Lynch and Stanley Kubrick. Indeed, Sletaune is not shy about calling Kubrick's *The Shining* 'the world's best ever film' (Sletaune 2016). The hotel of the Kubrick classic comes to life through staging, setting, cinematography, editing and sound design: the empty ballroom suddenly bustles with life, and a vacated hotel room is mysteriously inhabited by a woman after all. In Polanski's *Repulsion* walls crack open, rooms become impossible to understand, and the front door is nailed shut from the inside, all reminiscent of the mysterious apartment in *Next Door*. Both *Repulsion* and its Norwegian relative *Next Door* are impossible tales of dread that are told through the careful staging of impossible spaces, and where the inward escape is connoted by locked doors. The expression of John's condition and the construction of the film's horrors depend on Sletaune giving the viewer an experience of spatiotemporal disorientation. While the physical isolation in the slasher accommodates the deadly hunt for innocent victims, mental and emotional isolation is what terrorises the main characters of the psychological horror movie.

The house lives. The mind wavers. Persons appear out of nowhere like ghosts. The psychological horror film is full of what is often called the *uncanny*. Extrapolated from Sigmund Freud's term *unheimlich*, it might better be translated to English as the *unhomely* (Fisher 2016: 9). It is familiar, and yet it is strange. In her important work on horror film and the experience of the unhomely, Cynthia A. Freeland outlined and explained the concept as 'a disembodied, vague state of affairs' (2000: 215), attempting to describe that which is 'eerie yet enticing, strange yet familiar, creepy yet not horrific' (2004: 88). In short, this is a type of horror that emanates from an eerily off-kilter experience of everyday settings and situations, a slight twisting of time and place, with no psychopathic killer breaking in from the outside.

The places where horror happens, be it the American house on the hill or the Norwegian mountain lodge, are often a visualisation of inner states: a seemingly endless row of rooms, steep staircases, a dark and secret dungeon. The way that spaces are created and explored in *Next Door* can be traced to horror movies like *The Shining* and *The Haunting* (Robert Wise, 1963). Characters arrive at places that should be unknown to them, but that still have 'a familiarity about [them] that makes no rational sense' (Hutchings 2004: 73). This is how it feels for Jack Torrance in the Overlook Hotel, and also how it feels for John in the apartment next door. John's lack of grip on reality, or his refusal to accept such a thing, leads to his own apartment becoming alien to him while next door becomes strangely familiar.

Severin Eskeland's *Lust* is another example of this application of unhomely spaces in Norwegian horror cinema. *Lust* is a low-budget independent film in which Eskeland stages the post-traumatic breakdown of controversial author Lisa (Magdalena From Delis). She writes novels that depict explicit sex and violence, but she falls into desperate paranoia after suffering a brutal assault and rape. Lisa then locks herself in her apartment, seeking solace in bottles of pills and red wine. Eskeland exploits the very limited setting by turning the apartment into a character of its own that seems to live and breathe, building slowly to extreme bursts of violence in which Lisa maims and kills male characters either for real or in her own imagination. *Lust* is a rare Norwegian rape-revenge story draped in the conventions of psychological horror, although the ending suggests that the violent revenge of the woman is merely a paranoid fantasy. The experience of watching the film is just as much dependent on engaging with the cramped apartment as with the main character, the unhomely space of Lisa's living quarters seeming like an entity that has witnessed dark secrets.

Peter Hutchings writes that 'a recurrent feature of the horror genre is the house that contains secrets from the past, with the characters in these films often discovering that a familiar domestic setting is not so familiar after all' (Ibid.: 74). There is a touch of this in Eskeland's *Lust*, and more overtly so in Reinert Kiil's independent feature *The House* and Carl Christian Raabe's *Haunted*. The significance of the unhomely spaces is obvious in Sletaune's *Next Door*, and certainly also in Norwegian cinema's most typically generic example of this horror film motif: Øie's *Hidden*.

Hidden tells the story of Kai Koss, known as KK (Kristoffer Joner), returning to his hometown in rural Norway for the funeral of his estranged mother. He inherits her house, the place where KK grew up, but it quickly becomes apparent that he has dark and traumatic memories of both his mother and the house. KK claims to have been held prisoner in a room in the basement as a young boy, and he believes that his mother also kept another boy locked up there, unbeknownst to everyone, after KK himself escaped. When KK revisits the now defunct home of his mother, it becomes clear that the unhomely house has a life of its own, the subjective gothic nightmare being staged as a building that breathes with dark secrets.

KK attempts to burn the old house down but is foiled by the sheriff (Cecilie Mosli). He checks into a local hotel, situated close to a beautiful waterfall, the spectacular Vøringsfossen in Western Norway, which immediately suggests David Lynch's classic TV series *Twin Peaks* (1990–1991) as a source of inspiration. KK seems to be the only guest in the hotel, and the mysterious receptionist Miriam (Karin Park) tells him that the place is currently being refurbished. Trouble mounts when KK discovers that his hotel room's landline telephone connects automatically to a telephone in his mother's old house, and an unknown man in a red hooded sweater lurks in the shadows of both the house and the surrounding forest. When this mystery man kills two teenagers on a camping trip, KK warns the town that this must be the boy who grew up hidden in his mother's basement. The sheriff disbelieves KK's story, and suspicion falls on KK himself. The theme of dual identities is as strong in *Hidden* as in *Twin Peaks*, and the question is whether an unknown man is truly wandering the forest, or if KK is a murderous schizophrenic. The double Ks of the character's abbreviated name seem to suggest Øie's intention.

Hidden is aesthetically similar to the Norwegian slashers in the way that Øie constructs scares at a high rate. The unhomely house is a place of constant emotion markers that elicit the audience's startle response. The house also seems to be a sublime presence in itself that possesses KK like the Overlook Hotel possesses Jack Torrance in *The Shining*. The mystery man in the hooded sweater symbolises how KK never really left the house, even though he fled town. Like Jack was always the spiritual caretaker of the Overlook, KK's spirit has always remained wandering in the shadows of his mother's house. Even so, Øie ends the film on an ambiguous note, leaving room for interpretation. Such ambiguity is a hallmark of psychological horror, as is the intersection of different worlds, including the subjective and the potentially spiritual. The narrative of psychological horror movies is often meant to remain unresolved: a character's subjective mind filters events and recollections, and the plot becomes unreliable, even impossible. As a storyteller, Pål Øie seems more comfortable in the realm of these mysteries than in the material world of the slasher.

The houses in the woods and wilderness of Norway can be either the terrible places of slasher films or the unhomely spaces of psychological horror films, with both *Hidden* and Øie's later *Dark Woods 2* (*Villmark 2*, 2015) being examples of the overlapping fields of the two subgenres and their applications of particular settings. The *Dark Woods* sequel will be discussed in Chapter 8 as a prime example of the continued importance of water to the Norwegian horror cinema, while the upcoming Chapter 6 will show that even Norway's psychological horror films are rife with the same motif, despite their urban settings.

The psychological horror films of Norway have attracted smaller domestic audiences than the slashers. *Next Door* was the most commercially successful at 113,125 tickets sold, *Hidden* managed 83,822, while *The Monitor* ended up at a relatively modest 78,901 tickets despite being directed by an acclaimed Norwegian auteur and starring Noomi Rapace at the height of her initial fame (*Film & Kino* 2013: 61–3). Reasons are open to speculation, but *The Monitor* certainly did less well with Norwegian critics than Sletaune's films usually do (Reiersen 2011). Nonetheless, *The Monitor* is one of the most aesthetically and thematically interesting films of the Norwegian horror tradition, taking Norway's psychological horror subgenre into territory that has since only been matched by Joachim Trier's *Thelma* and Eskil Vogt's *The Innocents*. All three films are about characters with supernatural abilities that can both hurt and heal.

6. HEALING POWER

Anna must help the ghost of a murdered boy to find rest. Thelma must learn how to focus her powers into healing instead of hurting others. Ida must convince her autistic sister to use her otherworldly abilities of the mind to influence physical reality and oppose evil deeds. *The Monitor* (*Babycall*, Pål Sletaune, 2011), *Thelma* (Joachim Trier, 2017) and *The Innocents* (*De uskyldige*, Eskil Vogt, 2021) are examples in Norwegian horror cinema of characters not just experiencing the fantastic, but actually wielding supernatural powers.

These three films are psychological horror tales that take place in settings typical of the urbanised Norway's modern social democracy, but where not everything is right and bright. There is a hidden darkness in the woods and mountains of this country, but also in the city, where the rich and successful mingle with the less so. Supernatural lead characters Anna, Thelma and Ida are plunged into the very heart of this urban umbra.

If the wilderness of *Cold Prey* (*Fritt vilt*, Roar Uthaug, 2006) represents a slasher fantasy of Norwegian darkness, the cityscapes of *The Monitor*, *Thelma* and *The Innocents* put into focus the smaller and more seemingly realistic premises of stories that even so carry the weight of the supernatural. The gothic influence is traditionally strong in the psychological horror subgenre, and the Norwegian kind is no exception to the rule.

Norwegian gothic: *The Monitor*

All horror has gothic roots. As Fred Botting writes, the gothic was originally a kind of negative aesthetics where darkness provided an opposition to the Enlightenment of the mid-1700s. In particular, it is easy to recognise the psychological horror movie, including the Norwegian branch of the subgenre, in Botting's succinct definition of the gothic: 'Gothic texts are, overtly but ambiguously, not rational, depicting disturbances of sanity and security, from superstitious beliefs in ghosts and demons, displays of uncontrolled passion, violent emotion or flights of fancy to portrayals of perversion and obsession' (2014: 2). Pål Sletaune handled some aspects of this definition in *Next Door* (*Naboer*, 2005), and he would deal with yet more of them in his subsequent horror feature.

The Monitor is the story of Anna (Noomi Rapace), a troubled mother who moves into an anonymous apartment in suburban Oslo with her depressed son Anders (Vetle Qvenild Werring), to hide from her ex-husband. Anna claims that he has attempted to kill the boy, but a final decision in the custody case is pending. Two social workers are monitoring Anna, while she herself monitors the sleeping Anders with a baby alarm that she purchases from the shy but friendly Helge (Kristoffer Joner) in a nearby electronics store. Anna's state of mind is a point of contention, but things reach a tipping point when the baby alarm picks up sounds that appear to be a young boy's screams in the night: 'No! I don't want to! Let go of me!' Helge tells her that the device is capable of picking up signals from other monitors, and Anna becomes convinced that she has unwittingly listened in on a criminal and life-threatening act somewhere in her apartment block.

Anna admits to Helge, the only person she considers a friend, that she experiences memory loss. She also tells him that she sees 'things that I know are not real. It happens every day.' Indeed, when she plays the monitor recording for Helge, there is nothing there but the normal sound of a child crying. Meanwhile, her son Anders befriends a mysterious boy with whom he seems to share a sense of spiritual awareness, as well as a dark history of being abused by adults. Anna's investigation into what she perceives as criminal mistreatment of a child next door is cut short by the authorities' decision to grant her ex-husband custody of Anders. In desperation she attacks the social worker Ole (Stig R. Amdam) with a pair of scissors and jumps from her fifth-floor window with Anders in her arms. Anna dies from the fall, but Anders is gone without a trace. Helge learns from the police that the boy was killed by his father two years earlier, and that much of Anna's existence must have been delusion. However, doubt lingers. Helge himself has met Anders' mystery friend, and this young boy is soon found murdered in the woods thanks to clues that Anna inexplicably left behind.

As in *Next Door*, Sletaune opens with sound before the first shot. We hear Helge's voice from the end of the movie: 'Anna, where is Anders?' When we first meet Anna, she is all alone in the back seat of a car, while Anders seems to appear from out of nowhere when Anna exits the car and stands in front of her new apartment block. At certain points in the movie Sletaune also edits in a way that makes it seem as though social workers Ole and Grete (Maria Bock) disappear into thin air. Rather than seeing them exit through a door, we lose them from one shot to the next, while Anna is standing still in the same spot. It is not too obvious, but for the perceptive viewer it will seem uncanny and portentous. We are led to wonder if they exist at all, and whether or not Anders is real or imagined.

The abused boy who befriends Anders complicates the story of *The Monitor* to a degree that goes beyond either *Next Door* or *Hidden* (*Skjult*, Pål Øie, 2009). He is not merely a figment of Anna's imagination, because we also see him interact with Helge. Moreover, at that point in the film's story the boy is actually dead. In this way the film adds a layer that transcends the question of Anna's state of mind: this is the realm of the supernatural, and the boy is a ghost who visits Helge from the hereafter. We also learn that the sounds Anna heard on the monitor were not a delusion. Somehow, she heard the real murder of a real boy, she saw the body being carried into the parking garage, and she saw the boy's father covering the grave in the woods. Why can Helge also see the dead boy? Within Sletaune's fictional universe it seems logical that he can: Anna is marked by death through the murder of her son, and Helge's mother is awaiting death in her hospital bed. Together they are able to see the other side, to reveal the murder, and help the dead boy to be found. This seems to have been Anna's purpose, to heal the wound of a dead boy who is not yet at peace.

The return of the dead is one of the most, if not *the* most common motifs in horror film. James Kendrick writes that 'the most popular narrative in spiritual horror is a variation on this "return of the repressed" theme in which an unjustly murdered person makes contact with the living in order to solve the mystery of his or her death' (2010: 153). At the turn of the millennium, filmmaker M. Night Shyamalan made his name and reputation with the psychological horror movie *The Sixth Sense* (1999), which tells the story of how a child psychologist tries to help a young boy who claims that he sees dead people. The twist of the story is that the psychologist, Malcolm Crowe (Bruce Willis), is himself dead, and he needs the help of young Cole (Haley Joel Osment) to find peace, in much the same way that the dead boy in *The Monitor* needs the help of Anna and Helge.

A hallmark of the early gothic tale is the prominence of the supernatural, like ghosts or vampires. The gothic *elsewhen* of the classic literature from approximately 1760–1820 formed part of the basis for some of the most

Figure 6.1 Anna and Helge communicate with the dead via baby monitor. (Screenshot from *The Monitor*)

celebrated horror movie cycles: the American Universal films in the 1930s and the British Hammer films in the late 1950s. As David Punter has pointed out, the gothic tale has also been modernised, through the work of authors like Flannery O'Connor and John Hawkes, to arrive in settings closer to our own time and place: 'This "New American Gothic" is said to deal in landscapes of the mind, settings which are distorted by the pressure of the principal characters' psychological obsessions. [...] Violence, rape and breakdown are the key motifs; the crucial tone is one of desensitised acquiescence in the horror of obsession and prevalent insanity' (Punter 1980: 3). Pål Sletaune's psychological horror films can easily be identified in this description of the new gothic. *Next Door* and *The Monitor* are both narrated through a prism of subjective psychological states, and they both deal with the classic gothic motif of the returning dead.

Film critic Tonje Skar Reiersen has pointed out the gothic hallmarks of Sletaune's horror movies, comparing *Next Door* to Edgar Allan Poe's 'The Tell-Tale Heart' (1843) and *The Monitor* to Charlotte Perkins Gilman's 'The Yellow Wallpaper' (1892). Reiersen writes that the narrative twist of *Next Door* is not the real point of the film, but rather the immersion of the viewer in the psychosis of the main character. The attempt to shut something out, or to shut oneself in, is typical of this type of gothic tale: 'Like the killer in "The Tell-Tale Heart" fails to shut out the heartbeat of the dead body, and so is revealed to the police, John fails to cover up his deed. They are both driven to madness because of their crimes, and this – being inside a disoriented, desperate mind – is what gives the story its nerve' (Reiersen 2011).

The Monitor is a rarity in Norwegian horror cinema. First, because it is a ghost story, and second, because it is about a direct threat to the family unit. While the latter is a common motif in horror cinema history, only *The Monitor* and *Ragnarok* (*Gåten Ragnarok*, Mikkel Brænne Sandemose, 2013) play explicitly to this theme of all Norwegian horror-related movies, while *Thelma* and *The Innocents* can be said to hover on its fringes. With this, and through the combination of Anna's and Helge's narrative points of view, *The Monitor* becomes a very different psychological horror film from *Next Door*. Another difference is the way Sletaune clearly structures *The Monitor* as a three-act story. The first act culminates in the reception of a strange radio signal on Anna's baby monitor. The second act mid-point comes when Anna takes Anders on a hike to a lake in the woods: the lake is gone, replaced by a parking lot, and Anders runs from the scene after accusing his mother of lying to him. The turn into the third act is Anna's experience of seeing Anders' friend being drowned in the lake (now there again) by his father. When Anna dies eighty minutes into the film, it is up to Helge to resolve the story. In the film's denouement he follows a drawing that Anna has left behind and finds the boy buried in the woods.

Next Door and *The Monitor* have a significantly lower number of emotion markers than the Norwegian slasher films. They both construct about five such markers, which tells us that they do not attempt to elicit strong and precise emotions as regularly as the slashers do. Psychological horror movies are made to give the audience a different kind of horror experience: the unhomely and creepy sense of unease that builds at a lower tempo and highlights the characters' inner disorientation rather than a threat of physical violence. The spiritual dimension of *The Monitor* is about dead people lingering in the land of the living, ghosts that need help to find peace, and Sletaune's contemplative style effectively underpins his film's thematic issues. Settings are a key to this stylistic thematisation.

Sletaune has told the author that he likes to place his stories in somewhat indistinct settings, meaning that the milieu could be located almost anywhere, at least anywhere Scandinavian. At the same time, it was important to him that the settings of *The Monitor* remained recognisable as a Norwegian suburbia (Sletaune 2016). Like all of Sletaune's movies, the setting of *The Monitor* can be described as a kind of *urban no-particular-place*. The spaces of the film are a grey and dull Oslo, but this is of no particular importance: Anna's story takes place anywhere and nowhere special at the same time. If the settings of *Manhunt* can be described as a mythic rural *Texas, Norway* with no particular geographical anchoring (Iversen 2009), then *Next Door* can be said to take place in an urban *Manchester, Norway*. The spaces of the story could be any Northern European city when Sletaune steers clear of distinguishing geographical or architectural landmarks and shoots mostly interiors. *The Monitor* continues this setting of the indistinct to a point, but people familiar with the eastern parts of Oslo will be able to nail it down this

Figure 6.2 The empty windows of suburban Oslo stare out at Anna as she investigates the source of sounds on her baby alarm. (Screenshot from *The Monitor*)

time: the outskirts of the city, in the Grorud Valley, on the threshold between urban living and nature.

Anna settles in a suburban apartment block, very different from the gothic *elsewhen* with its ancient castles and haunted mansions. In *The Monitor*, hallways and stairwells have a sense of institution, like a hospital, all sterile walls and non-descript doors. On the outside the building is a face of windows, more than 100 of them staring from a grey wall, much like Poe's description of the Usher house's 'vacant eye-like windows' (Vidler 1992: 17). The eyes of Anna's new home look inwards, not out, which is brought to light by Anna's drawing of the building: she draws what is happening on the inside of it, and she cannot stand having her curtains open. Like John in *Next Door* she shuts herself in, but the house has a terrible secret, even if it seems peaceful on the outside. An icy Scandinavian reserve is in evidence, the notion that one should keep to oneself and not stick one's nose in anyone's business, or at the very least not be seen doing it. Draw the curtains and stay quiet.

The motif of staring windows is repeated in the electronics store where Helge works. Dozens of TV screens are mounted on the walls. They are monitors and also a means of communication, technology imbued with mysterious agency in a fundamentally eerie fashion (Fisher 2016: 11). At one point their black and empty windows are staring at Anna, while at a later point a dying woman in a hospital is staring out from the screens at Helge, a painful reminder of his own dying mother. At the end of the film, the conclusion to Anna's and Helge's common story is staring out into the empty store: a news report tells of the dead boy being found and his parents arrested.

This *urban no-particular-place* with its constant presence of staring windows is contrasted in the woods not far from Anna's building. This is Anna's breathing space, hidden from staring eyes, but also the place where the dead boy is buried. She visits the woods several times, and twice she finds the lake that does not really exist. The third time she approaches the edge of the water is after her own death, as Helge narrates a happy ending to Anna's story and she sits down with Anders, enjoying the peace and quiet at last. A fun footnote to the setting is that Sletaune filmed at the same lake that was used for the original *Lake of the Dead* many decades previously (Sletaune 2016).

Traces of gothic literature are plentiful in psychological horror. Some of this is connected to space and time, the settings of the film and how they are utilised, as Kendrick writes about gothic literature: 'an emphasis on the past, the exploration of the aesthetics of fear, and the merging of fantasy and reality' (2010: 147). *Hidden* might be the most obvious example of this in the Norwegian psychological horror subgenre, but *Next Door* and *The Monitor* also mine the gothic depths. Even if their stories unfold in our present time and place, they are thematically gothic tales. Not least are they gothic in terms of their focus on traumatic past events that are repressed and resurfacing, in how characters' rational relationship with the world around them is challenged, and in the way that ghosts and imagined persons interact with the living characters of the story.

Anders' mysterious friend shows up for the first time the day after Anna hears him being murdered on the baby monitor. Since Anders is also dead, it makes sense that only another dead boy can befriend him. The murdered boy needs Anna's help to be found, and Anders provides the link between the boy and his own mother. The connection between the two boys is the horrifying fact that they have both been murdered by their fathers. 'We help each other', they say quietly to one another. Anders also adopts the other boy's bruises. When Anna confronts him about them, Anders says, 'It doesn't hurt. They're not mine.'

The apprehensive relationship between Anna and Helge is founded on the fact that she is an over-protective mother and he is an over-protected son. They understand each other, and during a dinner at Anna's apartment Helge tells her that he grew up in the same building where she now lives. On this occasion Helge also meets the mystery boy, thinking that he is Anders. The boy has knowledge of things about Helge and his dying mother that he cannot possibly know, and Helge leaves in anger, thinking that Anna has told the boy things that she and Helge spoke of in confidence. Right after this, Helge decides to take the doctor's advice to turn off the respirator and let his mother pass away in the hospital. From this point until Anna's death towards the end of the film, Sletaune intensifies Anna's subjective delusions about the threat that she and her son are under. Desperation grows, but spaces do not become distorted the way they were in *Next Door*. Anna's surroundings remain the sober and neutral *urban no-particular-place* where her tragic inner battle is set. In the end Anna writes what amounts to a suicide letter:

> The only thing I must think of is Anders. Without him I do not belong to the world. When they placed him in my lap, I thought: 'Run, Anna! Take him with you and run! Only you can save him!' But I did not. Next time I will run. It will be soon.

She jumps to her death from the window in her son's room, the window that she has covered with curtains in a neurotic fashion ever since she moved in.

The disorientation in *The Monitor* is more temporal than spatial. The spaces of the story remain realistic and perspicuous, even if they are sometimes occupied by people who are not really there. Furthermore, the movie is about the transgression of one world upon another, the real and the spiritual colliding, like so many psychological horror films. Anders and his friend do not belong to the world of the living. The Anders that Anna clings to is from a different time, a time that ceased to be when Anders was murdered two years previously. Sletaune substantiates the temporal disorientation by elliptical edits. Time is contracted, sometimes in a way that makes it seem like persons in the room suddenly appear, sometimes in a way that makes them suddenly disappear. This is strongly reminiscent of one of Sletaune's favourite movies, *The Shining*, which is about 'not simply problems among people but disorientations in time' (Freeland 2000: 234). Where *Next Door* paints the main problem of the story through manipulation of spaces, the distortion of rooms, the problem in *The Monitor* is staged through temporal confusion.

Sletaune has freely admitted that he took major cues from both *The Shining* and early Polanski when crafting his horror genre movies (Brown 2010). However, while Polanski's horror thrillers are clearly geographically fixed, Sletaune always stuck with the *urban no-particular-place* as setting for his psychological horror films. *Next Door* was set almost entirely in two apartments in a non-descript Oslo, although we learned that the apartment next door to John's was not real. Changing from one scene to the next, it was riddled with narrow corridors, impossible angles, and endless amounts of doors and rooms. John was not only taunted by Anne and Kim and their uncanny knowledge of him and his life; he was also haunted by the murder of his great love at his own hands. The walls closed in on John, he found no way to unlock doors, and no way to escape the next-door labyrinth.

The mysterious and distorted neighbouring apartment in *Next Door* echoes Polanski's *Repulsion*, but *The Monitor* has a studied coolness about it which is essential Kubrick. *The Monitor* is shot in a realistic and neutral style where the cold winter daylight provides a grey and sombre tone, the absence of shadows eerily recalling the hotel of *The Shining*. There is nowhere to hide in the impersonal places of the story, and Anna is trapped in broad daylight because the locked room is her own mind. She is also under constant watch by eyes that do not really see, by rows of TV monitors and hundreds of windows on imposing building façades. In his two psychological horror films, Pål Sletaune constructs fundamentally different experiences of dread. In *Next Door* he creates disorientation of space through manipulation of sets and props, while he creates disorientation of time in *The Monitor* by occasional editorial manipulation, and the portrayal of Anna, the supernaturally gifted main character, throughout the movie (Andresen 2017a: 64–5).

Ultimately, Anna heals the hurt of her immediate surroundings. She channels her dead son and is able to communicate clues from the afterlife to Helge, in turn enabling Helge to find the body of the murdered neighbour boy. When Anna dies, her son Anders is also finally at rest. This concept of characters with supernatural powers, people who pass through traumatic experiences in order to arrive at a point of healing the hurts of others, is taken even further in a more recent Norwegian horror film. Joachim Trier's *Thelma* has several points of connection with *The Monitor*, but it is also quite different in the way that it aims to elicit audience reactions to its main character.

Empathy with the Devil: *Thelma* and *The Innocents*

The father who Thelma has come to hate sits in his rowing boat in the middle of the lake, pondering the dark fate of his infant son and the threat of his young adult daughter's paranormal gifts. He smokes his way through a cigarette in quiet preparation for the dreadful act he now sees as inevitable: killing Thelma, his own daughter. It is too late, however, as her newly refocused powers catch up with him. He suddenly bursts into flames and falls into the cold lake to his death, apparently killed from afar. Thelma walks to the lake, dives into the dark water, and vomits a living blackbird when she crawls back ashore. Then she returns to her paralysed mother in the family's country house. Putting a hand on her mother's thigh, Thelma says nothing, then turns and leaves. Before realising it, the mother has stood up from her wheelchair and followed Thelma on her way out of the house. Healed, inexplicably.

The combustion scene and its coda of supernatural healing is the dramatic climax of Joachim Trier's psychological horror film *Thelma* from 2017, and it might seem curious that audiences should cheer Thelma in an act of murder, even when tempered by the act of healing. There is, however, a logic and a method behind this experience, a way of structuring the story and its characters that establishes a sense of empathic engagement with Thelma which is unique in the Norwegian horror genre.

Joachim Trier (born 1974) was educated at the National Film and Television School in England and made his feature film debut in 2006 with *Reprise*, a poetically challenging character drama that won several international awards and established Trier as a young director to watch. His national and international reputation was further enhanced by his subsequent two features, *Oslo,*

August 31st (*Oslo 31. august*) in 2011 and *Louder Than Bombs* in 2015. It might have been unexpected that an acclaimed filmmaker of Trier's type would embark on a genre project, but looking beyond Norway's cinematic traditions, there have been classic examples of directors with seriously artistic and even modernist leanings having a go at horror movies: Roman Polanski doing *Rosemary's Baby*, William Friedkin making *The Exorcist* and Stanley Kubrick creating *The Shining*, to name but a few. They all brought something fresh to an old genre, and Trier would do the same for a Norwegian horror tradition that could be said to have stagnated at the point when *Thelma* appeared.

Thelma (Eili Harboe) grew up in a deeply religious protestant family in rural south-western Norway, and she experiences a great change in her life when she travels to Oslo for university studies. She falls in love with Anja (Kaya Wilkins) and starts to suffer violent seizures that a doctor thinks could have some kind of connection to Thelma's past. As her relationship with Anja intensifies, it becomes apparent that Thelma has supernatural powers: her emotions can affect physical reality. In fact, they have done so before to tragic effect. Her sense of rejection upon the birth of her baby brother led to feelings of jealousy that killed him by displacing him from the family's house into the nearby frozen lake, trapped inside the ice. Thelma's parents fear that her dangerous gift will manifest itself again, a deadly ability that they see in terms of a satanic religious darkness, and they privately weigh the horrible option of saving themselves by killing their daughter.

Thelma's shame about her own feelings of homosexual arousal, triggered by Anja, makes her wish that the object of her feelings was removed, and Anja disappears without trace. Thelma discovers that her own grandmother had the same gift of influencing reality with her emotions, and that the old woman Thelma thought was dead has in fact been silenced in a drug-induced torpor at an institution. Thelma's parents decide to bring Thelma back home in order to drug and kill her, and two questions crystalise: will Thelma survive her parents' murder attempt, and is there a way for her to transcend fear and apply her powers for the good of others?

Thelma essentially destroys her father and heals her mother, being liberated from oppression and taking up her independent life. Many of her actions cannot be evaluated as good or positive, including the taking of her father's life. The viewer's experience of the scenes, the way we root for Thelma in the face of adversity, is founded on two premises: an understanding of the horror genre that Trier utilises for his story, and an empathic engagement with the main character and her traumatic situation.

Trier is known for his portraits of conditions, not for any overtly generic plotting of his films. *Thelma*, however, is clearly a plot-conscious psychological horror movie, yet it still maintains Trier's characteristic interest in probing emotional states and subjective experiences of time, place and events. Trier

Figure 6.3 Thelma crawls from the lake and regurgitates a blackbird, shortly after her father spontaneously combusts and dies in the cold water. (Screenshot from *Thelma*)

and co-screenwriter Eskil Vogt deliberately crafted a story that would adhere to thriller and horror traditions of genre cinema, citing Dario Argento, Alfred Hitchcock and Brian De Palma as inspirations. According to the filmmakers, they wanted to make a plot-driven film. At the same time, the title of the interview appendix to their published screenplay reveals their sharp focus on character in their exploration of the visceral experiences of adolescence: 'Making horror with a view to humanity' (Vogt and Trier 2017: 183–5, 201–3; Andresen 2019: 227–8).

Empathy means feeling a strong emotional connection to somebody else's situation without necessarily making a sympathetic moral evaluation. In short, empathy is *feeling* with them without necessarily *agreeing* with them, a kind of gut-level reaction to someone else's plight. In a review of research on the experience of empathic engagement with fiction, Margrethe Bruun Vaage (2010) suggests a conceptual division into *imaginary* and *bodily* empathy, where the former is clearly cognitively driven, and the latter is much less so. In terms of Norwegian horror cinema, as a viewer, I feel very strongly that Jannicke must survive *Cold Prey*, which is a straight-forward emotional preference. However, I engage more deeply with Thelma, as her interaction with the world and the people around her engenders more complicated emotional conflicts and spiritual consequences.

The film starts with a scene in which the dad (Henrik Rafaelsen) takes aim at six-year-old Thelma with a hunting rifle. He does not pull the trigger, but the viewer's curiosity is certainly piqued. Also, this opening establishes a gut-level empathic connection with Thelma (no matter what a child has done, killing in retribution seems horrifically out of proportion), while at the same time putting the viewer out of alignment with her (she does not see what nearly happens, so we know more about her situation than she does). I might be able to share her emotional states and reactions later in the film, based on how Trier sets up the character and her surroundings, despite not having experienced such things myself. I will argue that three scenes early in the movie are decisive in structuring and accommodating the viewer's empathic connection with the main character, laying the groundwork for the drama that follows (Andresen 2019: 230). Within the first ten minutes, Trier creates this trio of small but important scenes that launch Thelma's arc and provide a starting point for her journey. This ultimately leads to the violent, but also liberating, ending previously discussed.

The first essential launching scene is Thelma's arrival at the University of Oslo, where her tiny person is slowly picked up in a wide shot of the myriad crowd of people in the campus courtyard. She is nearly invisible among all the students and others, lonely but not alone. In the second essential launching scene, her parents call from back home to check on Thelma, asking what she is making for dinner in her apartment that night. The place where Thelma lives is nearly void of personal effects, the grey and impersonal mise-en-scène tells of a lack of belonging. Mother and Father want to know details about her lecture schedules, and this near interrogation creates a sense that Thelma is neither allowed the independence of adulthood, nor to choose her solitude. The third essential launching scene of this three-part sequence is Thelma's violent seizure in the students' reading hall. This happens when she meets Anja for the very first time, at a moment when Thelma is truly seen. Thelma clearly has a medical problem that she does not seem to be aware of, and Trier adds horror tropes to the scene by having a flock of birds smash into the reading hall windows. The other characters in the hall see and hear the birds – this is not staged as Thelma's subjective impression, which effectively positions *Thelma* as a supernatural horror film.

Thelma, as is common for films in the psychological horror subgenre, is certainly open to narrative interpretation. However, this is first and foremost a film about a main character with supernatural abilities, and this character and her experiences represent a new turn in Norwegian horror cinema, a direction that co-screenwriter Vogt would further pursue with *The Innocents* a few years later. While *Thelma* is a psychological horror movie with elements of the supernatural or paranormal, it is also the story of a character's coming of age. This type of tale is uncommon in Norwegian horror, although it is prominent in the transnational subgenre of psychological horror, Brian De Palma's *Carrie* being a classic example. The filmmakers opt to situate the potentially evil force of the story inside the main character herself, imbuing the aesthetics of their predefined genre with a character arc that positions the viewer in a clearly empathic relationship with her (Vogt and Trier 2017: 183–203).

Why would the viewer empathise with Thelma when her supernatural powers have cost the life of her baby brother? It is evident that the audience often cheers the hero on to fight and even kill bad guys, the action film being a prime example. Thelma is also no more than six years old at the time of her brother's death, meaning that she does not understand the horrific potential of her powers. Thelma can do great harm, but the story is about her journey of discovery: her power can also be used for the good of others.

This journey, however, is filled with the anxiety and humiliation that provides the viewer with cause for empathic engagement. In *The Monitor*, Anna's situation is that she has experienced the trauma of her son's father seriously hurting the boy. In fact, Anna claims that the father has tried to kill Anders. She is currently in hiding with her son, but her neurotically over-protective and paranoid behaviour drains all sense of joy from his everyday life. It is hard for the viewer to actually like Anna, despite sympathising with her situation. The difference in *Thelma* is that we are exposed to many scenes where Thelma is smart and funny and kind, while regularly being ridiculed or humiliated for either her religious faith or her independent thoughts and opinions. The viewer engages empathically with her in these situations, particularly because Trier portrays her as a person with many positive attributes, in contrast to the overwhelmingly neurotic possessiveness that dominates the Anna character.

In a very important and very humiliating scene early in the film, Mother (Ellen Dorrit Petersen) and Father visit Thelma in Oslo. They travel there from their home in the south-west of Norway, the region of the country known as the Norwegian Bible Belt, and the three of them have dinner at a Chinese restaurant. Thelma talks about her frustration with the way many Christians believe that the Earth was created 6,000 years ago. The notion is absurd to her, but her father stops her dead in the tracks: "You talk like you know everything." Thelma's attempt at meaningful conversation falls completely flat, her parents reinforcing a central tenet of her upbringing: that she should not think she is better than others. However, she is undeniably different from others.

Uncomfortably for Thelma's parents, seated at the next table is a homosexual male couple. Being devout Protestant Christians from the most conservatively religious region of Norway, it presumably grieves them that their own daughter is a lesbian. In a film history perspective, moreover, *Thelma* highlights an issue of under-representation: Thelma is one of very few homosexual main characters to be found in the history of Norwegian cinema. In fact, she is the only homosexual main character identified in the past decade of cinematic features in Norway (Norwegian Film Institute 2020). This disturbing reality, coupled with the unique way in which Trier tells Thelma's story in both sympathetic and empathetic terms, makes the character and the film a truly rare kind of Norwegian horror experience.

The friendship between Thelma and Anja turns romantic and sexual, and Thelma enjoys being a young and independent adult, for once. However, this process includes drinking alcohol, which she immediately feels very guilty about and confesses to her father on the telephone. In a manipulative and controlling conversation, her father forgives her this trespass, and Thelma falls apart in heart-breaking sobs as soon as she puts the phone down. The control that Thelma's parents command over her is clearly a kind of emotional abuse. Trier intensifies this sense of devaluation and humiliation when Anja mysteriously disappears, seemingly the result of Thelma willing away that which arouses her. Thelma travels home to her parents in the rural southwest and is subjected to a ritual of repentance by her father, who claims that Anja must surely have fallen in love with Thelma because Thelma willed it to happen, not because Anja truly loves her. The homosexual attraction between the two young women is unnatural in his eyes. As her father watches, Thelma sits on her knees, facing the kitchen wall, and prays that the Lord 'create in me a pure heart'.

This type of emotional abuse is one-of-a-kind in Norwegian horror cinema, although Trier is careful not to portray Thelma's parents as one-dimensional monsters. Their sense of loss, dread and perplexity is understandable, but their abuse of Thelma reinforces our empathy with her, and eventually it crosses a physical border too. A subsequent scene in which the father bathes his drugged and naked adult daughter is mercifully brief, but still makes a ghastly impression. The viewer's empathy with Thelma, the bodily sense of her fundamentally unfair shame and humiliation, is strengthened manifold by this delicately tactile addition of physical abuse to her already overwhelming distress.

This clearly builds to the purge that becomes necessary for Thelma to find her way and turn her powers to the aid of others: the killing of the father. Horror films are inherently violent, and such ways of overcoming repression are more easily accepted here than in less fantastic genres. Her father's seeming self-combustion and drowning is not explicitly staged as Thelma's doing, but the implication is clear enough at this point in the story. Her act of supernatural murder is a case of self-preservation, in line with genre conventions. Her parents have agreed to kill her, and Thelma must survive. Once the deed is done, Thelma proceeds to heal her paralysed mother and then leaves for a fresh start in Oslo. Anja reappears to join her once this balance and purpose in Thelma's life is finally achieved.

The southwest of Norway is a region of the country where religious beliefs and dogma remain particularly strong. Trier's use of religious motifs in *Thelma* is certainly a hallmark of the international horror genre, but his is actually the only overtly thematic use of this in Norwegian horror cinema. The coming-of-age story is also a classic horror narrative, and yet *Thelma* is the only such example in Norwegian horror to date. A further distinction for *Thelma* in terms of Norwegian horror is the portrayal of its main character. Anna in *The Monitor* is an unreliable source of story information, something she even admits herself, and we also get the clear impression that her overreactions and paranoia impair the quality of life for her young son. The only time that Thelma, on the other hand, does something bad to another person is when she is a girl of only six years. Apart from this, she is routinely humiliated and dominated as a young adult, while struggling to be kind to others and find her own direction in life.

If *Thelma* touches on the morally challenging issue of frightened adults judging a six-year-old girl for the deed that killed her baby brother, *The Innocents* bases most of its drama on the heart-wrenching notion that children can cause great harm without being evil. The film centres on Ida (Rakel Lenora Fløttum), who is nine years old and moving to a new apartment in suburban Oslo with her parents and her autistic older sister Anna (Alva Brynsmo Ramstad), during the lazy days of summer vacation. Ida is frustrated with her parents' expectations that she act beyond her years in taking care of her sister, but she makes a new and mysterious friend, Ben (Sam Ashraf). At the same time, Anna experiences a strong bond with Aisha (Mina Yasmin Bremseth Asheim), and all four children go about exploring their new friendships, as well as the apartment blocks and woods in their neighbourhood.

As the children's games turn deadly serious, it becomes apparent that some of them wield supernatural powers. Ben has the telekinetic ability to move objects without physically touching them, which extends to influencing other people's minds and bodies from afar, sometimes to gruesome effect. Aisha, for her part, is able to communicate telepathically with Anna, which soon results in the first coherent words and sentences that her family has ever heard from her. Darkness descends when Ben channels his abilities into murdering a playground bully and his own depressed single mother. In a horrific scene Ben also influences the murder of Aisha at the hands of her own mother, the rage within him attempting to remove all checks on its power. Ida attempts to kill Ben in order to put a stop to the spiralling events, but in the end it is her sister Anna who reveals powers equal to Ben's, effectively shutting down his body in the film's emotionally devastating climax.

Eskil Vogt (born 1974) has made his name as writer and director of the drama film *Blind* (2014), and the acclaimed co-screenwriter on all of Joachim Trier's feature films: *Reprise*, *Oslo, August 31st*, *Louder Than Bombs*, *Thelma*, and most recently *The Worst Person in the World*, a 2021 (arguably) romantic comedy that was selected for the main programme at the Cannes Film Festival in France. *Louder Than Bombs* also received this nomination in 2015, but *The Worst Person in the World* was the first Norwegian language film to be selected for the Cannes main programme since Anja Breien's *Next of Kin* (*Arven*) in 1979. *The Innocents* itself, written and directed by Vogt, was simultaneously selected for the festival's 'Un Certain Regard' programme, reaffirming Vogt's national and international standing as a filmmaker.

Figure 6.4 Ben and Anna's trial face-off in the woods in Eskil Vogt's supernatural thriller, foreshadowing the final showdown. (Screenshot from *The Innocents*)

The early idea for *The Innocents* was hatched when Vogt was working on the concept that would ultimately become *Thelma*, and it developed out of the filmmaker's thoughts about how his young son saw the world so differently from his jaded adult self (Vogt 2021). Thus, the fantastic is completely real to the children of *The Innocents*, and supernatural events like the final showdown between Anna and Ben are sensed by children and animals, but not by the adults around them. The philosophical issue at the heart of the film is massive, as Vogt explained to *The Hollywood Reporter*: 'Are we born as innocent angels? Or are we born as egomaniac sociopaths and then have to learn morals and empathy and be part of the social contract?' (Ritman 2021). The film seems to say that the latter is Vogt's view.

The setting for the story of *The Innocents* is very similar to what we saw earlier in *The Monitor*. In fact, the films were both shot in the Grorud Valley of eastern Oslo, and the people of the story are in both cases the less well-off inhabitants of the modern Norwegian social democracy. Another similarity with *The Monitor*, and also with *Thelma*, is that the premise of the dramatic situation is the main characters' relocation and an attempt to establish a new everyday life. The biggest difference is that the main characters of *The Innocents* are four children at the ages of 9 to 11, and that two of them, Ben and Aisha, are of a minority immigrant background. The latter is a representational rarity in Norwegian cinema, and although *The Innocents* has been on the receiving end of criticism for portraying the children and families of immigrant backgrounds in a way that could propagate stereotypes, it is commendable as a first in Norwegian horror's character gallery.

Vogt's film depicts the clashing and overlapping of different worlds, in a way reminiscent of the thrillers of M. Night Shyamalan. The director works well with celebrated cinematographer Sturla Brandth Grøvlen in creating what I will call borderline images. There is the simple yet effective shot of the apartment block exterior, a sheer wall of concrete and windows, so uncomfortably close to the forest that looms right at the edge of the apparent safety of homes, threatening to invade the known with the darkness of the unknown. There is the overhead shot of the locked front door to Ida and Anna's apartment, Anna gripping the handle on one side while Aisha silently grips the other side, their minds meeting while their physical bodies are unseen to each other. These borderline images contribute to creating a dense field of tension in which the secret world of the children reaches magical and horrifying depths of expression.

Vogt achieves this without resorting to clichés. A case in point is how *The Innocents* eschews predictable tropes of horror sound design in favour of a subtly layered soundscape, courtesy of sound designer Gisle Tveito, which is sometimes built around the sound of Anna's spinning of casserole lids on the floor. For example, the clanging and whirring of the spinning lids is made into a tense sound effect in the scene where Ben applies his mental powers to fatally wound his mother: he makes a frying pan fly across the room to knock her unconscious, and then tips a pot of sausages to splash boiling water over her legs on the floor, all to the steadily intensifying sound of whirring lids. Much like the absence of jump scares throughout the film gives it a low-key feel, the originality of the sound design makes the tale of *The Innocents* seem realistic, somehow, to an uncomfortable degree. Vogt avoids cheaply generic emotion markers to elicit audience reactions, and so he builds an unusually strong sense of cognitively driven empathy with the four troubled children at the film's core, including the one who could on the surface be seen as the story's antagonist: Ben.

The depiction of Ben and his situation, a nagging and unsupportive single mother and the absence of any apparent father figure exacerbating his loneliness, makes it impossible to judge him for the abuse of his supernatural powers. The viewer's empathic engagement with children who suffer difficult circumstances makes the horrific violence of the story and the fatal showdown where Ben dies delicately ambiguous experiences. Enthralling yet horrific, exciting yet tragic. Moreover, Vogt's film adds weight to the question of horror fiction set in a successful social democracy: is modern Norway truly a classless society, and is the welfare state equally safe and supportive for all citizens of the realm? The answer is no, and here lies a seed of nightmares that underpin much of the last two decades of Norwegian horror cinema.

Social-democratic nightmares

Both Ben and Aisha are children of the Norwegian modern-day working class, born to parents of immigrant backgrounds and limited means, and living in the traditionally working-class parts of eastern suburban Oslo. In the shadow that is cast by the towering image of the prosperous and equitable social-democratic Norwegian society, it remains an empirical fact that the rich have gotten much richer while the poor have stayed relatively poor.

Since I have asked in earlier chapters what are the hallmarks of Norwegian horror, the key answer to which is the use of nature and landscapes as the source and site of horror, one could reasonably ask what these films might tell us about the particulars of horror in a social-democratic society. The Nordic welfare model is internationally well-known, if sometimes deeply misunderstood, and these films are produced in such a country. As I pointed out in Chapter 1, through my discussion of Nordic noir and its relation to Nordic horror, social criticism is a hallmark of such crime fiction, in particular a lament for the apparent end of the Nordic welfare model's golden age in the decades from 1950 to 1980. As I explained in the opening chapter, Norway is certainly a generally prosperous and wealthy country, especially in the wake of discovering oil in the 1960s. However, the income and particularly the wealth is not evenly distributed throughout the population. In fact, inequality increases steadily.

Since the 1980s, income and wealth distribution in Norway has increasingly favoured the country's richest people, and particularly those with large and growing, often inherited, fortunes. After several post-war decades dominated by the Labour Party and the construction and expansion of the welfare state, the 1980s saw a political shift to the right, away from leftist ideas of collective programs and towards an apparently British- and American-influenced brand of capitalism and neoliberalism inspired by the governments of Margaret Thatcher and Ronald Reagan. In the forty years since the reorientation effected by the centre-right government of Prime Minister Kåre Willoch, who was in office from 1981 to 1986, the people of Norway have become increasingly unequal in terms of income and particularly wealth, the richest few steadily pulling ahead of everyone else. The available statistics show this quite clearly, even if the numbers are inevitably obscured by the fact that the richest Norwegians hide much of their wealth in tax havens abroad (Statistics Norway 2018 and 2020; Gitmark 2021).

Meanwhile, common Norwegians suffer the humiliation of not being able to afford proper dental care, professional eye care or psychological treatments. Although Norwegian health care is universal on paper, dentists and opticians are not covered by the public system, leaving most people's teeth and eyes dependent on the availability of private funds. Psychological treatment is covered by the health care system, but psychologists for public coverage are few and far between, leaving those who cannot afford private clinics to wait in line for months on end. Over the past decade, lower-income families with children have particularly seen their purchasing power decline in general (Lorch-Falch and Tomter 2021).

Similarly, working-class people in Norway experience greater difficulty buying homes in a perpetually booming housing market, particularly in the bigger cities and especially in Oslo. A schism widens between those who can afford to buy their homes and those forced to rent them. Young people with well-off parents who can aid them in securing increasingly expensive homes easily pull away from those who have less, contributing further to the growing inequity of wealth in Norway. Recent research by Norwegian sociologists Marianne Nordli Hansen and Maren Toft states it quite clearly: who your parents are, and how much money they have, matters more to the distribution of Norwegian wealth than it has done in a long time. This mechanism has grown much stronger in the past twenty-five years due to lenient or absent taxation of wealth and inheritance. In short, the attainment of capital versus the acquisition of debt strongly promotes and increases the dominance of 'the sons and daughters of the economic upper class' (Hansen and Toft 2021).

The social-democratic nightmare is the realisation that social democracy is broken. Or worse, that it does not exist anymore. Simply put, in our days of globalised capitalism, the social-democratic Scandinavian and Nordic ideal may be just a fading memory. The nightmare is waking up from a dream to find that the outwardly national-romantic utopia is something else on the inside, a dystopia beneath the surface. Norway is a paradise for the wealthy, but not all Norwegians are wealthy, let alone super-wealthy. In short, Norway is not what the equitable image of the country makes it out to be. The social-democratic nightmare is that the social-democratic dream of equality is a thing of the past.

These things are represented in *The Monitor* by Anna being a low-income single mother, in *Thelma* by its title character coming from a modest background and embarking on a higher education that might increase her income but not likely her wealth, and by the main characters of *The Innocents* being children of parents with limited means and little to pass on that could help their kids advance up the social ladder. These are thematic threads through some of the Norwegian horror cinema, and they are certainly universal issues, but the question remains: what is the unique appeal of Norwegian, and thereby social-democratic, horror?

The water, snow and ice of *Dark Woods* and *Cold Prey* are aesthetic hallmarks of Norwegian horror, while locating thematic hallmarks is considerably more complicated. After all, the emergence of Norwegian horror cinema after 2000 was influenced chiefly by American, and to some extent European, subgenres of horror. Granted, the typically Norwegian high level of trust in authorities is reflected in the lack of, say, police bad guys. *The Monitor* adds to this a story about a woman who is practically in the care of government officials who deal with her housing and general welfare. That film also portrays a bleak suburban setting dominated by non-descript exteriors and sterile interiors in a way that both Norwegians and Swedes would generally recognise as authentically Scandinavian. Anna of *The Monitor* seems to somehow disappear into this grey non-place where her individuality remains unseen by the cold mechanics of bureaucracy. Certainly, *The Monitor* and *The Innocents* both shed their particular light on the dark side of a deceptively glorious modern Norway, where utopia is increasingly reserved only for the few.

On the other hand, even if a character like John in *Next Door* lives in social-democratic Norway, it is hard to see his crime and psychosis as particular. Even the more exterior-bound *The Monitor* seems to handle national specificity in a somewhat superficial way, as does *The Innocents*, as a clearly interesting setting for fundamentally universal stories and characters. Indeed, as I have pointed out, such tales of psychological horror have a long tradition not only in the cinema, but also in the literature of gothic authors like Edgar Allan Poe. If *The Monitor* successfully creates a social-democratic gothic landscape, its resonance with audiences both at home and abroad would clearly depend greatly on the universality of its story and plot. Viewers in Norway have been drawn to their national horror cinema at least partially because of its adherence to transnational genre aesthetics, while viewers abroad would likely be attracted to not just the exotic Nordic settings, but also the generically recognisable and applicable stories and characters. As I showed in Chapters 3 and 4, the Norwegian slashers are not that different even from classic American forebears, except for their settings and landscapes.

There might not be a profound answer to the question of social-democratic hallmarks in the Norwegian horror cinema tradition, beyond the simple fact that bad things also happen in good places. Happy countries also have unhappy people and terrible violence. Indeed, it is clear from recent studies in Norway that general national wealth does not necessarily equal happiness (Nes et al 2021). Despite material prosperity and the protection of the welfare state, Norwegians are like anyone else in their search for meaning: it will not be found in wealth alone, not even in the Nordic absence of unrest. What horror films have always treated is the dark side of human nature. A Nordic utopia could not neuter human nature, even if such a utopia truly existed, and the dark side exists in Norway and Norwegians just like anywhere and anyone else. What the Norwegian horror cinema ultimately achieves, at least in the slasher and psychological horror subgenres discussed so far, is to pinpoint not so much the dark side of a modern social democracy, but how the dark side of human nature *works* and *feels* and *looks* and *sounds* in a peaceful country like modern-day Norway.

Norwegian horror appeals because it is sufficiently universal, not because it is altogether unique. It wraps fairly universal tales and characters in the landscapes and settings of a modern Nordic country on the edge of the Arctic. These aesthetic hallmarks would also feature prominently in the crossbreed type of horror that has come to dominate Norwegian horror cinema in recent years, but they would be amped up in terms of the fantastic. The creatures, motifs and settings of Norwegian folktales and sagas would play a major part in the growing line of Norwegian horror hybrids.

7. FANTASTIC HORROR HYBRIDS

The turn to genre in Norwegian cinema after 2000 created a tradition of Norwegian horror. The slasher film in particular had proven popular with national audiences, but the psychological horror subgenre had also provided commercially and artistically successful films. Taking the entertainment value further, filmmakers would soon rip another leaf out of Hollywood's book and combine horror tropes with comedy, action-adventure and found footage in high-concept genre hybrids. The debate about Norwegian cinema's relationship with Hollywood would continue, while audiences in Norway flocked to genre entertainment.

There is much genre fiction among the most popular films in Norwegian film history, examples being the animated comedy *The Pinchcliffe Grand Prix* (*Flåklypa Grand Prix*, Ivo Caprino, 1975), the action movie *Pathfinder* (*Veiviseren*, Nils Gaup, 1987), the comedy *Elling* (Petter Næss, 2001), the war film *Max Manus* (Joachim Rønning and Espen Sandberg, 2008) and the disaster movie *The Wave* (*Bølgen*, Roar Uthaug, 2015). The Norwegian horror movies are no commercial match for these, but some of them make an impressive showing in cinemas. In particular, horror tropes have seeped into broader cinema entertainment in the form of genre hybrids.

Tommy Wirkola's *Dead Snow* (*Død snø*) from 2009 was a zombie movie where dark humour mixed with splatter horror, and André Øvredal's *Troll Hunter* (*Trolljegeren*) from 2010 was a found-footage mockumentary that also mixed comedy and horror. Furthermore, the action adventure was combined with monster horror in Mikkel Brænne Sandemose's *Ragnarok* (*Gåten Ragnarok*) from 2013. Indeed, when horror has taken part in Norwegian genre hybrids, it has usually done so in the shape of monsters.

The monsters of Norway: Trolls and zombies

One might think that trolls have been regulars in Norwegian cinema, but they have not. Apart from the puppet short films of animator Ivo Caprino in the 1960s, these mythical beasts of the wilderness have been conspicuously absent from Norwegian movies. Most likely they would have been too complicated and costly to realise in the days before CGI, but perhaps one also needs to view Norwegian culture, history and folklore from the outside to appreciate their significance and uniqueness. These creatures have finally entered Norwegian cinema with a new generation of filmmakers who are more naturally attuned to Hollywood aesthetics than before. Unlike the unconventional Swedish troll tale of recent years – *Border* (2018) by Ali Abbasi – Norway's first troll tales would sit unapologetically in the category of high concept entertainment. After their long absence, trolls roared into their Norwegian live-action cinema debut with André Øvredal's *Troll Hunter* in 2010.

In legends and folklore, trolls are fantastic creatures that dwell in the Nordic woods and mountains. In the Middle Ages, such beasts were seen as detrimental to religious virtue, and Norwegian law in the late 1200s demanded harsh punishment for anyone who nurtured contact with trolls. These laws were part of the Christian conquest of the country, and the opposition between civilised Christianity and the barbaric trolls of heathen folklore endures in the modern notion of trolls as hostile to people in general, and Christians in particular. During the European witch hunts in the Middle Ages, the accused in Norway were actually labelled *troll folk*, not witches. Most creatures of Nordic folklore were thus demonised, but trolls made a national-romantic comeback as powerful symbols of Norwegian wilderness with the literary collection of folktales during the 1800s. However, could they be more than fantasy?

André Øvredal (born 1973) was educated at the former Brooks Institute of Photography in California, and he was a prolific commercials director before turning his attention to feature film. The found footage that comprises Øvredal's debut *Troll Hunter* is the video recordings that have been left behind by currently missing students from Volda University College in western Norway, a real-world school that has educated journalists and documentary filmmakers since the 1990s.

The recordings show the students investigating what appears to be illegal bear killings in the area, trailing the suspected poacher Hans (Otto Jespersen). The journalist Thomas (Glenn Erland Tosterud), sound technician Johanna (Johanna Mørck) and photographer Kalle (Tomas Alf Larsen) follow Hans around the tangibly Norwegian autumn landscapes of fjords, woods and mountains, all draped in drizzling rain and orange foliage. The case takes an unexpected turn when local hunters suggest that bear cadavers have in fact been dumped around the countryside. Does Norway really have an escalating bear problem, or does the officially sanctioned bear story cover up something else entirely?

One dark night the students lose sight of Hans in the woods, but after a while he suddenly comes running towards them from out of the tall trees, shouting: 'Trolls!' Indeed, Hans claims that he is not hunting bears, but trolls. Furthermore, he is doing so in a job for the Norwegian government. Increasingly frustrated with life as a secret agent tasked with keeping the Norwegian troll stock in check, Hans invites the documentary students to follow him around as he attempts to deal with a disturbance that drives trolls out of their natural and protected remote habitats and into populated areas of the country.

The sceptical students go about documenting Hans' nocturnal journeys around the fjords and mountains of western Norway, their camera and microphone providing him with an opportunity to tell the tale of Norway's biggest secret: the actual existence of trolls. He claims to work for the Secret Troll Service, stating that his job is 'to kill all trolls that break out of their territory and get close to people'. This is a lonely and unglamorous chore, and Hans feels that it is time to reveal to the public what is really going on, partially to serve the greater good and partially to give the troll authorities their comeuppance for underpaying him.

With the students on Hans' tail, and the bureaucrat Finn (Hans Morten Hansen) being agitated by this potential disclosure of a state secret, the hunt for escaping trolls steadily becomes more and more dangerous. Camera operator Kalle is secretly a devout Christian, and it is well-known from folktales that trolls hate Christians and can smell Christian blood in their vicinity. Consequently, Kalle comes to a grisly end when a group of Mountain Kings catch his scent in a cave. Kalle is replaced by Malica (Urmila Berg-Domaas), who might fare better on account of being Muslim, and Hans brings the students onto the high plateau of the Dovre mountains to confront the ultimate cause of the unrest: a raging, giant Jötunn troll who has chased all other types of trolls out of their habitats. We do not learn what ultimately becomes of Hans and the students, as several agents of the Secret Troll Service arrive to pursue them and shut down the documentary project. The students attempt to flee, and their camera drops to the ground. Text on the screen tells us that the footage we have seen is all that is left of those who set out to reveal the truth about Norway's biggest secret.

Troll Hunter is a horror comedy, a film on the fringe of the horror genre. Fear and amusement are two quite fundamental human emotions, and it should come as no surprise that both horror and comedy are enduring and consistently

FANTASTIC HORROR HYBRIDS

Figure 7.1 Norway's biggest secret, quite literally, is revealed to be the Jötunn troll, itself a mountain in the mountains of Dovre. (Screenshot from *Troll Hunter*)

popular film genres, as is the horror comedy combination (Hallenbeck 2009: afterword). The comedy has always been a highly adaptive genre, being easily applied to parodies of other genres and just as easily coupled with other genres into hybrids (Neale 2000: 66). As far back as James Whale's horror classic *Frankenstein* in 1931 there was a touch of comedy in the characterisation and performance of the Fritz character as played by Dwight Frye, and the same director fine-tuned this genre hybridisation in the less well-known *The Old Dark House* in 1932.

Trolls would also show up in the Norwegian-Canadian animated children's film *Troll: The Tale of a Tail* (Kevin Munroe and Kristian Kamp, 2018), an adventure story with both comedic and scary elements in the mix. At the time of writing, these terrifying creatures are set to have another high-concept action outing in Roar Uthaug's forthcoming monster movie *Troll* (2022) on Netflix, but Øvredal's *Troll Hunter* will remain a curiously ground-breaking genre hybrid and also a technological pioneering work. What sets it apart in terms of tone is the highly successful blend of horror and comedy. Øvredal's film takes delicious advantage of the comic timing expertise of Norwegian comedians like Otto Jespersen as Hans, and Robert Stoltenberg as the Polish bear hunter who supplies cadavers to cover up the troll problem. At the same time, it handles its preposterous premise with a straight face and is all the funnier, and scarier, for it.

Comedy and horror share a particular formal trait: the episodic escalation of the narrative tension (Paul 1994: 416–17). Both humour and fear are often built in tableaux, from the early chuckle or shudder to the climactic orgies of

NORWEGIAN NIGHTMARES

Figure 7.2 Hans the troll hunter, underplayed by comedian Otto Jespersen. (Screenshot from *Troll Hunter*)

laughter or fright, moving from one set piece to the next in the tradition of what Tom Gunning has called 'the cinema of attraction' ([1986] 2006). In *Troll Hunter*, every episode within the film is built around Hans' attempts to handle and neutralise the trolls, culminating in his confrontation with the giant Jötunn at Dovre. The film utilises the large physical size and savage temperament of these fantastic creatures of Norwegian folklore, and then juxtaposes this against the understated humour of Jespersen's performance. 'You can forget the fairytales,' he says, 'trolls are animals, carnivores.' Director Øvredal achieves a delicate balance of horror and comedy in the way that Jespersen approaches every incredible situation with a stoic and even jaded sense of routine, while the frighteningly photo-realistic trolls threaten death and destruction upon the students, and possibly the entire nation, if left unchecked.

The film's creatures are based on the troll drawings and paintings of artist Theodor Kittelsen, whose works from the early 1900s often accompany the classic folktale collections of authors Peter Christen Asbjørnsen and Jørgen Moe. These representations of trolls are souvenir mainstays in the Norwegian tourist industry, and *Troll Hunter* elegantly exploits this motif of national romanticism. In fact, the characters and plots of the folktales are often horrific: the trolls feed on rocks, they smell Christian blood from afar, and sunlight makes them either burst or turn to stone. Here is located both the threat and the solution. A gigantic lamp mounted on Hans' jeep is capable of projecting enough ultraviolet light to disable the angriest trolls.

FANTASTIC HORROR HYBRIDS

Figure 7.3 'The troll that ponders how old it is' ('Trollet som grunner på hvor gammelt det er'), by artist Theodor Kittelsen in 1911, is one of the significant templates for the modern visualisation of trolls. (Public domain)

The film's humour is mostly created by the friction between the wide-eyed documentary students and the laconic and world-weary Hans. There is also a comic juxtaposition of the utterly fantastic trolls on one side and Finn's carboard-dry bureaucratic approach to the problem on the other. Bear attacks and tornadoes are lied into existence to cover up the truth, and high-voltage power lines run in incomprehensible circles across the mountain plateau to fence in the giant Jötunn. Hans is incredulous at people's willingness to believe every smokescreen that Finn conjures: 'That people don't even *notice* huge beasts *thundering* across the fields and *razing* the woods like this ...', Hans trails off.

Troll Hunter garnered significant interest in the UK and the US, and it was subsequently optioned for a potential Hollywood remake. That project never materialised, but Øvredal soon embarked on a Hollywood career of his own, and he has to date directed the American horror films *The Autopsy of Jane Doe* (2016) and *Scary Stories to Tell in the Dark* (2019), while also making the fantasy action film *Mortal* (*Torden*, 2020) in his native Norway. With *Troll*

Hunter, Øvredal created a mockumentary that not only brought mythical creatures to life on the big screen, but also succeeded both at home and abroad through the use of authentic Norwegian exteriors.

The settings are of paramount importance to the staging of *Troll Hunter*'s one-of-a-kind premise: western Norway, the Jotunheimen mountain range and the Dovre plateau, drenched in the permanently grey weather of autumn and early winter. Norwegians will certainly recognise the settings as authentic, and audiences abroad will most likely pick up on how they are different from what you would expect from American films of the same kind. The realistic settings and the found footage aesthetic underpin the film's biggest attraction, the audio-visual appearance of photo-realistic trolls. These monsters are specifically Nordic in their origin, hailing all the way back to Norse mythology, but found their modern form in the folktale traditions of the 1800s and particularly in Kittelsen's enduring illustrations.

However, more international monsters have also appeared in the horror cinema of Norway. The living dead have been a feature of the horror film for about ninety years, at least since Victor Halperin's *White Zombie* in 1932, starring Bela Lugosi in the leading role (Kay [2008] 2012: 5). As Rikke Schubart has written, the cinema precursor to the zombie creature is the somnambulist in *The Cabinet of Dr. Caligari*, 'the nightmare of a human being that loses their identity' (1993: 25). Other early examples of this particular horror monster can be seen in such diverse films as *The Ghost Breakers* (George Marshall, 1940), *I Walked with a Zombie* (Jacques Tourneur, 1943) and *Invasion of the Body Snatchers* (Don Siegel, 1956), and the zombie phenomenon would often be related to voodoo possession and magical reanimation of dead bodies. However, cinema zombies as we know them today were to a large extent invented by George A. Romero in *Night of the Living Dead* in 1968, a groundbreaking low-budget feature that set the standard for the diverse and extensive subgenre that has subsequently come to be known as the zombie film. These creatures either rise from the dead or are infected by mind-altering viruses, and they are in either case reduced to non-thinking killing machines that also tend to have an appetite for human flesh. Zombie movies often combine splatter horror with science fiction, apocalyptic or post-apocalyptic stories and settings, and sometimes comedy.

Tommy Wirkola (born 1979) made his feature film debut in 2007 with a parody of Quentin Tarantino's 2003 martial arts drama *Kill Bill*, titled *Kill Buljo*. His early work was marked by a sure grip of genre aesthetics and a willingness to apply a sense of ridiculous exaggeration to sinister and violent premises. In many ways Wirkola was the right filmmaker for the right time, and his *Dead Snow* (*Død snø*, 2009) could certainly not have happened a decade earlier. *Dead Snow* gorges on extreme and bloody violence, brutal maiming and death, the losing of limbs and the squirting of body fluids.

In short, Wirkola's breakthrough movie revels in the disgusting opening of bodies beyond repair. It is not just a zombie film but also a splatter exercise, a horror subtype that does not necessarily aim to scare its audience, but rather 'to *mortify* them with scenes of explicit gore' (McCarty 1984: 1). In the 1980s and 1990s, the very attraction of the splatter movie lay beyond the borders of public funding that Norwegian filmmakers relied on, cast away to the dark underbelly of video culture by the censorship laws of a largely genre-incompetent Norwegian establishment society.

With the liberalisation of censorship laws and the political effort to cultivate a more commercially viable Norwegian film production, major cultural shifts that were outlined in Chapter 2, audiences welcomed Wirkola's zombie splatter. *Dead Snow* combined several attractions that proved popular: a playful handling of genre conventions and the expectations of its genre-competent target audience, massive amounts of blood and gore, and the black and tasteless irony-laden humour that often accompanies the bodily destructions of the splatter. Wirkola aimed at eliciting laughter and discomfort simultaneously, applying black humour to the gore-fest, 'that form of humour which, using cruelty, bitterness, and sometimes despair, underlines the absurdity of the world [...]' (O'Neill [1983] 2010: 81). Unlike the fatigued audience perceptions of violent action movies with little relief, the experience of bloody and gory splatter horror is often balanced by the ironic distance that comes with dark humour and disgusting exaggerations (Sjögren 1993: 121–2). Wirkola was clearly and mischievously aware of this dynamic.

The premise is instantly reminiscent of the then-recent Norwegian slasher success *Cold Prey*: A group of medical students heads into the mountains of Finnmark in northern Norway to spend their Easter vacation together. Hanna (Charlotte Frogner) and Martin (Vegar Hoel) are dating, Roy (Stig Frode Henriksen) is single with a big mouth, Liv (Evy Kasseth Røsten) is single and humble, while Chris (Jenny Skavlan) and Erlend (Jeppe Beck Laursen) are single film nerds who soon get attracted to each other. Upon arriving at their cabin in the snowy wilderness of Arctic Norway they expect to meet Vegard's (Lasse Valdal) girlfriend Sara (Ane Dahl Torp), who is supposed to have gotten there ahead of them.

The number of characters involved, no less than eight friends sharing a quite crowded vacation, is necessary for Wirkola to stage as many gruesome attacks on the body as he can think of. The group gets into drinking while waiting for the seemingly delayed Sara, but they are soon interrupted by a mysterious local man (Bjørn Sundquist) who claims to bring them a warning. He tells them a tragic story from the days of the Second World War about a troop of German Nazi soldiers who wreaked havoc in the area under the dreaded Colonel Herzog (Ørjan Gamst). They tortured and killed at will, and they tried to make off with the locals' gold and valuables when the war ended. The locals revolted and chased Herzog and his men to their deaths in the wilderness. The mysterious visiting local warns the students not to disturb the sleeping evil of the mountains. Then he returns to his tent out on the snowy plains, where he is attacked and killed by someone or something unknown.

The next day, as Vegard takes off on a snow scooter in search of his missing girlfriend Sara, the rest of the students uncover a chest of old valuables beneath the cabin's floor boards. That night the cabin is attacked by zombies, and Chris and Erlend (conventionally having just had sex) are killed in horrific ways. The surviving students barricade themselves in the cabin, while Vegard discovers a cave containing both Nazi soldier helmets and Sara's severed head. Herzog's Nazi zombies are now hunting the students to reclaim their loot from the Second World War. Liv gets her intestines torn out while she is still alive, Vegard is killed by having all his limbs cut off, Martin accidentally kills his girlfriend Hanna in the confusion, and Roy meets a grisly end when hundreds of Nazi zombies rise from the snow to do battle. Martin gets bitten by one of them and cuts off his own arm with a chainsaw to avoid zombie infection. He hands Herzog the chest of valuables and makes his way to the car, all set to escape the slaughter. Then, as he is about to start the engine, a misplaced gold coin falls from his pocket, and Herzog smashes the car window with his fist.

The DVD cover for *Dead Snow* labels the film a 'Nazi-zombie-horror-splatter-comedy'. Wirkola's first horror film aims as much to elicit laughter and head-shaking recognition of genre conventions as it aims to scare, and thus sets itself far apart from contemporary Norwegian horror movies like *Cold Prey* and *The Monitor*. Even so, it shares *Cold Prey*'s premise of a group of young people meeting their horrible fate in the snowy mountains of the Norwegian holiday tradition, adding Norwegian war history to the base of its story in a way similar to *Dark Woods* and *Dark Woods 2*. The signalling of national motifs gets going as Edvard Grieg's world-famous 'In the Hall of the Mountain King' is played over the opening sequence, in which the Nazi zombies hunt the person we later realise is Sara through the snow. The similarities to *Cold Prey* extend to how the filmmakers establish a group of characters by having them be either romantic couples or frustrated singles, and of course there is no mobile phone signal in this particular area.

However, the meta level of action and dialogue in *Dead Snow* sits far from the earnest and straight-forward storytelling of either *Dark Woods* or *Cold Prey*. On the way to the cabin, Erlend exclaims: 'How many movies start with a group of people on a trip without cell phone signals?' Chris, sporting the androgynous name that conventionally belongs to a slasher survivor, name-checks the obscure *April Fool's Day*, probably thinking of the 2008 remake of the 1986 mobile phone-less original. She subsequently becomes the first person in the film to die, rather than the film's final girl. She has sex with Erlend in the

FANTASTIC HORROR HYBRIDS

outhouse and is consequently attacked, pulled down into the loo and doused in urine and excrement.

The slasher's return of the repressed takes the shape of a monstrous human killer who is nearly impossible to disarm or overcome, like the resurrected Mountain Man in *Cold Prey II*. In the psychological thriller the mind can suppress the horrors of reality only up to a point, as John experiences in *Next Door*, or ghosts might reach out from the beyond, like the dead boys who appear in the story of *The Monitor*. The repressed in Wirkola's zombie movie literally rise from the dead: these were monsters in life, and they are monsters in death, or more to the point, they are undead Nazi zombies that break free from the shackles of snowy graves. From the moment that the Sundquist character delivers the unheeded warning, an extremely rare occurrence in Norwegian horror of the conventional old community character warning the young community of danger, *Dead Snow* becomes a movie unrelentingly made up of explicit emotion markers. This violent and darkly comic orgy of blood and gore was the first of its kind in Norwegian mainstream cinema, and also garnered enough praise in the US for its director to embark on a combined Hollywood and Norway career that to date includes the action fantasy *Hansel & Gretel: Witch Hunters* (2013) and the sci-fi crime thriller *What Happened to Monday* (2017) in America, as well as the Norwegian action comedy *The Trip* (*I onde dager*, 2021).

The American interest in *Dead Snow* and its director makes a strong mark on the sequel. Wirkola's *Dead Snow 2* (*Død snø 2*, 2014) picks up the pieces right where the first film ends, like *Halloween 2* and *Cold Prey II*, and eschews

Figure 7.4 A Nazi zombie emerges from the Arctic snow. (Screenshot from *Dead Snow*)

115

much of its Norwegian characteristics in favour of several American actors and mostly English dialogue. To a large degree the sequel keeps piling on the gore like its predecessor, but the settings become a little less original, as the mountain landscapes are exchanged for a more conventional suburbia-like small town with its quiet streets and shops, its peaceful church and graveyard. Where the first film had a climactic scene set to Norwegian rock icon Åge Aleksandersen's hit song 'My Day' ('Min dag') from 1993, the sequel aims at transnational nostalgia with Bonnie Tyler's 1983 worldwide smash 'Total Eclipse of the Heart'. *Dead Snow 2* was shot in Iceland in both a Norwegian language and an English language version, clearly being primed for an international market from its inception (Thorkildsen 2014).

A more recent take on Norwegian zombies was seen in Henrik Martin Dahlsbakken's *Project Z* (2021), a meta-style found footage horror comedy about a group of film students who bring three professional actors to a remote defunct motel in rural Norway to shoot a low-budget zombie film. While the amateurish production is ongoing, Earth is subjected to violent hails of meteorites. Soon enough, the shower of space rocks somehow leads to a true zombie infestation, and the film shoot disintegrates into real horror.

Project Z playfully references such different horror classics as *The Shining* and *The Blair Witch Project*, and Dahlsbakken stages effective sequences involving everything from meteorite-stricken cars in motion to *Alien*-like eggs in the dark woods being unwisely probed by hand. There is, however, a sense that perhaps the film would have been more engaging as a straight horror fiction than the found footage hybrid Dahlsbakken creates, the juxtaposition of the film-within-the-film and the 'real world' zombie attack remaining an uneasy fit to the end. In addition, the film assumes the audience's familiarity with Norwegian actors and previous horror genre works of Norwegian cinema: lead actors in the film are Eili Harboe (previously seen in 2017's *Thelma*), Iben Akerlie (previously seen in 2019's *Lake of Death*), Arthur Berning (previously seen in 2009's *Hidden* and 2010's *Cold Prey III*), as well as the older and internationally acclaimed Dennis Storhøi.

Henrik Martin Dahlsbakken (born 1989) is an impressively productive and versatile filmmaker, having directed eight feature films at the time of writing and being in some state of production on at least a further two. One of his upcoming projects, set for 2022, is the psychological horror film *Possession*, a 1918 supernatural story in which settlers from the South clash with Sami culture in Northern Norway. Dahlsbakken previously touched on horror motifs in *Cave* (2016), a tensely simplistic thriller about underground cave exploration, while his amalgamation of comedy and zombie horror in *Project Z* proved less artistically and generically successful.

However, not all zombie films from Norway attempt the horror-comedy genre hybridisation. The second Norwegian zombie film to play in cinemas nationwide, in-between the two *Dead Snow* movies, was of a very different kind than the others. The sombre and satirical *Dark Souls* (*Mørke sjeler*, 2011) by Mathieu Peteul and César Ducasse took aim at the very foundation of Norwegian wealth: the oil industry. Produced entirely outside the system of public funding, it was an early example of a change in Norway's genre film distribution: independent Norwegian low-budget features finding their way to cinemas through positive word-of-mouth generated at festivals and similar screenings.

The story is incited when the young woman Johanna (Johanna Gustavsson) is assaulted on a jogging trip in her hometown of Oslo. A masked man in an orange coverall drills a hole in her head and leaves her in the woods, seemingly for dead. However, Johanna comes back to life on the autopsy table, vomits a black and sticky liquid, and returns home to her very worried father, Morten (Morten Rudå). Doctors ascertain that Johanna is breathing but does not have a pulse, a fate shared by many young people around the city who have had black liquid injected into their skulls. Police inspector Richard Askestad (Kyrre Haugen Sydness) is tasked with investigating the case and bringing the perpetrators to justice.

Clues lead Askestad to the headquarters of the oil company Hydro+, where coverall-wearing and oil-drinking murderers work under orders from an elderly, suited gentleman (Gustav-Adolf Hegh). A former North Sea diver (Karl Sundby) warns Askestad not to go up against the oil drinkers, telling him how the divers once found something in the depths of the ocean: 'I have seen the powers of darkness,' one of his diver colleagues once said, 'they are inside me.' Askestad does not heed this warning, enters the premises of Hydro+, and is consequently killed. Norway succumbs to the rise of the oil zombies, and the modern Norwegian apocalypse is a fact.

What *Dark Souls* suggests is that *we* have become the monsters, that the curse of finding black gold is the apocalyptic state of a generation of young people staring blankly into computer screens while silently crying out for help. Something else entirely was also dragged up out of the dark ocean depths, a desensitising greed that destroys the world around us while it also destroys us on the inside, us being the people of modern Norway. Anachronisms in the film's mise-en-scène underlines the point: even if the action is set in the years immediately after 2000, we see 8mm film projections used in meeting rooms, a photo camera loaded with celluloid film, and even an old Radionette unit in working order. These are relics from the time when modern Norway was shaped by the discovery of oil in its offshore waters. This direct criticism of Norway's social and political reality in the age of the current global climate crisis is the main storytelling ambition of *Dark Souls*, and it sets the film far apart from the entertainment-oriented majority of horror-related genre hybrids in Norwegian cinema. Audiences, however, would seem to prefer the escapism of less relatable monsters.

Figure 7.5 Feeding on fossil fuel, in a rare socio-political satire depicting Norwegians as helpless oil junkies. (Screenshot from *Dark Souls*)

Creatures of Myth and CGI: Ragnarok Americanised?

During the production of his first feature film *Thale* (2013), director Alexander Nordaas explained his motivation and ambition for the project: 'It is high time that we start dealing with this part of our history. *Troll Hunter* has broken new ground for Norwegian folklore in the movies, at home and abroad, and *Thale* is taking up the baton' (Budalen 2012). His movie dealt with the folklore creature known as the *hulder*, a perilously seductive young woman who lures unsuspecting men into the woods, sometimes trapping them in the shadowland of the blue mountains.

Leo (Jon Sigve Skard) and Elvis (Erlend Nervold) are at the scene of a death. Leo owns and runs No Shit Cleaning Service, specialising in cleaning up the sites of either crimes or natural deaths. On this particular job the two men are faced with the decayed body of a Swedish military officer, and they come across a hidden basement in which they find the young hulder Thale (Silje Reinåmo) submerged in a tub filled with a milk-like liquid. Thale is proof of the existence of supernatural creatures in the Norwegian woods, and she has been held captive in the officer's house since she was a small child. While Leo and Elvis try to figure out how to handle their discovery, it soon becomes apparent that both a paramilitary group and Thale's goblin family are trying to find and capture her. In the end, her people save Leo and Elvis from certain death at the hands of soldiers, and Thale also effects the healing of Leo's terminal cancer disease, recalling the healing powers of *The Monitor* and *Thelma*.

Thale was essentially a chamber piece in which the title character and her family supplied the supernatural elements of horror. Nordaas seemed more interested in mining the folklore material than he was in creating a genre-conscious feature. However, audiences in Norway still seemed to prefer such fantastic tales and creatures wrapped in recognisably generic structures, as evidenced by another successful genre hybrid with significant horror elements.

If one were to combine the two Steven Spielberg movies *Raiders of the Lost Ark* (1981) and *Jurassic Park* (1993), the result would pretty much be a blueprint for Mikkel Brænne Sandemose's action-adventure *Ragnarok* from 2013. The story kicks off with an exotic hunt for treasure, and it ends in a desperate flight from a prehistoric monster. The shift in the situation and personality of action heroes is also conspicuous from the 1981 to the 1993 Spielberg films: where Indiana Jones (Harrison Ford) does not relate himself to children or family connections, Alan Grant (Sam Neill) is trapped on the dinosaur island with two kids who are both vying for his attention and care, leading to Grant eventually accepting his role as a father figure to them. The main character of *Ragnarok*, Sigurd (Pål Sverre Hagen), is a single father struggling to take care of his two kids in the aftermath of his wife's death. Anne Gjelsvik has pointed out how the American action hero changed from a relatively carefree bundle of muscles in the 1980s into a modern man with more realistic problems, a description which also fits the *Ragnarok* hero: '[In] contemporary American cinema, a true hero must be a good father, or rather he must learn how to become one' (2013: 91). The love story subplot of the traditional action movie has to a large degree been replaced by a family subplot.

Sigurd is an archaeologist on the trail of a long-forgotten secret. The discovery of the Oseberg Viking ship and the earthly remains of a Viking queen has led him to speculate that the concept of Ragnarok, the Norse term for the apocalypse, is not a divination about the end of the world but a message to the future about a significant historical event. Sigurd's colleague Allan (Nicolai Cleve Broch) discovers a runestone in northern Norway suggesting that the Oseberg Vikings possibly sailed much further north than previously believed. Sigurd takes his children Ragnhild (Maria Annette Tanderø Berglyd) and Brage (Julian Podolski) with him on what everyone, and Allan in particular, believes will be a treasure hunt.

The group is joined by Swedish scientist Elisabeth (Sofia Helin) and local guide Leif (Bjørn Sundquist), as they venture into the wilderness of no man's land on the border between Norway and Russia. In a deep cave, on an island in the middle of a lake, they find what they were hoping for: cultural treasures of Viking heritage. However, they come to learn that the runic message Sigurd has been slowly deciphering is actually a warning. Before Sigurd manages to complete the puzzle, their guide Leif takes off with the treasure. The rest of the group is abandoned at the bottom of the cave, slowly realising that many people have once fought and died there. Meanwhile, Leif's raft is intercepted and attacked by something that hides in the darkness of the lake. Both Leif and the treasure disappear in the deep.

The lake in no man's land contains the secret that the Viking queen Åsa (Vera Rudi) discovered over a thousand years earlier, a threat that she attempted to warn the world about: a gigantic sea serpent, no less than the very real Midgard Serpent of Norse mythology, a harbinger of Ragnarok, the Norse Armageddon. Now Sigurd's group must fight for their lives in a desperate attempt to escape the island before the serpent kills them all. Unfortunately, Allan is overcome by his greed, wanting to keep a newly hatched (and presumably dizzyingly valuable) baby serpent, thereby further endangering them all. Allan pays for this transgression with his life, while Sigurd finally escapes with his children and Elisabeth.

Mikkel Brænne Sandemose (born 1974) made his feature film debut with *Cold Prey III* in 2010 and stayed with producers Fantefilm for *Ragnarok* in 2013, a film that proved very popular in Norway. The director would later move on to fantasy and action-adventure based on Norwegian folktales with two *The Ash Lad* movies, *In the Hall of the Mountain King* (2017) and *In Search of the Golden Castle* (2019). The latter two were also commercially successful, but *Ragnarok* remains his most generically sure-handed work to date. *Ragnarok* was a high-concept fantasy and action-adventure film, mixed with elements of monster horror that would not have been possible to achieve before the age of CGI. Along with *Troll Hunter*, Sandemose's monster movie marked the point in time when horror tropes and conventions were integrated into broader cinema entertainment in Norway, a trend that would develop further with the coming of the Norwegian disaster blockbuster in 2015. *Ragnarok* was broad family entertainment, its 11 rating allowing children as young as seven years old to attend screenings in the company of adults who would probably also enjoy the spectacle.

The lure of the unknown can be a strong inciter for cinematic storytelling. 'Man knows little', Sigurd reads from the mysterious runes left behind by Queen Åsa and her contemporaries. He looks at the unimpressed gathering of financiers who have come to hear his pitch for further investigation of the Oseberg riddles. 'So, what did they know, that we know not?' It may not accurately portray how Norwegian museums are organised in reality, but the film clearly wants to cast Sigurd as the man in opposition to commercial interests, much like Harrison Ford's professor Jones and his iconic mantra: 'It belongs in a museum!'

As the main protagonist, Sigurd has to handle the dangerous action of hunting historical secrets, while also struggling to maintain a connection with his daughter Ragnhild. The younger brother Brage looks up to his father as a hero, but Ragnhild has a much less favourable opinion of a father who seems

FANTASTIC HORROR HYBRIDS

Figure 7.6 It could have been a Hollywood dinosaur, but it is the CGI Midgard Serpent of Norse mythology. (Screenshot from *Ragnarok*)

to be more engaged by ancient mysteries than by his kids. Sigurd is undoubtedly a workaholic, spending all his time and energy on the secrets of the Oseberg discovery in an effort to dull the pain of his wife's passing. Sandemose takes several cues from Spielberg movies that put the frictions and dynamics of the modern family into the centre of the plot. The absence of either a father or a mother is a key problem at the heart of *E. T. the Extra-Terrestrial* (1982) and *The Lost World: Jurassic Park* (1997), the latter being a sequel to the equally father figure-obsessed original *Jurassic Park*. Even Indiana Jones would be thrust into the roles of either father figure or scorned and resentful son in Spielberg's sequels *The Temple of Doom* (1984), *The Last Crusade* (1989) and *The Kingdom of the Crystal Skull* (2008).

The audio-visual inspiration for *Ragnarok* is evident in the design and application of the mythological monster that dwells in the lake but is equally at ease on land. The unwise theft of the baby serpent is akin to the egg-theft in Joe Johnstone's *Jurassic Park III* (2001), and Sandemose also quotes other major genre movies either consciously or not, like Ridley Scott's science fiction and horror masterpiece *Alien* from 1979. When the archaeologists and the kids approach the ultimate secret of the grotto, they break through a membrane of water to uncover the slimy eggs of the serpent mother. This crosses a threshold, breaks a barrier, much like the astronauts break the layer of mist that protects the extra-terrestrial eggs in *Alien*.

Ragnarok was produced by the same company that had previously produced the *Cold Prey* series, Fantefilm, led by producers Martin Sundland and Are Heidenstrøm. In 2013, Norway's population numbers had passed 5,050,000, and *Ragnarok* sold 252,375 tickets, which was considered a success. Fantefilm

121

had thus been responsible for a diecast slasher trilogy, of which *Cold Prey* had sold 257,001 tickets and *Cold Prey II* had sold 268,427, and they had also succeeded with a genre hybrid of action-adventure and monster horror. Once again, for many readers these numbers will seem miniscule, but they were solid and sustainable in light of the general cinema attendance in Norway and the reality of financing and producing motion pictures in a small country that relies on public funding. Ultimately, only the competing *Troll Hunter* with its 279,090 tickets sold would have the edge in terms of horror fiction's appeal to national audiences (*Film & Kino* 2014: 59).

In addition to the political and cultural factors that facilitate more commercially oriented filmmaking in Norway these days, digital effects technology has also reached a point where monsters and action on a large scale previously associated with Hollywood filmmaking is finally achievable for Norwegian filmmakers. Along with the domestic success of the *Cold Prey* horror series, genre movies like the war film *Max Manus*, the historical drama *Kon-Tiki* (Joachim Rønning and Espen Sandberg, 2012), the action comedy *Børning* (Hallvard Bræin, 2014), and the horror-tinged *Troll Hunter* and *Ragnarok*, would all further fuel the persistent debate about a perceived Americanisation of Norwegian cinema.

Film genres are transnational. None of them were conceived in a Hollywood vacuum by North American filmmakers alone. Even so, Hollywood cinema enjoys a decisive position in genre history, and comparisons are inevitable when genre filmmaking becomes common and systematised in the cinemas of smaller nations like Norway. In the Norwegian films on the fringe of the horror genre – the hybrids – we can detect obvious American models: zombie films, horror comedy, monster action and found footage. At the same time, the Norwegian specifics and aesthetics are clearly visible and audible: the backstory and setting of *Dead Snow*, the oil motif of *Dark Souls*, and the folklore foundation that makes *Troll Hunter* much more than a copy of *The Blair Witch Project* or *Cloverfield* (Matt Reeves, 2008).

There exists a constant friction between two different but related assumptions concerning Norwegian cinema. The first is the assumption that there is something particularly Norwegian that can be projected through filmmaking, and the second is the assumption that certain types of filmmaking are best suited to engage a large audience. A lot of contemporary Norwegian filmmaking takes place in this crossfire. To give some perspective to these assumptions, one could consider Henrik Ibsen, an internationally well-known Norwegian classic author. His body of work is often cited as one of the pillars of the definition of the typically Norwegian in storytelling and temperament, the texts being of fundamental national significance. However, Ibsen crafted some of his most acclaimed works during long stays abroad, and his stage plays are among the founding materials of the classical narrative cinema that is first and foremost associated with Hollywood. Furthermore, his grandson Tancred Ibsen brought these classical Hollywood impulses back to Norway when he became the most important director of Norwegian cinema in the 1930s. The typically Norwegian and the typically American, at least in terms of cinema, are clearly interwoven categories.

Claims of Americanisation in Norwegian cinema will often be founded on the application of certain generic models of storytelling. On the other hand, the use of particular settings, narratives involving certain characters or supernatural creatures, as well as backstories from national history, will all tend to be hailed as Norwegian specifics. The transnational is a fundamental trait of genre history, and the Norwegian horror movies are additions to their genre that invite debate about the national, the transnational and the concept of Americanisation in the cinema. These films exist in the border region of the Norwegian and the generic, in the field of tension where transnational genre conventions meet nationally specific traits of characters, settings and history. Most important to this creative collision is the filmmakers' use of landscapes, that which I have discussed as Norwegian spaces throughout the book. The following chapter will elaborate on the significance of this concept. As Roar Uthaug's 2015 disaster movie *The Wave* launched a new genre trend in Norwegian cinema that would largely displace mainstream horror, the originator of modern Norwegian horror, Pål Øie, returned to the landscapes and thematic motifs of dead water with *Dark Woods 2*.

8. DEAD WATER

Norwegian horror cinema has divided itself into three main trends. The major subgenres of the slasher film and the psychological horror film were apparent from the outset, and soon after a wave of genre hybrids saw horror combined with other genres like comedy and action adventure to great popular effect.

In later years, a fourth trend has also come to the fore. The mainstream horror film has been eclipsed, almost completely, not only by the big budget disaster movie, but also by the independent and very low-budget underground horror previously consigned to DVD releases and genre festival appearances. This emergence of underground horror in cinemas nationwide rides on the back of digital distribution technology, exploiting the genre entertainment awareness that has marked the behaviour of Norwegian audiences throughout the period covered in this book.

However, Norwegian horror cinema seems unwilling to let go of its roots. The return to the source of horror in 2019's *Lake of Death* (*De dødes tjern*, Nini Bull Robsahm), and also the unexpected sequel *Dark Woods 2* (*Villmark 2*, Pål Øie) in 2015, suggests that Norwegian horror, despite the thematic and stylistic advances made in *The Monitor* (*Babycall*, Pål Sletaune, 2011), *Thelma* (Joachim Trier, 2017) and *The Innocents* (*De uskyldige*, Eskil Vogt, 2021), might never part from certain premises. The most important of these seems to be the notion that darkness and evil always emanate from nature, from wilderness, and most particularly from dead water.

'No life, no oxygen': Back to the *Dark Woods*

Dark Woods 2 (also known as *Villmark: Asylum* internationally) is Pål Øie's sequel to his own ground-breaking genre film *Dark Woods* (*Villmark*, 2003), but it does not follow the surviving characters from that story. Instead, although the film is not a prequel, it digs into the backstory of the lake and the dark events of the past that were hinted at in the first film. In doing so, Øie turns up the intensity and increases the threat from dead water. This time around, terrifying things do not merely come out of the water, but the water itself becomes an active threat, seeping into the action with violent force.

The setting for *Dark Woods 2* might be described as a contemporary Norwegian version of the gothic castle. The building seen in the movie is a real-life abandoned sanatorium, situated not far from the location of the lake filmed for the original *Dark Woods*. When combined with the industrial ruins that Øie used for interiors, the hallmarks of gothic 'tales of mystery and horror' become clearly visible and audible, if updated: 'wild and desolate landscapes, dark forests, ruined abbeys, feudal halls and medieval castles with dungeons, secret passages, winding stairways, oubliettes, sliding panels and torture chambers' (Cuddon [1976] 1998: 356). The original gothic tropes are adapted to modern Norway in *Dark Woods 2* and given the dead water treatment, which is essentially the defining narrative and stylistic trait of Norwegian horror cinema.

A company called Deco is sending an inspection team of five people to a defunct sanatorium in preparation for its demolition. Led by Live (Ellen Dorrit Petersen) they have the tightly scheduled mission of inspecting 312 rooms and 4 kilometers of piping in just three days. Junior team member Even (Mads Sjøgård Pettersen) exclaims that the inside of the sanatorium seems 'like a cathedral!' The building has previously served as a hospital and insane asylum, but it has been abandoned since 1978 and is now left in the care of Karl the janitor (Baard Owe). Karl feigns unawareness of the impending demolition, letting Live know that she can tell her company 'that *I* take care of this building'. The only structure in an otherwise desolate mountainside, the sanatorium proves to have a life and will of its own, stubbornly refusing to be torn down, feeding off the water that flows through its pipes like blood through veins.

The lake of the original film is not prominent here, but the water most certainly is. The lake feeds the asylum, its water pumps noisily through the piping system, pregnant with terrible portents, carrying the certainty of destruction, what Gaston Bachelard has called 'blood accursed, like blood which bears death' ([1942] 1983: 49). And bear death it does. The inspection team is doomed, unlike the team in the previous *Dark Woods* film. Where the original allowed most of the characters to survive, the sequel is far more sinister. Water pours into the sanatorium as senior team member Frank (Tomas Norström)

Figure 8.1 The contemporary Norwegian gothic castle. (Screenshot from *Dark Woods 2*)

cracks open a water pipe. Closing the stop valve is no use, and soon another pipe bursts as well, allowing water to saturate the building, infecting it with death. Pipes and drains make terrible groaning sounds – the deathly voice of the asylum – and as the story progresses the horror of the lake in the woods becomes inescapable.

The inspection team comes to realise that the sanatorium is supplied with water from the very lake that hid the deadly secrets of the original *Dark Woods*, although they don't know the dark events of its recent past. Live asks Ole (Anders Baasmo Christiansen) to analyse water samples, and he concludes that the water in the pipes is anoxic. Live responds in disbelief, 'dead water?', to which Ole replies that indeed, the water has 'no life, no oxygen', but 'lots of sulphur'. As for how this phenomenon could have manifested itself in a seemingly healthy mountain lake, Ole can only speculate: 'Lord knows how many patients have drowned themselves up there.' The legacy of *Lake of the Dead* (*De dødes tjern*, Kåre Bergstrøm, 1958) lives on in Øie's *Dark Woods* sequel.

The Deco inspection team find that Karl the janitor is not the only resident. A mysterious nurse (Éva Magyar) seems to assist Karl in dubious medical experiments, and Live also discovers that Karl is hiding his own adult son in the asylum. The attentive viewer might recognise the son (Torstein Løning) as the mysterious background figure in *Dark Woods* that we came to suspect was the real murderer. Tenuous though the connection would be for a general audience, Øie nevertheless steers this bridging character into the gloomy backstory of the tale. In the horror genre tradition of returning the repressed, Øie dives deeper into a dark national past to reveal torture and murder on a horrifying scale. Although Øie's story is fictional, it shines its light into very dark corners of Norway's recent history.

In old documents discovered by junior team member Synne (Renate Reinsve) the history of the sanatorium is explained: forty-four war children and their mothers were interned there after the war and subjected to barbaric tuberculosis vaccine experiments. Karl the janitor appears to have been one of these children, the son of a German pilot who crashed in the lake during the war. In the original *Dark Woods*, Gunnar the producer tells the tale of a war-time plane crash and how it turned the lake into a legend of dread. Now Karl tells Synne that the pilot survived the crash, only to be tortured and drowned by the Norwegian resistance, a horrific treatment which included stabbing his eyes out.

On this point, *Dark Woods II* manifests a clear alternative to the modern Norwegian war film and its consistently heroic portrayal of Norway's war history and the perceived purity of the resistance effort. Films and series in the war genre inevitably focus on the invasion and occupation of Norway by Nazi Germany in the years 1940 to 1945, but there has been much critical debate concerning the kinds of stories that tend to dominate the retelling of events from this traumatic and formative period of Norwegian history in the steadily growing corpus of post-2000 war films and series. *Max Manus* (Joachim Rønning and Espen Sandberg) set the template in 2008, highlighting the titular resistance agent's personal sacrifice in the covert fight against Nazi occupation, and becoming hugely popular and successful for it. A later example is the television series *The Heavy Water War* (*Kampen om tungtvannet*, Per-Olav Sørensen), also known as *The Saboteurs*. The series dramatised the Norwegian resistance's efforts to sabotage the Nazis' heavy water production in Norway, and it attracted a huge audience on its *NRK* premiere in early 2015. Like *Max Manus*, it was a hero-centric story.

There has also been the Emmy Award-winning but controversial series *Atlantic Crossing* (Alexander Eik, 2020), based on the true story of the wartime friendship between Norwegian Crown Princess Märtha and American president Franklin D. Roosevelt. In this case, what attracted considerable criticism was the series makers' narrative manipulation of the Norwegian royal, granting her an inaccurately decisive role in terms of influencing Roosevelt's choice to have the US enter the war. Another royal whose life and times provide engaging source material for entertainment fiction is King Haakon VII. He was the King of Norway from the end of the Swedish-Norwegian union in 1905 until his death in 1957, including the turbulent war years when he remained King of Norway in British exile. The 2016 feature film *The King's Choice* (*Kongens nei*, Erik Poppe), unlike many other war films and series, stuck remarkably close to historic facts, following the beleaguered King through the days of the German invasion that culminated in his refusal to comply with German demands to appoint Nazi leader Vidkun Quisling as Prime Minister.

All of these tales are hero stories, focusing largely on men of honour (a woman in the case of *Atlantic Crossing*) who stand up against evil and tyranny to save Norway, freedom and democracy, usually at great personal risk. An extreme example of this heroic tale is *The 12th Man* (*Den 12. Mann*, Harald Zwart, 2017), based on the real experiences of Norwegian resistance agent Jan Baalsrud. These events were previously depicted in Arne Skouen's Academy Award-nominated *Nine Lives* (*Ni liv*, 1957), a modernist interpretation of Baalsrud's journey. *The 12th Man*, however, is an out-and-out action movie that showcases the current state of genre-driven Norwegian cinema in contrast to the Skouen classic of sixty years earlier. The 2017 adaptation pits selfless Norwegians against merciless Nazis who could just as well have been characters in an Indiana Jones movie. Baalsrud must escape their evil clutches into safety across the Swedish border, and he suffers immense physical and emotional pain on his way through the overwhelming Norwegian winter landscapes. He finally makes it across the border, not least because of the numerous everyperson helpers along the way, folks who are loyal and self-sacrificing to a fault, the very definition of selfless solidarity. As much as there is a gripping real-life story at the heart of *The 12th Man*, the film overemphasises Baalsrud's physical disintegration (many scenes being visually akin to the horror genre) and the simplistic streamlining of good guys and bad guys.

Treatments of the immense shadow of the Second World War in Norwegian popular culture should certainly not be limited to cardboard Nazi villains and naively heroic resistance fighters, and a contrasting television series about Quisling is in the works. However, it is perhaps telling that *Dark Woods*, and in particular *Dark Woods 2*, suggest that an alternative take on the Norwegian experience of war, a non-heroic inspection of dark secrets, is possible outside the domain of war films and series. As Øie's horror sequel progresses, the inspection team's mounting realisation of the area's past misery and war-related suffering is matched by the ever-increasing masses of water dripping from the ceilings and surging through the piping. From out of the woodland lake, through the ghostly sanatorium's abandoned rooms, and into the very foundations of the building, dark history and dead water descends.

On Karl the janitor's original building plans there is a floor previously unknown to the inspection team, a sub-basement beneath the lowest floor in their updated plans. Frank and Synne head into the deep bowels of the building to investigate the secret basement. What they find is a perfectly captured image of unhomely horror, as seen on this book's cover: a tent, the very symbol of Norwegian nature's freedom of movement and recreation, erected inside a dark concrete hall, practically entombed inside a bunker-like underground cavern. Its blood red colour matches the one that Øie also uses for key props throughout the movie. String, rope and measuring lasers are all marked by the colour of blood, highlighted by Øie's choice of changing the original film's green and yellow tent to a luminous red. In *Dark Woods* it was Lasse who at one point became trapped in the tent, assaulted by someone on the outside, and in *Dark Woods 2* it is Synne who experiences the same terror of being trapped inside the very symbol of bucolic Norwegian freedom. After being saved by Live, a terrified Synne can barely muster the words to describe her ordeal: 'We found the tent. [. . .] Someone pulled me out, and into the water.' She is safe for the time being, but the climax of the movie plunges both her and Live into the lowest basement again, which is flooded with dead water.

Dark Woods 2, Pål Øie's third horror film following *Dark Woods* and *Hidden* (*Skjult*, 2009), is one of the most visually complex films of Norwegian horror cinema, the director and his regular cinematographer Sjur Aarthun eschewing the original movie's video style for something much more sophisticated. It might be narratively frustrating if one is looking for answers, as it sticks to the impossibility of the psychological horror tale. Linear clarity does not seem to have been Øie's priority. Quite the contrary, the film is uncompromising in its dissertation of the dread and terror that can be mined from the mysterious landscapes of Norway, revelling in the sensual exploration of spaces, and excelling as a horrific meditation on evil and the depths of dead water. Live is the last of the team standing, fighting to the death with the mute nurse of the sanatorium, ultimately victorious. However, as was the case with Camilla in *Manhunt* (*Rovdyr*, Patrik Syversen, 2008), there is little reason to assume that Live survives. She meets a young girl who leads her through the maze of corridors to a door that opens into the woods. As the lake of the original movie comes into view, the girl raises a huge needle into a stabbing position and the film cuts to black.

Bachelard describes water as the element of dreams, and as such it also carries with it a potential for nightmares. The dead water of Pål Øie's *Dark Woods* movies becomes a powerful symbol of the promise or threat that the repressed will inevitably return, that the danger and evil hidden beneath the surface will eventually reveal its dark and deadly secrets. Nature, wilderness, woods and mountains are the terrible places of Norwegian horror cinema, the unfathomable and sublime spaces that engender Norwegian, Nordic and Arctic nightmares in a remarkably consistent line of films from 2003 up until the present time.

In *Cold Prey* (*Fritt vilt*, Roar Uthaug, 2006), water has become snow that will become death. To stress the point, Uthaug stages a scene where the killer, the Mountain Man, seems to attack a victim by rising out of the ground, out of the snow, like a living rock coming to life and going in for the kill. The slasher movie conventions are ideally suited for removal to the Norwegian wilderness, but even in the psychological thrillers of the horror tradition in Norway, dead water flows.

The arguably most important of these films, with predominantly urban settings, are *The Monitor* and *Thelma*. Both movies explore the subjective states and experiences of a woman – Anna in the former and Thelma in the latter. It is highly interesting that both movies have decisive turning points in and around lakes, even if they are primarily set in the city of Oslo. The pivotal scene in Anna's desperate investigation is when she dives into a mysterious lake in the woods in a hopeless effort to save an unknown boy's life. Even this urban *nowhere in particular* has dead water at the heart of its drama. As Anna wades into the water, she also dives into her own repressed memories, her own trauma, again exemplifying what Bachelard sees in Poe: 'The past life of the soul is itself a deep water' (Bachelard [1942] 1983: 52).

The horror of Thelma's repressed mind is centred on the lake, the site of the past tragedy and the object of her father's routine visits in a small boat. Throughout the film, Thelma is apparently comfortable in a swimming pool (although she tellingly gets trapped in one), and at the climax of the story she accepts and takes command of her abilities by literally sacrificing her father to the deep water of the lake and healing her paralysed mother. In the words of Bachelard, 'could an image of *full depth* ever be obtained without a meditation in the presence of deep water?' (Ibid.). Even in these examples of generally urban Norwegian horror films, the tactile settings and landscapes include some form of gothic dead water.

The terrible places in Norwegian horror movies are often the lakes, the rivers, the woods and the mountains. Less culture, more nature. As Norway's modern identity was crafted on the notion that Norway was a more rural country than both Denmark and Sweden, so has Norwegian horror cinema gone to the same source with a different intention: to reveal the dread, to unmask the terror, to find the terrible danger of death and destruction that hides out there. This is the dark side of Norway, informed by the horror of folktales, the dystopia that lurks beneath the surface of utopia, the horrible reality of a country that was once a true social democracy but no longer upholds the ideals that made it world-renowned.

While Pål Øie's movies are not set in the cartographically defined Arctic region, they capture and communicate a sense of the overwhelmingly sublime Nordic nature and wilderness in the context of the horror movie genre, and thus provide Norwegian horror cinema with a distinguishing feature that matches an aesthetic and sensory definition of the Arctic, as well as the notion of the Arctic (and thus the Nordic and Norwegian) as a state of mind. As Luis Rocha Antuñes writes: 'There is no single answer to exactly *what* or *where* the North is. [...] [It] is perhaps more accurately described as a dynamic play of energies that are not necessarily defined in strict geographical terms' (2016: 132–3). These energies certainly include the audio-visual representation of people in the grip of sublime landscapes, what Øie himself previously described as the cold and stylised sounds and images of something slow but massive.

The Norwegian horror cinema has appropriated this representation successfully, since its very genre permits the filmmakers to exaggerate and conjure the fantastic on film. Horror movies lend themselves to imagining and conceptualising not only evil, as Cynthia Freeland has convincingly argued, but also the North. The Nordic and the Arctic can be discussed as what historian Kenneth Coates has called *spatial constructs*, one of the ways in which he suggests that we can define the North (1994: 20). The dark and violent fantasies of Norwegian horror cinema are more often than not tied to the sensual experience of landscapes, those spaces of the North that are desolate, and where isolation itself constitutes a threat.

The Arctic as concept has always been subject to different kinds of accounts, produced within and outside the region, including fictional audio-visual representations that help shape a 'historical perception of the Arctic and the far north' (Ryall et al 2010: ix). A big part of this perception involves how the region, or its mythical representation, looks and sounds and feels. Norway's horror cinema delves into a mythical space: Norwegian, Nordic and Arctic spaces intertwined, a conceptual perception which provides the source of madness, death and destruction, a myth fully counter to the liberty and regeneration that remain more traditional connotations of such spaces in Norwegian film history.

The woods and mountains of Norway have served as fertile ground for a national horror cinema tradition that most of all seems preoccupied with the deep and dark mysteries of dead water. The Arctic nightmares of Øie's two excursions into the *Dark Woods* are tales of death and water that could not simply have been conceived and staged *wherever*. They clearly demand a conceptually specific place in which to unfold, a setting which is much more than a backdrop, a landscape which provides visual and thematic cohesion for these tales of horror in a country that fits the description of being cold, dark and still.

The properties that Øie himself pointed to in Chapter 2, his interest in the aesthetic experience of something cold, dark and still, is what defines his horror movies as being somehow specifically Norwegian, Nordic or even Arctic. These properties are also applicable to other Norwegian horror films like the more action-packed *Cold Prey* slasher series, as well as several films of the psychological horror subgenre. The dangers and threats of Norwegian horror cinema are *cold, dark and still*. At least they are still, waiting in silence, until they come creeping out of deep waters or rising from the snow, infecting landscapes and characters with overwhelmingly sublime dread and terror. In short, Norwegian horror cinema has turned the regenerative and peaceful landscapes of national romanticism into sites and sources of national nightmares.

In certain ways, things are as they always have been in the horror of Norway. Yet, in other ways, a lot has changed from its inception up to its current incarnation. A comparative look at the two adaptations of André Bjerke's novel *Lake of the Dead* will highlight some key points of development.

Lakes of death, 61 years apart

The legendary poet and playwright Henrik Ibsen is often cited as one of the major inspirations behind the classical narrative cinema of Hollywood, and his work has also been essential to the idea of Norway, Norwegians and Norwegian drama in the 1800s, through the 1900s and beyond. In fact, director Kåre Bergstrøm's original *Lake of the Dead* from 1958 opens with an Ibsen quote that seems in retrospect to be a harbinger of the Norwegian horror cinema tradition in our time:

> Child, beware the tarn-fed stream.
> Danger, danger, there to dream!
> Though the sprite pretends to sleep,
> and above the lilies peep.
> (Verse from the poem 'With a Water-lily', Henrik Ibsen, 1871)

Danger from the deep, the return of the repressed, the horror of dead water seeping into both the subconscious realm of dreams and memories as well as physical reality. All of it is summed up in this quote, the threat of destruction and apocalypse hiding just beneath a tranquil surface. The very first Norwegian horror film already manifested it.

Lake of the Dead begins in a way that remains immediately recognisable in terms of the later Norwegian horror genre. A group of friends are headed out of the city by train. They are to spend a few days of summer in a remote cabin in the woods, somewhere in the Østerdalen valley north of Oslo. Bernhard Borge (Henki Kolstad) and Sonja (Bjørg Engh) are a married couple, while Harald Gran (Georg Richter) and Liljan (Henny Moan) are engaged to be married. Joining them on the expedition are the literary critic Mørk (André Bjerke, real-life author of the 1942 book that the film is based on) and the psychologist Bugge (Erling Lindahl), the latter two being frequently at loggerheads over questions of rational psychology versus more occult readings of people and the world. The group are expecting to meet Liljan's twin brother Bjørn Werner (Per Lillo-Stenberg) at the cabin, but they find it deserted with no sign of Bjørn except disturbing passages in the diary he has left behind.

When Bjørn's dog is found killed on the nearby lakeside, near a man's footprints apparently leading into the water but not back, the group of friends and the local sheriff (Øyvind Øyen) are faced with a mystery: has Bjørn taken his own life, has he been murdered, or is there something supernatural going on in the dark woods? The lake in question is called Blue Lake, and the sheriff can relate a tale of horror concerning its past. A man called Tore Gråvik, previous owner of the cabin, once killed his sister and her lover in this area, dumping their bodies in Blue Lake. Torn apart by his deeds he then proceeded to drown himself in the lake, and his lingering evil spirit is said to possess cabin visitors with a mysterious urge to follow him into the darkness of the water. Indeed, many people have in fact disappeared in the apparently bottomless Blue Lake over the years, never to be recovered, the sheriff admits.

Liljan has recently had distressing dreams and premonitions about herself, her brother, and a mysterious lake, and Bugge, the psychologist, has been attempting to reveal the source of her discomfort through psychoanalytic therapy sessions. Now that her brother has disappeared in or around a lake in the woods, Liljan approaches a nervous breakdown. Gran, a lawyer by trade, is convinced that something more sinister than suicide is the cause of Bjørn's disappearance, advocating the theory of murder. Mørk, on the other hand, is prone to believing in the supernatural force of the lake. Meanwhile, Bugge divulges to Bernhard, a crime author who is utterly confused about what to think, the fact that Bjørn Werner has harboured romantic and erotic feelings for his twin sister Liljan.

When staying alone in the cabin near the lake, it seems that Bjørn's dark desires have been enhanced by the ghost of Gråvik, as the schizophrenic ramblings in his diary would indicate. He writes that he is drawn to the deep and still darkness of the lake, and that he has to go in, that he has to know what happens when the water closes around him. According to the myth, the lake will work to draw Liljan in after him, joining them in death beyond the reach of civilisation's laws or morals.

The 1958 *Lake of the Dead* seems to have inspired Pål Øie's *Dark Woods* many decades later in ways much deeper than the mere surface of woods and waters. This is highlighted by how the legend that Øie placed in the dead waters of the lake resonates with the inception of the original story: there is a downed Nazi fighter plane in the lake of *Dark Woods*, while the original Norwegian lake of horror was conceived in André Bjerke's novel, which was written during the Nazi occupation of Norway and published in 1942. Some might be tempted to read Bjerke's novel, and consequently Bergstrøm's film adaptation, as a subtle allegory where the darkness of the lake is Nazism, and the purity and innocence of its intended female victim is Norway. Whether that was truly the case or not with Bjerke's tale, Øie's duo of *Dark Woods* films in the new millennium would dig in their heels on the point of both Nazi brutality and resistance horror hidden in the deep waters of history.

As it happens, Bjørn Werner has staged his own disappearance, and one dark night he assaults Liljan's fiancé Gran, dumping his dead body in the lake.

Apparently, Bjørn is consumed by the same rage of incestuous jealousy that led Gråvik to commit the terrible murders of his sister and her lover. Bugge takes charge of setting a trap for Bjørn, luring him to the lake at night with the help of the excellent swimmer Sonja posing as Liljan and diving into the black waters. Ultimately, Bjørn throws himself into the lake and disappears, and Bugge seems satisfied that he has secured the rational explanation for the horrific events: a man gone insane with the unnatural desire for his own sister. Bjørn's diary outlines how his psychosis was triggered by reading August Strindberg's autobiographical novel *Inferno* (1898), eventually shifting to the hypnotic power of the nearby lake as a locus of obsession, where the ghost of Gråvik consumed him.

Certainly, *Lake of the Dead* has a lot of crime trappings to it, mainly the mysterious current disappearance of a troubled man and the question of whether he has committed suicide or has in fact been murdered. The presence of the sheriff adds weight to the crime and suspense aspect, but other attributes of the story tie the film, as the book, to the genre of horror. Setting these in motion is the storytelling by the fire, where the sheriff suggests to the group the folktale-like ghost of Gråvik. Such a spectre is not a common trait of modern crime fiction, and this edges the film towards horror territory. The background of incest and murderous jealousy, however, would fit neatly in a modern story of Nordic noir, but it is perhaps a little startling as a taboo component in a 1958 cinematic feature. There is also the meta-level aspect of the story's framing device to support the potentially supernatural view of the deadly events: the author Borge later puts the drama into a crime novel, himself being less than convinced of the rational, psychoanalytic approach to what has transpired.

Bugge, the psychologist, effectively personifies the very horror-relevant notion of returning the repressed to the surface, as he literally tries to do in his treatment of Liljan. Sigmund Freud's psychoanalysis had been groundbreaking in the treatment of psychological and emotional distress, and the method was making significant impressions in Norway at the time of Bjerke's novel in 1942. As it turns out, Bugge has also been treating her brother Bjørn and has a head start on everyone else when it comes to understanding the ominous incestuous background to current events. The combination of Bugge's treatment of the siblings and the discovery of Bjørn's dark descent as elaborated in his diary, a text that Bugge says describes 'a man's spiritual catastrophe', creates a perfect horror movie character. Director Bergstrøm enhances this impression by depicting several of Bjørn's experiences in flashbacks: the confused man is haunted by the ghost of Gråvik (Leif Sommerstad) appearing out of the lake. To further emphasise the supernatural element, at least Bjørn's own impression of it, the Gråvik spectre apparently transforms into the shape of a one-legged crow, the man himself having lost his leg in real life.

The occultist Mørk, played by the author of the source novel, expounds for a minute on a concept that points ahead to the post-2000 Norwegian horror wave in succinct fashion, as he berates Bugge and the others for what he thinks is an irrational belief in the rational. Mørk complains that modern Europeans imagine that they possess 'the full truth' about the world and everything in it, trusting even their minds to scientific rationality, but that we in reality are more like ignorant children, what Mørk condescendingly labels 'spiritual bushmen'. He laments our civilisation's lack of acceptance for 'creepiness', a fixation with 'cosiness' and a neurotic need to explain everything, making us blind to much in heaven and earth that cannot be explained by rational thought alone. The transformation of the cosy national-romantic wilderness into the creepy wilderness of Norwegian horror cinema is predicted here in Mørk's indictment of our preoccupation with what is safe and rational. It cannot last, because it is fundamentally unnatural in its denial of darker and deeper truths.

Watching Bergstrøm's *Lake of the Dead* today, more than sixty years later, is in some ways a surprising experience. The pace and tone of the film appear more modern than one would probably expect in a 1958 horror movie from a country that never made horror movies. Stylistically, *Lake of the Dead* sits comfortably in the tradition of the classical narrative cinema first and foremost associated with Hollywood. It was the first Norwegian feature to be shot in cinemascope, and it is also remarkably sure-footed as a work of genre filmmaking. On the other hand, certain attributes of the film are no doubt signs of the time in which it was made. Chief among these is the frequently overbearing and condescending attitude towards the women of the story, seemingly the hysterical sex in need of rational male guidance. This attitude extends to the narrative itself, where there is a slight sense of irony, a cynical distance to the characters and story at times, partly initiated and supported by the fact that Bernhard Borge (Kolstad's main character) is an author who sits down to adapt the tale into a novel in the opening framing scene of the film. However, this tone is rather successfully adjusted by the ambiguous ending, where Borge finds himself defending the psychoanalytic conclusion to the story while holding an eerily unexplained crow's feather in his hand.

Sixty-one years later, director Nini Bull Robsahm (born 1981) would create a re-adaptation of the André Bjerke source novel, slightly adjusting the English title of the work to *Lake of Death* (2019). Robsahm's horror credentials included co-writing and starring in 2008's *Manhunt*, as well as writing and directing the relationship thriller *Amnesia* (2014), and she both wrote and directed the new Bjerke adaptation. In the process, Robsahm would become one of very few female Norwegian horror cinema directors, the only others being Astrid Thorvaldsen, who directed the low-budget student film *Myling: The Myth Awakens (Utburd)* in 2014, and Kjersti Helen Rasmussen, who directed the 2022 psychological horror movie *The Nightmare (Marerittet)*.

The two major differences between *Lake of the Dead* in 1958 and *Lake of Death* in 2019 are detectable in the latter's gender portrayals and its subgeneric aesthetics. In the first instance, the female lead character becomes gradually more active, as opposed to the statically passive women of the original film. In the second instance, however, the new film becomes more predictable and less engaging than the original because of its affiliation with the modern subgenre of slasher movies. An example of the latter is the updated composition of the group of friends who head into the countryside for a weekend getaway.

Lake of Death does not have the slightly reassuring framing device of the previous adaptation, opening instead with the train journey into the (by now) well-established rural wilderness, which is all but the omnipresent prerequisite of any Norwegian horror story. Lillian (Iben Akerlie) is travelling with her ex-boyfriend and psychologist Gabriel (Jonathan Harboe), the romantic couple Harald (Elias Munk) and Sonja (Sophia Lie), and the podcaster Bernhard (Jakob Schøyen Andersen). The group meets up with the Swedish ranger Kai (Ulric von der Esch), another ex-boyfriend of Lillian's, and is set to spend some days in the remote lakeside house that Lillian co-owns with her twin brother Bjørn (Patrick Walshe McBride), who has been missing following a sudden disappearance one year earlier. Lillian is looking to face the trauma of losing him and selling the house to achieve emotional closure.

The first thing to notice about the cast is that it's pan-Scandinavian, a common occurrence in these days of international co-productions. Beside the Norwegians there are two Danes (Gabriel and Harald) and one Swede (Kai). Lillian's brother Bjørn is also played by the British actor McBride, but since Bjørn is mute there is no issue with language. This mix of nationalities is believable enough, but the generically required dynamics of friction makes for a very unlikely group of friends. Several of them seem to dislike each other to such a degree that it frankly becomes impossible to accept that they would agree to spend time together in the wilderness.

An early example of this friction-driven dynamic comes in the very first scene, aboard the train. Bernhard has his nose in a novel, and Sonja proceeds to slap the book with her hand, right in front of his face, merely chuckling at his annoyance. Compared with the early scene of admittedly confrontational but still good-humoured banter in 1958's *Lake of the Dead*, this set-up scene in 2019's *Lake of Death* appears primitive and ineffective. It is a sign of everything to come: we don't see any of these characters doing anything good or nice for each other, the creation of tension taking complete precedence over the audience's potential engagement with fairly well-rounded characters and their plight.

The apparent reason for this approach to the story is the teachings of the slasher subgenre of horror films, as discussed in Chapters 3 and 4 of this book, where the composition of a group of people has the ultimate aim of providing fodder for a killer. With the genre awareness in modern Norwegian cinema also comes an inevitable target audience awareness. As the group that comprises the young community in *Lake of Death* reaches the wild, the film seems anxious to nudge its presumably genre-aware audience. There is an overt reference to *The Blair Witch Project* (Daniel Myrick and Eduardo Sánchez, 1999), and at one point Sonja imitates Freddy Krueger from the *A Nightmare on Elm Street* franchise, intoning 'I'm your boyfriend now, Nancy.' However, the question is whether this appeals at all to a target audience in the heavily cinema-going 15 to 25 bracket, or if, as seems more likely, such references are ultimately aimed at people over 40 who have a nostalgic relationship to the films in question. Indeed, at one point an excited Bernhard exclaims, 'This is completely *Evil Dead*', as they discover the entrance to the secret basement. In any case, the age and hipness of the cast of characters is clearly tuned into the slasher movie mode of our age. Engagement and marriage are not concepts in this story, unlike the previous adaptation, and the audience is asked to relate to a group of basically overgrown kids. This set-up misses a key point of engagement with genre fiction: audiences enjoy seeing characters they *would like to resemble*, the people they *want to be*, as much as people actually resembling themselves.

It is unclear why Lillian would bring Bernhard, Harald and Sonja with her on this expedition. The only character with a clear purpose related to Lillian is Gabriel, replacing Bugge as the psychologist who labours to understand and cure the emotional ailment of the central female character. The new aspect of this patient-doctor relationship is a romantic involvement in the recent past, which understandably would have been unheard of in the novel or in the original adaptation of it. Admittedly, Bernhard has an interest in the occult, replacing the critic Mørk of the original film, and so he finds the haunted house qualities of Lillian's old home fascinating as material for his podcast. Harald and Sonja, on the other hand, seem to serve no other function than causing friction when things get spooky. Although their names were also present in *Lake of the Dead*, this time they are brought together as a couple for the apparent reason that King Harald of Norway is married to Queen Sonja. It's nothing but a curious aside, and once things in the house start to go wrong, Harald is anything but a calm and considerate presence: he quickly loses his cool, angrily confronting both Bernhard (who he accuses of foul play in the interest of creating a scary podcast) and Lillian (who he simply calls 'a witch').

The trigger for this credibility-defying eruption of conflict is Lillian's habit of sleepwalking, long kept at bay but now returning upon her revisit to the old house. One morning the group find the breakfast table set when they wake up, each assuming one of the others has arranged it. When it becomes apparent that no one is responsible for this seemingly selfless act, not surprising considering their blatantly self-centred attitudes, Harald in particular gets upset and confrontational. The creaky house seems to live a life of its own, possibly hiding secrets that relate to Lillian's past, and nerves fray.

With Bjørn having been lost since the previous year, there is no current disappearance and no criminal investigation going on in *Lake of Death*. There is no police presence in the story, although Bjørn reappears like he does in the original adaptation, having somehow survived undetected for a whole year until his sister returns to their house in the company of several people who will fuel Bjørn's incestuous jealousy. Bjørn is hiding in a secret basement of the house, one that even Lillian never knew about, and the background myth of the lake is not as central to the story as it was in 1958. In fact, there is a forced dialogue of exposition about the lake when Bernhard asks, 'Do you know how deep it is, by the way?', and Lillian answers, 'No one knows. They say it's bottomless.' Kai the ranger joins the group by the lakeside and tells the story of Tore Gruvik (adjusted back to the name in the novel, after the alternative Gråvik was used in the first film), a troubled war veteran who lived in the woods by the lake with his wife and son in the 1920s. He became entranced by the lake, some say possessed by it, and his frustrated wife took a young lover to make up for the lack of marital affection. Gruvik then allowed the dark power of the lake to overcome him and murdered both the lover and his own wife, later drowning himself in the lake. It should be noted that there is no hint of incest in the lake's myth this time, but Robsahm still intensifies this aspect in a different way as the story unfolds.

In lieu of the current mystery of disappearance that the story revolves around in *Lake of the Dead*, Robsahm's *Lake of Death* homes in on the psychological trauma of Lillian. Her dreams and visions are made explicit here, not merely related as they were in the previous adaptation. Lillian has vivid dreams and visions of dark, dead water creeping from the lake and coming out of the house's faucets and even infecting bodies. She dreams of a black liquid crawling down the walls and covering her body, and she actually sees a sickly dark shape on Harald's chest. The supernatural, or the paranormal, is indisputably present here, not ambiguously implied as it was in the 1958 version: when an upset Harald storms out of the living room to leave the house, he stops at a mirror and sees the dark liquid filling his own eyes. This black, oily water taints Lillian in her dreams and visions, but it also marks others for death. It seems that Gruvik's spirit has become the lake, and that Bjørn might have been literally taken by Gruvik when he disappeared the year before. Gruvik's evil spectre then reappears as Bjørn, rising out of the basement of the old house, to claim his victim: the already marked Harald, who accuses Bjørn's sister of witchcraft. Bjørn has presumably already assaulted Kai. The ranger's car is found in the woods, empty and blood-stained. The next to be targeted is Gabriel the psychologist. Both he and Kai are rival contenders for Lillian's affection, and this Bjørn cannot accept.

The very first frame of the movie is the reflection of Lillian and Bjørn in the water of the lake. The camera tilts up to reveal the siblings sitting in a rowing boat. Bjørn is fascinated by their mirror images in the water, and he asks Lillian if she thinks it is true that there is a different person in one's reflection. The twins proceed to do a kind of dance with each other, acting like each other's mirror and moving in unison. This overt symbolism of twins, mirrors and the water surface lays bare a certain artistic ambition that goes beyond the rather simple narrative momentum of the 1958 version. However, Lillian is there with what Bjørn feels is very bad news: she is leaving, with Kai. This short scene is a little piece of the story's past event, in Vera Dika's meaning, and Robsahm cuts to the legend 'one year later . . .'

It is not until the end of the film that we learn what happened when Lillian gave Bjørn the bad news. Bjørn reacted by attempting to rape Lillian. In desperate self-defence, the one truly active (or reactive) moment in her character arc, Lillian grabbed an oar and swung it heavily at Bjørn's head. Dizzy and fainting, Bjørn fell into the lake, disappearing into what Lillian believed to be his death in the dark depths. Even if the incestuous aspect is removed from the Gruvik myth of the lake, it is intensified on screen in the story of the twins. Leading up to the denouement that includes the flashback rape attempt, this relationship goes as far as a kiss, just barely obscured by the camera angle but obviously a kiss, nonetheless. However, the illness is Bjørn's alone, not the lake's. This is curious, since removing the incest from the myth also removes the connection between Gruvik and Bjørn that was there in the 1958 version. In a similar way, the Gruvik cabin is no longer the place where the group stays. This time the house is Lillian's own, with no previous history outlined. In short, Robsahm's re-adaption plays down Gruvik's influence in favour of Bjørn's personal responsibility for his actions, while at the same time tying Lillian much closer to the power of the lake through her explicit dreams and visions.

Two main points emerge in the comparison of Robsahm's 2019 *Lake of Death* with Bergstrøm's 1958 *Lake of the Dead*. On the one hand, the new film is strongly akin to the relatively primitive tropes of the modern slasher subgenre of horror, even if *Lake of Death* is clearly a psychological horror film. Examples of this include the structure of past and present events coming together, the generically friction-oriented composition of the cast of characters, and the staging of the old dark house as the terrible place of the story. In *Lake of the Dead*, the house was still basically a safe and cosy place. In *Lake of Death*, it has become the creepy and unhomely terrible place of the slasher in American cinema: part haunted house and part killer's lair. The creaking floors, self-opening doors, deep shadows and shuffling footsteps are effective set-ups for slasher-typical jump scares. Inside this generally terrible place, the most specifically terrible place is of course the basement, reminiscent of the Mountain Man's lair in the basement of the hotel in *Cold Prey*, as discussed in Chapter 3. Here, in the deepest place of Lillian's haunted house, lies Bjørn's diary. The rambling scribbles therein betray a mind in apocalyptic distress, much like the diary did in *Lake of the Dead*. In *Lake of Death*, the still alive Bjørn becomes very much the subgeneric killer of the slasher, emerging from his hiding place to take the lives of members of the young community that has invaded his realm.

On the other hand, the new film shows a heightened sense of artistry in the motifs of waters and mirrors. Robsahm builds a kind of border world where Lillian sees and experiences both sides, an audio-visual ambition that was not present in the earlier *Lake of the Dead*. The concept of twins and dualities becomes quite overt in the staging of scenes, like the opening shot of the siblings' reflections in the lake. This motif is repeated in mirrors inside the old house, a significant example being the audience's fleeting views of the hiding Bjørn in a mirror as the unknowing Lillian investigates the secret basement. The mirror motif is coupled with the mud-like substance that creeps out of the lake, oozes from faucets and cracks in the walls, covers Lillian's body in her dreams and visions, and even infects Harald physically after he has survived an apparent attack while swimming in the lake. Ultimately, the mirror motif and Lillian's visions of the invading oily liquid can be taken to represent her sense of how her twin brother has been taken over by the murky darkness of the lake.

Essentially, what is hidden in *Lake of Death* is shame and guilt. Lillian suffers the deep shame of her twin brother's romantic and sexual feelings for her, and she doubles that shame with the secret of her own attack on Bjørn, thinking that she has in fact killed him. The lake represents not merely a distant past and a mythical threat of destruction, but Lillian's very recent

Figure 8.2 Lillian and her twin brother ponder their separation in a boat on the lake, in the film's traumatising past event. (Screenshot from *Lake of Death*)

experience of a shameful crisis. The juxtaposition of two different worlds is a hallmark of the psychological horror film, and *Lake of Death* stages this as being over and under the water, outside and inside the mirror. Lillian's mind fluctuates between the two sides, the two worlds, while her brother Bjørn has transgressed, crossed over, slipping under the water and into the mirror. The twins are separated. Such a separation means disorder, and it reminds Lillian of the separation of her and Bjørn as orphaned children. That trauma led to him becoming a mute and her becoming a sleepwalker. Lillian says that she has been carrying a heavy sense of grief ever since. The current separation intensifies her feeling of being lost between worlds: Bjørn has surrendered to the darkness, while Lillian resists it, although the ending of the film seems to suggest that Lillian has become one with the lake, thus reuniting the long-lost twins. There is indeed a different person in Lillian's reflection, a different her in the shadows of the other side, as the film's opening suggested.

Like Norway itself and Norwegians themselves, Norwegian horror cinema has changed a lot in the sixty-one years that separate the forebear *Lake of the Dead* and the current re-adaptation *Lake of Death*. Some of this is obvious: the very short and revealing nightgown that modern-day Lillian wears when she plunges into the lake while sleepwalking would surely never have appeared in a 1958 film. In other ways the changes are strongly tied to the development of the modern horror film. Norwegian directors, like Nini Bull Robsahm, have become accomplished in the art of creating modern horror genre entertainment. This means that *Lake of Death* expertly stages the prerequisite jump scares that are most clearly identified with the slasher film, even if it is quite obviously a psychological horror film. Even so, the modernised re-telling of André Bjerke's horror classic still relies on the dark secrets of dead water as the source of horror. This never changes.

What has changed in recent years, however, is Norwegian cinema branching out into the apocalyptic stories of the disaster film, which is clearly a horror-related type of genre entertainment. At the same time, some of the directors most intimately connected with the Norwegian horror tradition have made the leap to Hollywood, spreading the Norwegian doom and gloom in a way that was never before likely to happen. Their American movies have sometimes been hugely successful, but they are often lacking the tactile particularity that made their Norwegian output remarkable in the first place.

9. THE NORWEGIAN APOCALYPSE

All horror tales involve some kind of threat to that which is safe and familiar, a threat of upsetting an ostensibly natural, or at least preferable, order. This looming destruction and transformation has the potential to bring about a figurative or even literal end to the world as the main characters know it, taking audiences on a journey into the unknown and beyond. Inherently, such tales are about either transgression or transcendence: whether they portray the attacks on innocent victims by a masked killer, or the discovery of spirit realms and supernatural powers, horror tales are fundamentally about exceeding limits and crossing borders. Indeed, all drama ultimately carries with it the threat of downfall, the possibility of passing a point of no return, a chance that the world will change forever. The horror genre simply amplifies this aspect of dramatic fiction.

In recent years, the wave of cinematic horror in Norway has subsided somewhat, in the sense that publicly funded mainstream horror productions have given way to an increase in the number of low-budget features that now achieve broad cinema distribution with digital ease. At the same time, the disaster film has emerged as a new (and clearly horror-related) Norwegian genre of destruction and transformation, gaining huge audience popularity. In a time when several Norwegian horror directors have found work and success in Hollywood, the Norwegian apocalypse, taking shape in either the horror or disaster genres, is as terrifyingly tantalising as it ever was.

The end of the world, Norwegian-style

As discussed at the end of Chapter 6, there are real existential threats to the social-democratic ideal, a true dark side to the Nordic utopian dream. The image of Norway as a beacon of equality and progress is fading with the increasing inequality of its citizens, the rich getting steadily richer and the less well-off enjoying ever less opportunity to climb social and professional ladders, particularly in terms of the wealth accumulation of the rich set against the debt accretion of the middle and lower classes. Norway is practically running to catch up with Sweden, once known as the world's most equitable country, where 'the social-democratic era has been erased' in the flurry of privatisation, commercialisation and wealth concentration that has taken place since the height of social-democratic Swedish politics in the early 1980s (Bredeveien 2019). A similar situation is developing in Denmark, where the widening gap between haves and have-nots, the differences in opportunities afforded by belonging to different economic and social classes, is quickly becoming more influential in people's lives than it has been in ages (Olsen et al 2021). In the Nordic and Scandinavian region of Europe, still hailed as being among the world's most peaceful and equitable countries, researchers are once again discussing social and economic developments in terms of class.

These things add up to the real-world nightmare of discovering that the social-democratic Nordic utopia no longer exists, if ever it did, whether this be the case of Sweden, Denmark or Norway. The crime fiction of Nordic noir, exemplified by the Swedish *Millennium* series from Stieg Larsson, often underpins the drama with this bleak social reality of seemingly prosperous countries where the post-war programs of collective rebuilding have been superseded in the last forty years by the neoliberal agenda of New Public Management, corporate capital and decreased wealth taxation. The Norwegian horror cinema, as I have shown throughout the book, is akin to this and expounds on it by imbuing the previously regenerative and romantic nature and wilderness so symbolic of Norway with sinister secrets of death and destruction, a dystopian darkness hidden beneath the utopian surface.

Imagining a Scandinavia where social-democratic politics are applied anew to re-establishing programs of equalisation seems difficult in this day and age, our collective and mediated perception of the world apparently leaving us unable to counter the momentum of neoliberal and capitalist politics of inequality. Ironically, the popular genre entertainment of recent years in Norway has shown that there is no lack of imagination, in the minds of filmmakers and audiences alike, when it comes to visualising and staging complete and utter cinematic catastrophes. Fictional disasters on an apocalyptic scale have partially replaced the attraction of smaller-scale horror stories. However, I will argue that the coming of the Norwegian disaster blockbuster is intrinsically linked with the Norwegian horror film, and that they both resonate with the post-social-democratic reality of modern Norway.

Christopher Sharrett has discussed the slasher movie forebear *The Texas Chain Saw Massacre* as a story about apocalypse, a depiction of the end of civilisation, in which 'myths of utopia' are ultimately revealed to be false illusions (1984: 301). Much of Norwegian horror cinema can be characterised in a similar way, for example *Dark Woods* (*Villmark*, Pål Øie, 2003), the *Cold Prey* (*Fritt vilt*, 2006–10) series and *Manhunt* (*Rovdyr*, Patrik Syversen, 2008), which are all examples of the generically apocalyptic slasher subgenre that Sharrett initially describes. However, there are other kinds of apocalypses in other kinds of Norwegian horror movies. In *Next Door* (*Naboer*, Pål Sletaune, 2005), John's world crumbles by way of a psychotic breakdown, and the titular character in *Thelma* (Joachim Trier, 2017) suffers humiliation and defeat while struggling to perceive her own supernatural powers as something other than a curse. She ultimately disintegrates to the point of giving herself up, only narrowly avoiding death at the hands of her father. There is also the more literal apocalypse of the Norwegian horror hybrids: a zombie invasion in *Dead Snow* (*Død snø*, Tommy Wirkola, 2009), a national disaster of ravaging monsters in *Troll Hunter* (*Trolljegeren*, André Øvredal, 2010) and the Midgard Serpent, quite literally a symbol of the end-time, in *Ragnarok* (*Gåten Ragnarok*, Mikkel Brænne Sandemose, 2013).

When the Norwegian horror originator Pål Øie ventured completely outside the horror genre to direct the 2019 biographical film *Catching the Flame* (*Astrup – Flammen over Jølster*), a historical drama about the early 1900s painter Nikolai Astrup, it became plain to see that the aesthetics of apocalypse remains a thread through all of Øie's work. The struggling painter in *Catching the Flame* yearns to capture a subjective and tactile sense of nature and culture in his native Western Norway, dismissing national romanticism and wanting to communicate the sublime mysteries of woods, lakes and mountains, much like Øie would do with his own horror films. Astrup is also fighting an asthmatic condition, as well as his vicar father's pious authority, inexorably leading him to the imminent personal crisis of losing his battles on all fronts. This dread of downfall is framed by the overwhelmingly beautiful landscapes of the real Astrup's actual home, the place where Øie himself grew up: Jølster in the west of Norway. The historical painter's personal disintegration happens in a place where the national-romantic image of Norway would suggest no such thing could happen, in the liberating and regenerating rural and wilderness. Astrup dies of pneumonia at the age of 47, a poor and broken man, completing his personal and artistic apocalypse.

Catching the Flame opens with a surprisingly direct voice-over where Astrup (portrayed by the Danish actor Thure Lindhardt) tells of a childhood dream, or perhaps a memory, that haunts him: 'The descent into hell. I walked down through a hole, and something that seemed like stairs.' It sets the tone for a meditation on the spiritual aspects of the Norwegian nature and farmland culture that both Astrup and Øie labour to understand and capture in paintings and moving images, respectively. The sun is reflected in the still water of a lake, and the flame of a bonfire dances in Astrup's eyes, in Øie's visualisation of the burning desire that drives the painter onward, but also, and inevitably, downward into disintegration. The real Nikolai Astrup was uncompromisingly at odds with contemporary national-romantic trends of art and nation-building, and he saw nature as something deeper and more profoundly meaningful than the rise and fall of nations and unions. In the film, his urge to capture and communicate this aesthetic is a race against time: his illness, coupled with a dependency on atropine tobacco and medicinal cognac, is slowly driving him ever further into anxiety and depression.

Øie stages the apocalypse in all his movies. As a director he is the auteur of the downfall. The most intimate and personal example is *Catching the Flame*, while the most overt and generic is probably the original *Dark Woods*. Yet another version is seen in the disaster film *The Tunnel* (2019), Øie's most realistically dramatic take on apocalypse. Road tunnels are certainly man-made, this is no natural disaster in the making, but they are built to overcome the challenge of transportation in a mountainous country. Norway is criss-crossed with tunnels for roads and railways, and the safety concerns are very real. In recent years, there have been potentially catastrophic fires in several of the country's long road tunnels, and only a combination of luck and outstanding work by fire personnel has prevented loss of life.

The Tunnel focuses on Stein (Thorbjørn Harr), a fireman charged with leading a rescue mission into the mountain when a tanker truck catches fire and traps many vehicles and people inside. One of the people in peril is his own daughter Elise (Ylva Fuglerud), escaping to the city on an outbound coach after a fight with her father. The family battling internal friction as well as a major external crisis is a core component of the disaster film genre, and Øie's characters are recognisably real and normal people. Indeed, for many Norwegians, the film will be all-too-familiar in its low-key portrayal of the everyday risk of tunnel travel gone horribly wrong. The generic story is framed in both this sense of narrative believability, and an outstanding cinematographic application of landscapes and roads: the majestic shots of snowy mountains in the film's opening scenes, masterfully filmed and edited by regular Øie collaborator Sjur Aarthun, are effectively juxtaposed with the claustrophobic tunnel where there is seemingly no escape from catastrophe. As in the horror of *Dark Woods*, the powerful nature of Norway is the site of apocalypse in Øie's disaster movie too.

The disaster film is often thought of as being about people who suffer natural disasters of some sort. A classic American example is *Earthquake*

(Mark Robson, 1974), and modern takes on the variant are seen in *Dante's Peak* (Roger Donaldson, 1997) and *San Andreas* (Brad Peyton, 2015). However, the genre has always included plot patterns as diverse as alien invasion, like the older *The War of the Worlds* (Byron Haskin, 1953) and the newer *Independence Day* (Roland Emmerich, 1996); hubris-driven and technology-dependent accidents, like *The Towering Inferno* (John Guillermin, 1974) and *Titanic* (James Cameron, 1997); epidemics and pandemics, like *Outbreak* (Wolfgang Petersen, 1995) and *Contagion* (Steven Soderbergh, 2011); experiences of war and terrorism, like *Saving Private Ryan* (Steven Spielberg, 1998) and *United 93* (Paul Greengrass, 2006); or global destruction from comets and asteroids, like *Deep Impact* (Mimi Leder, 1998) and *Armageddon* (Michael Bay, 1998). More recently, tragic natural disasters can also come in the form of apocalyptic environmental and climate disorders that are caused by humans, as in Roland Emmerich's two blockbusters about the issue, *The Day After Tomorrow* (2004) and *2012* (2009). Key generic components of the disaster film are most often action set-pieces, romantic and family drama, thriller-oriented suspense, science fiction trappings, and also horror motifs, as in the case of monster movies like *King Kong* (Merian C. Cooper and Ernest B. Schoedsack, 1933), *Cloverfield* (Matt Reeves, 2008) and *Jurassic World* (Colin Trevorrow, 2015). What these different types of disaster films all have in common is the portrayal of more or less ordinary people faced with terrifying accidents, invasions or disasters (Keane [2001] 2006).

In 2015, Roar Uthaug directed the movie that put the sublime Nordic and Arctic landscapes of Norway into apocalyptic action, launching the disaster tradition in Norwegian cinema. *The Wave* (*Bølgen*, 2015) was produced by Fantefilm, Uthaug's partners in the making of *Cold Prey* and *Escape* (*Flukt*, 2012), and it depicts the horrific effects of a massive rock avalanche plunging into a fjord in Western Norway. The resulting tsunami devastates the internationally well-known tourist town of Geiranger, a genre-defining tragic outcome of not heeding the warning of a scientist. *The Wave* sold 832,723 tickets in Norway, far outpacing anything mustered by the Norwegian horror tradition, and so put in place the groundwork for a new popular genre wave that is still rolling (*Film & Kino* 2015: 13).

The Wave bases its premise on the real Loen disasters of 1905 and 1936. In both cases, a huge chunk of Mount Ramnefjell plunged into Lovatnet Lake in the middle of the night, creating tsunamis that killed sixty-one persons in 1905 and seventy-four persons in 1936, utterly demolishing two lakeside villages. Forty people were killed in a similar disaster in Tafjord in 1934, adding grimly to the number of people lost to the devastating natural forces of colliding mountains and waters in Norway. In many parts of the country, people live with the constant threat of tall mountains that will inevitably shed massive amounts of rock, some of them dropping their weight into a lake or fjord where deadly waves can result. *The Wave* warns that it is only a matter of time before this happens again, and a matter of sufficient warning if people are going to survive. The film follows geologist Kristian (Kristoffer Joner, leading man for the start of Norwegian disaster cinema as he had previously been for the start of Norwegian horror with *Dark Woods*) as he is about to quit his job in Geiranger, where he is monitoring the mountain Åkerneset, and take his hotel manager wife Idun (Ane Dahl Torp) and their two kids to Stavanger for a new job and a new life. Needless to say, this doesn't happen without complications, and the heroic scientist must battle a natural disaster of truly epic proportions while also trying to save and unite his family.

Uthaug takes his time in building the suspense, much like he did in *Cold Prey*. Family scenes are interwoven with a growing anxiety about mysterious sensor readings from the mountain, and Kristian has a very hard time packing his bags and letting go of his previous responsibility of watching Åkerneset. In the disaster film, as in the horror film, the slowly but steadily increasing tension and the audience's anticipation of horrific events are key to the genres' ultimate emotional payoffs. Uthaug understands the importance of this dynamic and the need for a creeping sense of unease to carry the viewer along, built up through a combination of narrative information, character interactions, landscape vistas and ominously intensifying music cues. Spectacular helicopter shots of the fjords and mountains lead up to the point of apocalypse, wherein the beauty of the Norwegian landscape disintegrates in a violent symphony of CGI splendour that Norwegian cinema had never seen before. The crumbling mountain unleashes the monster wave, 80 meters tall, that Kristian has warned his less anxious colleagues about: '10 minutes later, Geiranger doesn't exist anymore.' The devastation is complete, and the viewer's engagement is all the more intense because of the authentic sense of people and places that Uthaug has orchestrated up to this point.

Ultimately, Uthaug did for the Norwegian disaster film what he had previously done for Norwegian horror. *The Wave* signalled the consolidation of a very popular disaster movie trend in Norwegian cinema, creating a blueprint that Fantefilm (and conceivably other producers interested in the genre) could use for future films. This particular blueprint was even more Hollywood-inspired than the one they had created with *Cold Prey*, and *The Wave* became a major game-changer in Norwegian cinema. Previously, the few Norwegian films that had touched on the disaster mode of cinematic storytelling had been decisively more modernist in their approach, even somewhat impressionist at times: the less expensive and less popular *Rising Tide* (*Havet stiger*, Oddvar Einarson, 1990), *Pax* (Annette Sjursen, 2010) and *People in the Sun* (*Mennesker i solen*, Per-Olav Sørensen, 2011) had all been false starts to the disaster genre in Norway. Now, in the wake of Fantefilm's successful pursuit of popular genre cinema, this trend would produce films from two of the directors who had earlier initiated the Norwegian horror tradition: Uthaug's *The Wave* and Øie's *The Tunnel*. The former was successful enough to warrant a sequel in 2018: *The Quake* (*Skjelvet*), directed by cinematographer turned director John Andreas Andersen. The same characters would now be caught in the middle of a shattering earthquake that destroys the Norwegian capital Oslo.

We meet Kristian (Joner again) three years after his heroic efforts to save Geiranger from a deadly tsunami. To the people and press of Norway he is a hero, but he has also become a bit of a hermit, living alone high up the mountainside on the outskirts of Geiranger. Kristian has grown a beard, as depressed and otherwise troubled hero characters tend to do, while popping pills to deal with post-traumatic stress and the self-inflicted obsessive guilt of not having saved more people than he did. Joner carries these clichés with conviction, excelling when Kristian fails to deal with a visit from his daughter Julia (Edith Haagenrud-Sande). When she tries to help her father out by making him breakfast in the morning, he promptly sends her back to her mother Idun (Torp again), who is now involved with running the skyscraping Hotel Plaza in downtown Oslo.

The early parts of the film thus re-establish the setting of Western Norway's fjords and mountains that was so effective in *The Wave*, only to ditch them for the less exotic and arguably less engaging urban cityscapes of Oslo, a kind of anywhere and nowhere in particular compared with the tactile specificity of Geiranger. Kristian goes to Oslo, partly to reconcile with his family and mostly to pursue his geologist obsession further. A fellow geologist working for the NORSAR foundation has been killed in a mysterious accident in a subsea road tunnel. It turns out that the man, Konrad Lindblom (Per Frisch), was trying to get in touch with Kristian over concerns about seismic activity in the Oslo region. Kristian shaves off his beard, follows up Konrad's leads and research, and enters into a protracted and ultimately doomed personal effort to get NORSAR to sound the warning for an impending earthquake disaster. Kristian is left with nothing to do but save his own family.

The payoff in *The Quake*, the ultimate destruction of Oslo, comes curiously late in the movie's running time, leaving very little time for the aftermath and reorientation that are structurally essential phases of the disaster movie's traditional narrative pattern. It happens about one hour and ten minutes into the film's one hour and forty-five minutes running time, when the ground breaks open and alternately swallows and upends Norway's biggest city. In fact, the destruction kicks off the film's third act, unlike the second act mid-point event in *The Wave*, and Kristian faces the personal apocalypse of losing his wife Idun in the disintegration of the Plaza hotel. The hotel's top floors stand upright like the deck of the stricken Titanic, and collapsing buildings throughout the cityscape bring to mind commonplace devastations in contemporary Hollywood disaster films and superhero movies. Julia's view of the disaster from the hotel's sky bar is undoubtedly awesome (if contrived), and the horrific action of CGI destruction, interwoven with Kristian's desperate efforts to save his daughter, makes for action that is amped up even compared with *The Wave*. However, the loss of Idun, wife and mother, emotionally outdoes anything else the filmmakers throw at the screen.

The structure of *The Quake* is quite different from that of John Andreas Andersen's subsequent disaster movie, *The North Sea* (*Nordsjøen*, 2021). In the latter film, where the catastrophic action is placed far out to sea in the oil and gas fields off the coast of Norway, the disaster has already started happening when the film opens, albeit off-screen in a not entirely satisfying move for a disaster film. Sofia (Kristine Kujath Torp) is an ROV operator working with the oil and gas industry in Western Norway. Out of the blue, Sofia and her assistant Arthur (Rolf Kristian Larsen) are called upon to apply their skills and their Eelume underwater robot (which exists in the real world) in a top-secret mission: an oil rig has foundered in the North Sea, possibly as a result of sudden seismic activity, and Sofia and Arthur have to send their robot into the wreckage to locate both the dead and the living, sadly without being able to save anyone. However, upon reviewing their footage they find what appears to be massive gas leaks in the ocean floor, a sign that the entire area has become unstable and might spawn multiple earthquakes and underwater avalanches. This could potentially disrupt and destroy all the oil and gas rigs of the North Sea in a disaster of truly apocalyptic proportions, tearing open more than 300 wells to the ocean and the world above.

A massive evacuation of all North Sea installations is initiated, but Sofia's boyfriend Stian (Henrik Bjelland) is left behind when he tries to manually seal a well on the Gullfaks A platform (also a real installation). No official rescue effort can be risked, so Sofia and Arthur embark on their own and very unofficial mission. In the meantime, with the entire North Sea in the throes of seismic disruption, the resulting oil spill takes on horrific dimensions. Oil company head honchos led by William Lie (Bjørn Floberg) reach the difficult decision, along with Norway's government, that their only viable option is to bomb the spill from the air to literally burn away the threat of catastrophic environmental damage to the sea and the mainland. If the industry and authorities are caught between the devil and the deep blue sea, Sofia and her friends are physically trapped on an offshore platform while all hell breaks loose around them.

There are certainly big things about *The North Sea*. Besides the enormity of the basic premise, the most expected is a new level of special effects mayhem that no previous Norwegian film has achieved, not even *The Wave* or *The Quake*. Somewhat less expected is the presence of a proper female action lead: Kristine Kujath Thorp is every bit the match for Kristoffer Joner in Fantefilm's previous two disaster movies, anchoring the spectacle in a believably realistic performance of human frailty and determination. Her performance is also reminiscent of Fantefilm's ultimate genre character: Ingrid Bolsø Berdal's final girl Jannicke in the first two *Cold Prey* films. If Jannicke was the Ellen Ripley of Norwegian cinema, Sofie might just be the Sarah Connor. *The North Sea* also has the potential to depict a Norwegian apocalypse that resonates on several levels of storytelling: besides the physical death and destruction of the entire Norwegian portion of the North Sea, there is the impending doom of climate catastrophe on Earth right here and right now. This is a real catastrophe in which Norwegian oil and gas production inevitably bears significant responsibility, but this national conundrum is an aspect that Andersen and his screenwriters sadly avoid addressing properly, even when it would have strengthened the genre intentions of their film.

Indeed, Andersen and Fantefilm are strikingly careful not to depict anyone in the oil industry as a villain. Institutional greed or personal ambitions are not factors in the present disaster. Floberg's character, emergency manager William Lie, is in fact set up as the perfect antagonist on the inside of the system, somewhat reminiscent of Vice President Becker (Kenneth Walsh) in *The Day After Tomorrow*. In *The North Sea*, however, Lie ultimately makes all the right calls in a job that is both technically and ethically demanding. This might be realistic, but it works against the tension of the disaster genre. Furthermore, it removes the contemporary sting that *The North Sea* could have delivered. Certainly, in order to gain the desired access and cooperation, both in terms of plot mechanics and commercial product placement, Fantefilm have to stay on the good side of any corporate or government entity they rely on. Paradoxically, in *The North Sea* this means sacrificing the generic tension they strive to create: criticism of Norway's oil industry and national fossil fuel politics is kept to a bare minimum and is even voiced by industry insider William Lie himself, effectively giving Norwegian oil and gas a conscientious voice within the film and providing a sufficiently green sheen for industry and filmmakers alike.

This approach to commerciality brings to mind Fantefilm's use of the real NORSAR research foundation in *The Quake*. NORSAR's work involves research and consulting in connection with infrastructure safety, climate change and energy production. According to their own pitch, they 'specialize in seismology and seismic monitoring', and 'Norwegian earthquake news' is a section of their norsar.no website. NORSAR lends credibility to the incredible story and plot of *The Quake*, and in return they get the opportunity to introduce themselves to a huge audience that had previously never heard of them. In addition, it is fair to speculate that the heightened public visibility and general earthquake awareness that comes with an exaggerated blockbuster such as *The Quake* could influence NORSAR's ability to secure both public and private funds. A critical question with regard to the lucrative hype is whether a magnitude 8 earthquake (a truly massive earthquake akin to the one depicted in the film) is likely at all in the Oslo region, when we know of no more than around magnitude 6 events (slight damage to infrastructure and buildings, around the scale of the 1904 Oslo earthquake that the film bases its premise on) in the history of Norwegian earthquakes. The problematic bottom line is that the marketing campaign for *The Quake* not only sold a fiction film, but also raised the profile of a real-world research institution, all based on the fictional account of a terrifying Norwegian apocalypse rendered realistic on the big screen (Andresen 2018, Müller 2018).

Fantefilm are no strangers to maximising budgets and profits through commercial smartness; in fact they have been masters of this art since the beginning. In his 2018 master's thesis, Vidar Tevasvold Aune surveyed Fantefilm's marketing philosophy with a focus on the *Cold Prey* horror series. Aune documented how Fantefilm consciously looked to American cinema for models on how to shape and apply marketing campaigns involving sponsors, product placement, poster art and trailers (Aune 2018). These strategies were successfully implemented with Fantefilm's first feature film, Roar Uthaug's *Cold Prey* in 2006, where trailers and posters closely mimicked the promotion materials of then current American slasher movies. Furthermore, the car manufacturer Fiat Chrysler and the fast-food franchise Burger King were on board for product placement and promotional tie-ins that would continue through many Fantefilm productions to come. Possibly the silliest instance of product placement in Norwegian horror would appear in 2010's *Cold Prey III*, where one member of the group on a wilderness excursion has packed Burger King Whoppers and proceeds to explain to his friends what the burgers consist of. The scene is perfectly awful, although it might explain why the film is set in 1988, the very year the franchise opened its first Norwegian restaurants. Much less narratively gratuitous, but arguably more intrusive, was the Burger King tie-ins for *The Quake*, where the floors of Burger King restaurants were decorated with 'cracks', and you could order an official '*Quake* Menu'. If the alleged Americanisation of Norwegian cinema was ever true, Fantefilm certainly brought it.

To be sure, this cynical production practice is all the more questionable in the case of *The North Sea*, since the industry and national politics at the plot's base are the real-life sources for the existential threat of Norwegian, and indeed global, apocalypse in our age of catastrophic climate change. *The North Sea* could have been the ultimate Norwegian disaster film, the entertainment blockbuster with a conscience that embraced a current global catastrophe in the way that *The Day After Tomorrow* had done before it. Unfortunately, it compromises its own genre ambitions and stops short of its potential, for apparently commercial reasons. However, this criticism might be missing the point, as commercial dominance in the marketplace is clearly one of Fantefilm's main objectives. Indeed, Fantefilm is a prime example of the current era of the producer in modern Norwegian cinema. It does not really matter much who wrote or directed *The North Sea*, it is clearly a Martin Sundland-produced Norwegian disaster movie. The brand has been successfully established through the company's horror films and taken further up the ladder of commercial success with their three apocalyptic visions of the Norwegian end-times.

Maybe such an apocalypse is better had as pure fantasy than a somewhat reality-based drama? The year 2022 sees the release of Roar Uthaug's Netflix feature *Troll*, a diecast monster movie in which a gigantic troll awakes from slumber deep inside the Dovre Mountains and proceeds to wreak havoc on its way south to Oslo. Not since *Troll Hunter* in 2010 has the mythological troll creature been such a threat, but unlike André Øvredal's humorous mockumentary, *Troll* takes American monster movies like *Godzilla* (Gareth Edwards, 2014) as its template. In the end, the threats in Norwegian disaster movies are usually forces of nature and creatures of folklore, but on a vastly bigger scale than the apocalyptic threats of downfall in the country's horror tradition. Meanwhile, at the opposite end of the size spectrum, there are also downfalls and violent endings in low-budget horror films.

Downfalls outside the mainstream

The mainstream Norwegian horror film has not disappeared, but the Norwegian nightmare has in recent years expanded into the much more overtly apocalyptic, and much more popular, disaster film. Recent horror movies like Nini Bull Robsahm's *Lake of Death* (2019) and Pål Øie's *Dark Woods 2* (2015) were made without production funding from the Norwegian Film Institute, unlike most horror movies in the formative period from 2003 to 2010. In fact, Øie has stated that his team saw no point in applying for such funding when they prepared the *Dark Woods* sequel (Øie 2015). After all, most of these genre movies are unlikely to receive funding based on artistic ambition and merit, and producers will have to argue instead that the film's box office potential warrants consideration.

However, the domestic popularity of Norwegian cinema in general has increased considerably following the film policy changes that were outlined in Chapter 2, and funding based on commercial potential thus requires a higher projected audience figure than before. Horror films, although surprisingly popular in the 2003 to 2010 period and still commercially viable, simply cannot compete with war epics or disaster movies. The Institute demands a potential for at least 200,000 tickets sold, numbers unseen by Norwegian horror (excepting some of the genre hybrids discussed in Chapter 7) since Mats Stenberg's *Cold Prey II* in 2008. Given the circumstances, it is no wonder that directors like Uthaug and producers like *Cold Prey*'s Fantefilm have moved on to disaster movies.

Even so, there is still a faithful (if small) audience for Norwegian horror cinema entertainment, and in place of the publicly funded mainstream films there has been an influx of low-budget horror making it to the big screen nationwide thanks to the ease of digital distribution and exhibition. An early example of these was the zombie satire *Dark Souls* (*Mørke sjeler*, 2011) by César Ducasse and Mathieu Péteul, which was discussed in Chapter 7. There has also been Astrid Thorvaldsen's psychological horror *Myling: The Myth Awakens* (*Utburd*, 2014), Frode Nordås' slasher *Bloody Water* (*Skjærgården*, 2016), Reinert Kiil's supernatural horror *The House* (*Huset*, 2016) and his slasher *Christmas Blood* (*Juleblod*, 2017), Severin Eskeland's psychological rape-revenge fantasy *Lust* (*Lyst*, 2017), Carl Christian Raabe's psychological thriller *Haunted* (*Hjemsøkt*, 2017), Geir Greni's slasher turned psychological horror *All Must Die* (*Alle må dø*, 2020), and Henrik Martin Dahlsbakken's zombie comedy *Project Z* (*Prosjekt Z*, 2021).

Horror elements also keep popping up in non-horror films of all sizes. Self-aware genre hybrids at the fringes of horror would happen only once in Norwegian cinema before 2000, in the slightly horrific and chiefly comedic *Something Completely Different* (*Noe helt annet*, Morten Kolstad, 1985), but following the breakthrough of horror that was engendered by film policy changes aiming at increased domestic popularity, they have been conspicuous. In addition to the films discussed in Chapter 7, there has been the thriller *Cave* (Henrik Martin Dahlsbakken, 2016), the mystery drama *Valley of Shadows* (*Skyggenes dal*, Jonas Matzow Gulbrandsen, 2017), and the horror comedy *Vidar the Vampire* (*VampyrVidar*, Thomas Aske Berg and Fredrik Waldeland, 2018), among others.

Then there are the films created completely outside the realm of Norwegian cinema, the straight-to-video and genre festival darlings that don't get to dip their toes in the mainstream. A kind of precursor to this, quite paradoxically, was produced by the public broadcaster NRK in the 1970s. A four-part miniseries titled *A Little Horror?* (1973–4) was constituted of vaguely horror-related short films written by, or based on works by, the well-respected authors André Bjerke, Roald Dahl, Hanns Heinz Ewers and (more obscurely) the Norwegian singer and songwriter Ole Paus. As NRK was the only broadcaster in Norway at the time, this was definitely not outside the mainstream, but it was still outside the film production intended for cinemas.

The notion of film production outside the mainstream is quite new in Norway. As Gunnar Iversen has explained, up until quite recently the only stream in Norwegian cinema was the mainstream, or in other words: everything that got produced and exhibited was mainstream. Norway has never really produced avant-garde cinema, and there has been no tradition of

B-movies being created alongside the dominant mainstream productions, no *cinema bis* alternative. The institutionalised notion of films in good taste, meaning what the average Norwegian would not be too offended by, has largely been upheld by the public funding of production and the public ownership of exhibition. There has been little or no incentive for ideas and projects that veer in the direction of 'the experimental, the tasteless, the indecent, or the shocking' (Iversen 2015).

The digital age, however, has helped change this. Deviating aesthetics have gained a larger foothold and a platform for reaching out, with the relative ease and democratic availability of digital video cameras, laptop software and digital distribution and exhibition technology that can either include or exclude traditional cinema programming. There were examples of so-called video nasties in Norway in the 1980s, but the start of the 2000s saw more accomplished low-budget exploitation films like *22* (Pål Aam and Eystein Hanssen, 2001) and *Bread and Circus* (*Brød & sirkus*, Martin Loke, 2003). Possibly the most prominent filmmaker in this underground segment of Norwegian horror has been Reinert Kiil, who made his name and reputation with *Whore* (*Hora*, 2009) and *Inside the Whore* (2011).

Another current trend that further changes the landscape of horror film production in Norway is the rise of global streaming services. HBO Max, Viaplay and Netflix have all established their own production of original content as well as purchases of independent content in the Nordic countries, and these international giants have access to a level of funding that far outmatches publicly funded or private-public co-financed Norwegian cinema productions. Netflix has recently co-produced and distributed the post-apocalyptic feature film *Cadaver* (*Kadaver*, Jarand Herdal, 2020) and the slightly horror-tinged crime comedy series *Post Mortem: No One Dies in Skarnes* (*Post Mortem: Ingen dør i Skarnes*, Harald Zwart et al, 2021). As previously noted, Netflix is also co-producing and distributing the 2022 monster movie *Troll* by Roar Uthaug. Even low-budget independent films made in Norway, like the psychological horror movie *The Psychics* (*De klarsynte*, Tomas Sem Løkke-Sørensen, 2019) and the post-apocalyptic thriller *Entombed* (Kjell Hammerø, 2020), have achieved digital streaming distribution despite not showing in Norwegian cinemas.

The broad streaming or cinema distribution of low-budget and amateur films has blurred the lines between mainstream and underground horror filmmaking in Norway, and what was previously the underground of independent horror for festivals and home video releases is now regularly exposed to nationwide audiences in cinemas or through global streaming services. Meanwhile, producers and directors of Norwegian mainstream horror have ventured elsewhere, sometimes into the genre of disaster movies. Some of them have even gone to Hollywood, their road ultimately leading them to the cradle of so much genre entertainment that had inspired their outlook and careers, and by extension had shaped the Norwegian horror tradition in the new millennium.

Norway's horror goes to Hollywood

Roar Uthaug told the author that the first call from Hollywood reached him as soon as the teaser trailer for *Cold Prey* was released in late 2005 (Uthaug 2015). This goes to show that producers and agents in Hollywood are ever on the look-out for international talent, and it also illustrates how Uthaug had successfully orchestrated the familiar generic beats of the slasher while imbuing it with a distinct style of his own. Uthaug chose to remain in Norway at the time, but the opportunity arose again after the huge domestic success of *The Wave*. The director travelled abroad and made his Hollywood debut in 2018 with a reboot of *Tomb Raider*, starring Alicia Vikander in the leading role as Lara Croft, previously popularised by Angelina Jolie in the 2001 Hollywood film based on the video game.

Uthaug has a sure hand with both characters and action in *Tomb Raider*, as would be expected of him. However, the film lacks the well-paced urgency and the tactile sense of places and people that have characterised his most important Norwegian feature work: *Cold Prey*, *Escape* and *The Wave*. Disappointingly, *Tomb Raider* feels more like an action movie made by committee, which might very well be an accurate enough description of a Warner Bros. Pictures production headed by a Norwegian director under the aegis of several credited producers. Uthaug dutifully hits all the expected beats of a Hollywood action-adventure, but *Tomb Raider* displays little of the distinct Uthaug-ness so successfully sported by his Norwegian output. While the reboot was fairly successful in commercial terms, it has not yet become the start of a new series, with no sequel plans materialising to date.

Besides Uthaug, many Norwegian genre directors have made Hollywood movies in the years since 2000. The best-known of them are probably Harald Zwart, Morten Tyldum and the directing team of Joachim Rønning and Espen Sandberg. The latter two had made the high-profile and hugely successful historical dramas *Max Manus* (2008) and *Kon-Tiki* (2012) in Norway, before heading west to direct Johnny Depp in *Pirates of the Caribbean: Dead Men Tell No Tales* (2017), the fifth instalment of the action-adventure series. Harald Zwart had gone to Hollywood long before, after making his feature debut with the Swedish action thriller *Hamilton* in 1998, based on author Jan Guillou's spy character. In America, Zwart would direct the comedies *One Night at McCool's* (2001), *Agent Cody Banks* (2003) and *The Pink Panther 2* (2009), as well as the commercially successful remake of *The Karate Kid* (2010) and the intended fantasy franchise kick-off *The Mortal Instruments: City of Bones* (2013), a commercial and critical failure. Morten Tyldum had helmed the Norwegian adaptation of author Jo Nesbø's crime thriller *Headhunters* (*Hodejegerne*) in 2011, before moving to Hollywood and finding great success with the Oscar-nominated biographical drama *The Imitation Game* in 2014. Subsequently, his 2016 science fiction film *Passengers* was less celebrated, but Tyldum remains attached to upcoming projects in Hollywood at the time of writing.

While none of these filmmakers are known for horror, Uthaug's fellow Norwegian horror directors would also flock to Hollywood. *Manhunt*'s director Patrik Syversen made the American low-budget independent horror movie *Prowl* in 2010, and he would later make the American direct-to-video fantasy film *Dragonheart: Battle for the Heartfire* in 2017, but the first Norwegian horror director to actually make the Hollywood leap was *Dead Snow*'s Tommy Wirkola. He made his Hollywood debut with the action horror comedy *Hansel & Gretel: Witch Hunters* in 2013, followed by the less formulaic science fiction thriller *What Happened to Monday* in 2017. The latter starred Noomi Rapace as seven sisters sharing one identity, in a dystopian near future of overpopulation and food shortage. In the context of Wirkola's filmography, *What Happened to Monday* is a slightly surprising and off-kilter suspense tale, showing that the shocks and laughs of his early exploitation-influenced Norwegian films are not the only colours in his filmic palette. The film's roll-out was split between cinema distribution in Europe and Asia and a Netflix release elsewhere.

There have also been Hollywood horror movies made by a Norwegian director who has in fact never directed a feature film in Norway: Lars Klevberg. His Norwegian horror short *Polaroid* (2015) led to a Hollywood feature remake, directed by Klevberg himself, which was finally released in 2019 after being delayed by the Harvey Weinstein scandals that affected the Dimension Films production company. By that point, Klevberg had already directed another horror remake, 2019's *Child's Play*, which was a new take on the murderous doll Chucky that first featured in Tom Holland's 1988 original.

Without a doubt, the Norwegian horror director with the most commercial success and critical acclaim in Hollywood is *Troll Hunter*'s André Øvredal. His first American feature was the supernatural horror *The Autopsy of Jane Doe* in 2017, in which Øvredal proved that he could master a serious horror story in a much more sophisticated style than the found footage horror comedy of his Norwegian debut. His Hollywood follow-up was the very different children's book adaptation *Scary Stories to Tell in the Dark*, released to great commercial success in 2019, a film which further established Øvredal as a versatile horror filmmaker. Being cited by Stephen King as a great horror film was undoubtedly an impressive feather in *Jane Doe*'s cap, and being patronised by *Scary Stories* producer (and world-class genre director in his own right) Guillermo del Toro is persuasive proof of Øvredal's international calibre. At the time of writing,

André Øvredal has been attached to the sequel *Scary Stories to Tell in the Dark 2*, and he is currently in production on the gothic horror film *Last Voyage of the Demeter*, which tells the story of the ship and crew that brought Count Dracula's coffin from Transylvania to London in Bram Stoker's 1897 novel.

Hollywood producers are clearly attracted to these Norwegian filmmakers because of their genre sensibilities, and most likely also because they have demonstrated through their Norwegian films that they can produce effective cinematic action, horror and suspense for a fraction of the cost that is common for Hollywood mid-budget films with equal production value. Norwegian horror films like *Cold Prey* were made for a mere tenth of the budget that went into the contemporary remake *The Texas Chainsaw Massacre* in the early 2000s. There are obviously many reasons why provincial Norwegian films are cheaper to produce than much more complicated Hollywood productions, but it is certainly hard to ignore how Roar Uthaug's *Cold Prey* looks, sounds and feels every bit as impressive, and arguably more authentic, than American slashers of the same era.

Norway is a peculiar country. Horror is a popular genre. Hopefully this book has helped to illuminate how and why Norwegian horror cinema came into being, what forms the genre has taken in Norway, and how the generic concepts of horror film travel across borders, to the point where some of the Norwegian filmmakers even become wanted in Hollywood. The reader might find points to debate in my analysis, but I am confident that the book has outlined a framework for understanding and discussing how a marginal Nordic country got good at making horror films.

Those films have been mostly of two kinds, the slasher and psychological horror subgenres, and some of their directors will go down in history as among the most influential in Norwegian cinema. What these films and filmmakers have illuminated, by design and also by the circumstances of developments in Norwegian genre filmmaking, is to some degree *the Norwegian condition*. The deepest fear of the Norwegian state of mind, the nightmare at the Nordic edge of the Arctic, is that nothing is what it seems, that utopia is a mirage. These stories resonate with domestic cinema audiences and also have the potential for successful travel across borders and oceans. But what remains in Norway, the key hallmark that does not follow these filmmakers to America, is the peculiarity of social-democratic nightmares, the particularly Norwegian apocalypse that the films of the Norwegian horror cinema tradition depict through their settings, landscapes, characters, histories and premises.

The films of Norway's horror cinema tradition are built on genre conventions largely associated with American cinema, but they also bear national hallmarks. Most importantly, they draw on the nature and wilderness of the country as source and setting for apocalyptic horror visions, making them particularly Norwegian nightmares in spite of the transnational generic framework. Directors like Uthaug and Øvredal found their way into Hollywood filmmaking through their expertise in juxtaposing the generic and the uniquely national, imbuing their horror visions with distinct styles that provide enough originality for their work to be interesting and effective in a transnational genre conversation.

In other words, American producers have an eye open for directors who can be trusted with mid-budget genre pictures, and many Norwegian directors have proven their trustworthiness by making successful Norwegian horror movies. Genres tend to travel easily, but the Norwegian horror cinema is not a mere copy of American genre patterns. The most prominent characteristic of this body of work remains the propensity with which it creates terrifying audio-visual portrayals of a deadly wilderness, revealing a potential apocalypse in every gloomy forest, in every dark lake, and in every abandoned mountain lodge.

FILMOGRAPHY

This is a chronological list of horror films and horror hybrids in Norway with a domestic general cinema release in the period from 1958 to 2022:

Lake of the Dead (De dødes tjern)
Subgenre: Psychological horror / crime
Premiere: 17 December 1958
Directed by Kåre Bergstrøm

Clocks by Moonlight (Klokker i måneskinn)
Subgenre: Anthology of psychological and supernatural tales
Premiere: 29 September 1964
Directed by Kåre Bergstrøm

Something Completely Different (Noe helt annet)
Subgenre: Surrealist comedy with horror elements
Premiere: 19 December 1985
Directed by Morten Kolstad

Isle of Darkness (Mørkets øy)
Subgenre: Crime drama with aesthetic intentions of horror
Premiere: 26 December 1997
Directed by Trygve Allister Diesen

Dark Woods (Villmark)
Subgenre: Slasher-related
Premiere: 21 February 2003
Directed by Pål Øie

Next Door (Naboer)
Subgenre: Psychological horror
Premiere: 11 March 2005
Directed by Pål Sletaune

Cold Prey (Fritt vilt)
Subgenre: Slasher
Premiere: 13 October 2006
Directed by Roar Uthaug

Manhunt (Rovdyr)
Subgenre: Slasher
Premiere: 11 January 2008
Directed by Patrik Syversen

Cold Prey II (Fritt vilt II)
Subgenre: Slasher
Premiere: 10 October 2008
Directed by Mats Stenberg

Dead Snow (Død snø)
Subgenre: Horror comedy / zombie / splatter
Premiere: 9 January 2009
Directed by Tommy Wirkola

Hidden (Skjult)
Subgenre: Psychological horror
Premiere: 3 April 2009
Directed by Pål Øie

Detour (Snarveien)
Subgenre: Slasher-related / snuff
Premiere: 31 July 2009
Directed by Severin Eskeland

Kurt Josef Wagle and the Legend of the Fjord Witch (Kurt Josef Wagle og legenden om Fjordheksa)
Subgenre: Horror comedy
Premiere: 5 March 2010
Directed by Tommy Wirkola

Cold Prey III (Fritt vilt III)
Subgenre: Slasher
Premiere: 15 October 2010
Directed by Mikkel Brænne Sandemose

Troll Hunter (Trolljegeren)
Subgenre: Horror comedy / fantasy / mockumentary
Premiere: 29 October 2010
Directed by André Øvredal

Dark Souls (Mørke sjeler)
Subgenre: Zombie / satire
Premiere: 14 January 2011
Directed by César Ducasse and Mathieu Péteul

The Monitor (Babycall)
Subgenre: Psychological horror
Premiere: 7 October 2011
Directed by Pål Sletaune

Thale
Subgenre: Fantasy
Premiere: 17 February 2013
Directed by Aleksander Nordaas

Ragnarok (Gåten Ragnarok)
Subgenre: Action-adventure / monster
Premiere: 4 October 2013
Directed by Mikkel Brænne Sandemose

Dead Snow 2 (Død snø 2)
Subgenre: Horror comedy / zombie / splatter
Premiere: 12 February 2014
Directed by Tommy Wirkola

Myling: The Myth Awakens (Utburd)
Subgenre: Psychological horror / fantasy
Premiere: 14 November 2014
Directed by Astrid Thorvaldsen

Dark Woods 2 (Villmark 2 aka *Vilmark Asylum)*
Subgenre: Psychological horror / slasher
Premiere: 9 October 2015
Directed by Pål Øie

Bloody Water (Skjærgården)
Subgenre: Slasher
Premiere: 8 January 2016
Directed by Frode Nordås

The House (Huset)
Subgenre: Psychological horror
Premiere: 4 March 2016
Directed by Reinert Kiil

Cave
Subgenre: Action / psychological horror
Premiere: 2 September 2016
Directed by Henrik Martin Dahlsbakken

Lust (Lyst)
Subgenre: Psychological horror / rape-revenge
Premiere: 21 April 2017
Directed by Severin Eskeland

Thelma
Subgenre: Psychological horror
Premiere: 15 September 2017
Directed by Joachim Trier

Valley of Shadows (Skyggenes dal)
Subgenre: Fantasy / mystery
Premiere: 20 October 2017
Directed by Jonas Matzow Gulbrandsen

Christmas Blood (Juleblod)
Subgenre: Slasher
Premiere: 2 November 2017
Directed by Reinert Kiil

Haunted (Hjemsøkt)
Subgenre: Psychological horror
Premiere: 24 November 2017
Directed by Carl Christian Raabe

Kurt Josef Wagle and the Murder Mystery (Kurt Josef Wagle og mordmysteriet på Hurtigruta)
Subgenre: Horror comedy / crime
Premiere: 24 November 2017
Directed by Stig Frode Henriksen

Vidar the Vampire (VampyrVidar)
Subgenre: Horror comedy
Premiere: 7 September 2018
Directed by Thomas Aske Berg and Fredrik Waldeland

Lake of Death (De dødes tjern)
Subgenre: Psychological horror
Premiere: 1 November 2019
Directed by Nini Bull Robsahm

All Must Die (Alle må dø)
Subgenre: Slasher / psychological horror
Premiere: 13 March 2020
Directed by Geir Greni

Project Z (Prosjekt Z)
Subgenre: Horror comedy / zombie
Premiere: 12 March 2021
Directed by Henrik Martin Dahlsbakken

The Innocents (De uskyldige)
Subgenre: Psychological horror
Premiere: 3 September 2021
Directed by Eskil Vogt

The Viking Wolf (Vikingulven)
Subgenre: Fantasy / monster
Premiere: TBA 2022
Directed by Stig Svendsen

Possession (Forbannelsen)
Subgenre: Psychological horror
Premiere: TBA 2022
Directed by Henrik Martin Dahlsbakken

The Nightmare (Marerittet)
Subgenre: Psychological horror
Premiere: TBA 2022
Directed by Kjersti Helen Rasmussen

BIBLIOGRAPHY

Allmer, Patricia, Brick, Emily and Huxley, David (eds) (2012), *European Nightmares: Horror Cinema in Europe Since 1945*. London and New York: Wallflower Press.
Altman, Rick (1999), *Film/Genre*. London: BFI.
Andresen, Christer Bakke (2016), *Åpen kropp og lukket sinn: Den norske grøsserfilmen fra 2003 til 2015* [*Open Bodies and Locked Minds: Norwegian Horror Cinema from 2003 to 2015*]. Trondheim: Norwegian University of Science and Technology.
Andresen, Christer Bakke (2017a), 'Deadly Wilderness: Norwegian Horror Cinema in the New Millennium', in *Panoptikum*, 17, pp. 54–76.
Andresen, Christer Bakke (2017b), 'From Hollywood to Norway and Back Again: The Transnational Horror Film and Norwegian Directors in America', in *Journal of Scandinavian Cinema*, 7:3, pp. 211–16.
Andresen, Christer Bakke (2019), '*Thelma*: Empathic Engagement and the Norwegian Horror Cinema', in *Journal of Scandinavian Cinema*, 9:2, pp. 227–33.
Antuñes, Luis R. (2016), 'Norwegian Arctic Cinema: Ecology, Temperature and the Aesthetics of Cold', in J. Dobson and J. Rayner (eds), *Mapping Cinematic Norths: International Interpretations in Film and Television,*. Oxford: Peter Lang.
Aune, Vidar Tevasvold (2018),'*Probably the most perfect slasher movie of all time*': *Markedsføringen av den norske skrekkfilmtrilogien* Fritt vilt [*Marketing the Norwegian horror film trilogy* Cold Prey] *(2006–2010)*. Trondheim: Norwegian University of Science and Technology.
Bachelard, Gaston ([1942] 1983), *Water and Dreams: An Essay on the Imagination of Matter*. Dallas: The Pegasus Foundation.
Badley, Linda (1995), *Film, Horror, and the Body Fantastic*. Westport and London: Greenwood Press.
Bergman, Kerstin (2014), *Swedish Crime Fiction: The Making of Nordic Noir*. Milano: Mimesis International.

Bomann-Larsen, Tor (2004), *Folket* [*The People*]: *Haakon & Maud II*. Oslo: Cappelen.
Botting, Fred (2014), *Gothic*. London: Routledge.
Braaten, Lars Thomas and Solum, Ove (1997), 'Tancred Ibsen og Hollywood-paradigmet. Noen tendenser i norsk film [Tancred Ibsen and the Hollywood Paradigm. Certain Trends in Norwegian Cinema]', in G. Iversen and O. Solum (eds), *Nærbilder: Artikler om norsk filmhistorie* [*Close-ups: Articles on Norwegian Film History*]. Oslo: Universitetsforlaget.
Bryn, Steinar (1992), *Norske Amerika-bilete. Om amerikanisering av norsk kultur* [*Images of Norwegian America. On the Americanisation of Norwegian Culture*]. Oslo: Det Norske Samlaget.
Bryn, Steinar (1993), *The Americanization of Norwegian Culture*. Minneapolis: University of Minnesota.
Clarens, Carlos (1967), *An Illustrated History of the Horror Film*. New York: G. P. Putnam's Sons.
Clover, Carol J. (1992), *Men, Women, and Chain Saws: Gender in the Modern Horror Film*. Princeton: Princeton University Press.
Coates, Kenneth (1994), 'The Discovery of the North: Towards a Conceptual Framework for the Study of Northern/Remote Regions', in *The Northern Review* 12/13, pp. 15–43.
Cuddon, J. A. ([1976] 1998), *The Penguin Dictionary of Literary Terms and Literary Theory*. London: Penguin Group.
Dahl, Hans Fredrik et al (1996), *Kinoens mørke, fjernsynets lys: Levende bilder i Norge gjennom hundre år* [*The Darkness of the Cinema, the Light of the Television: One Hundred Years of Live Images in Norway*]. Oslo: Gyldendal Norsk Forlag.
Dahl, Willy (1993), *Dødens fortellere: Den norske kriminal- og spenningslitteraturens historie* [*Narrators of Death: The History of Norwegian Crime and Thriller Literature*]. Bergen: Eide Forlag.
Day, William Patrick (1985), *In the Circles of Fear and Desire: A Study of Gothic Fantasy*. Chicago and London: The University of Chicago Press.
Dika, Vera (1990), *Games of Terror*: Halloween, Friday the 13th, *and the Films of the Stalker Cycle*. London and Toronto: Associated University Presses, Inc.
Engelstad, Audun (2006), *Losing Streak Stories: Mapping Norwegian Film Noir*. Oslo: University of Oslo.
Fisher, Mark (2016), *The Weird and the Eerie*. London: Repeater Books.
Forshaw, Barry (2012), *Death in a Cold Climate: A Guide to Scandinavian Crime Fiction*. Houndmills and New York: Palgrave Macmillan.
Freeland, Cynthia A. (1995), 'Realist Horror', in C. A. Freeland and T. E. Wartenberg (eds), *Philosophy and Film*. New York and London: Routledge.
Freeland, Cynthia A. (2000), *The Naked and the Undead: Evil and the Appeal of Horror*. Boulder: Westview Press.
Freeland, Cynthia A. (2004), 'Explaining the Uncanny in *The Double Life of Véronique*', in S. J. Schneider (ed.), *Horror Film and Psychoanalysis: Freud's Worst Nightmare*. Cambridge: Cambridge University Press.
Gjelsvik, Anne (2013), 'From Hard Bodies to Soft Daddies: Action Aesthetics and Masculine Values in Contemporary American Action Films', in K. Aukrust (ed.), *Assigning Cultural Values*. Frankfurt: Peter Lang GmbH.
Gunning, Tom (1991), 'Heard Over the Phone: The Lonely Villa and the de Lorde Tradition of the Terrors of Technology', in *Screen*, 32:2, pp. 184–96.
Gunning, Tom ([1986] 2006), 'The Cinema of Attraction[s]: Early Film, Its Spectator and the Avant-Garde', in W. Strauven (ed.), *The Cinema of Attractions Reloaded*. Amsterdam: Amsterdam University Press.

Gustafsson, Tommy and Kääpä, Pietari (2015), 'Introduction: Nordic Genre Film and Institutional History', in T. Gustafsson and P. Kääpä (eds), *Nordic Genre Film: Small Nation Film Cultures in the Global Marketplace*. Edinburgh: Edinburgh University Press.

Hallenbeck, Bruce G. (2009), *Comedy-Horror Films: A Chronological History, 1914–2008*. Jefferson: McFarland & Company, Inc.

Hanich, Julian (2010), *Cinematic Emotion in Horror Films and Thrillers: The Aesthetic Paradox of Pleasurable Fear*. New York and Oxon: Routledge.

Hansen, Kim Toft and Waade, Anne Marit (2017), *Locating Nordic Noir: From Beck to The Bridge*. Cham: Springer Nature / Palgrave Macmillan.

Hansen, Marianne Nordli and Maren Toft (2021), 'Wealth Accumulation and Opportunity Hoarding: Class-Origin Wealth Gaps over a Quarter of a Century in a Scandinavian Country', in *American Sociological Review 2021*, 86:4.

Harper, Jim (2004), *Legacy of Blood: A Comprehensive Guide to Slasher Movies*. Manchester: Headpress / Critical Vision.

Henlin-Strømme, Sabine Brigitte (2012), *Nature, Nation and the Global in Contemporary Norwegian Cinema*. Iowa City: The University of Iowa.

Hindrum, Tanja Aas (2018), *Fra undergrunnen til overflaten: Den norske undergrunnsskrekken* [From Underground to Surface: Norwegian Underground Horror]. Trondheim: Norwegian University of Science and Technology.

Hjort, Mette (2000), 'Themes of Nation', in M. Hjort and S. MacKenzie (eds), *Cinema & Nation*. London and New York: Routledge.

Hjort, Mette and Lindqvist, Ursula (2016), 'States of Cinema: Nordic Film Policy. Introduction' and 'Reinventing the Wheel: Transitions and Triumphs. Introduction', in M. Hjort and U. Lindqvist (eds), *A Companion to Nordic Cinema*. Malden, Oxford, Chichester: Wiley Blackwell.

Holst, Jan Erik (1995), '1970–1995: Børs og katedral [1970–1995: Stock or Cathedral]', in L. T. Braaten, J. E. Holst and J. H. Kortner (eds), *Filmen i Norge: Norske Kinofilmer gjennom 100 år* [Film in Norway: A Hundred Years of Norwegian Cinema]. Oslo: Ad Notam Gyldendal.

Hutchings, Peter (2004), *The Horror Film*. Harlow: Pearson Education Limited.

Iversen, Gunnar (1997), 'Norway', in T. Soila, A. S. Widding and G. Iversen (eds), *Nordic National Cinemas*. London and New York: Routledge.

Iversen, Gunnar (2009). 'Texas, Norway: Mythic Space in Recent Norwegian Crime Films', in R. Moine, B. Rollet and G. Sellier (eds), *Policiers et criminels: un genre populaire européen sur grand et petit écrans*. Paris: L'Harmattan.

Iversen, Gunnar (2011), *Norsk filmhistorie* [Norwegian Film History]. Oslo: Universitetsforlaget.

Iversen, Gunnar (2016), 'Between Art and Genre: New Nordic Horror Cinema', n M. Hjort and U. Lindqvist (eds), *A Companion to Nordic Cinema*. Malden, Oxford, Chichester: Wiley Blackwell.

Iversen, Gunnar and Solum, Ove (2010). *Den norske filmbølgen* [The Norwegian Film Wave]. Oslo: Universitetsforlaget.

Jerslev, Anne (1994), 'Iscenesættelse af kroppen i den moderne horrorfilm [Staging of the Body in the Modern Horror Film]', in A. Elgurén (ed.), *Det skrekkelige: Fra grøssere til splatter – seks essays om horror* [The Horrific: From Horror to Splatter – Six Essays on Horror]. Oslo: Aschehoug.

Karlyn, Kathleen Rowe (2009), 'Scream, Popular Culture, and Feminism's Third Wave', in H. Addison, M. K. Goodwin-Kelly and E. Roth (eds), *Motherhood Misconceived: Representing the Maternal in U.S. Films*. Albany: State University of New York Press.

Kay, Glenn ([2008] 2012), *Zombie Movies. The Ultimate Guide*. Chicago: Chicago Review Press, Inc.

Keane, Stephen ([2001] 2006), *Disaster Movies: The Cinema of Catastrophe*. London: Wallflower Press.
Kendrick, James (2010), 'A Return to the Graveyard: Notes on the Spiritual Horror Film', in S. Hantke (ed.), *American Horror Film: The Genre at the Turn of the Millennium*. Jackson: University Press of Mississippi.
Keskitalo, E. Carina H. (2009), 'The North – Is There Such a Thing? Deconstructing/Contesting Northern and Arctic Discourse', in H. Hansson and C. Norberg (eds), *Cold Matters: Cultural Perceptions of Snow, Ice and Cold*. Umeå: Umeå University and the Royal Skyttean Society.
Lismoen, Kjetil (2017), *Blant hodejegere og nazizombier: Generasjonen som gjenreiste norsk film* [*Among Headhunters and Nazi Zombies: The Generation that Resurrected Norwegian Cinema*]. Oslo: Tiden Norsk Forlag.
McCarty, John (1984), *Splatter Movies: Breaking the Last Taboo of the Screen*. Bromley: Columbus Books.
MacKenzie, Scott and Stenport, Anna Westerståhl (2015), 'Introduction: What Are Arctic Cinemas?', in S. MacKenzie and A. W. Stenport (eds), *Films on Ice: Cinemas of the Arctic*. Edinburgh: Edinburgh University Press.
Myrstad, Anne Marit (1997), '*Fante-Anne*: Det nasjonale gjennombrudd i norsk film [*Gypsy Anne*: The National Breakthrough in Norwegian Cinema]', in G. Iversen and O. Solum (eds), *Nærbilder: Artikler om norsk filmhistorie* [*Close-ups: Articles on Norwegian Film History*]. Oslo: Universitetsforlaget.
Ndalianis, Angela (2012), *The Horror Sensorium: Media and the Senses*. Jefferson and London: McFarland & Company, Inc., Publishers.
Neale, Steve (2000), *Genre and Hollywood*. London: Routledge.
Nilsson, Ørjan (2017), *Tears From a Stone: Conversations About a Work with Paul Waaktaar-Savoy*. Oslo: Falck Forlag.
Nordås, Frode Nesbø (2006), *Digital filmproduksjon i Noreg: Praktiske og estetiske konsekvensar* [*Digital film production in Norway: Practical and aesthetic consequences*]. Trondheim: Norwegian University of Science and Technology.
Norwegian Film Institute (2020), 'Mangfold på lerretet 2013–2020 [Diversity on screen 2013–2020]'. Oslo: Norwegian Film Institute.
Olsen, Lars et al (2021), *Rige børn leger best: Et portræt af det danske klassesamfund* [*Birds of an affluent feather flock together: A portrait of the Danish class society*]. Copenhagen: Gyldendal.
O'Neill, Patrick ([1983] 2010), 'The Comedy of Entropy: The Contexts of Black Humour', in H. Bloom (ed.), *Dark Humor*. New York: Bloom's Literary Criticism, Infobase Publishing.
Paul, William (1994), *Laughing Screaming: Modern Hollywood Horror and Comedy*. New York: Columbia University Press.
Petridis, Sotiris (2014), 'A Historical Approach to the Slasher Film', in *Film International*, 12:1, pp. 76–84.
Punter, David (1980), *The Literature of Terror: A History of Gothic Fictions from 1765 to the Present Day*. London and New York: Longman.
Ryall, Anka, Schimanski, Johan and Wærp, Henning Howlid (2010), 'Arctic Discourses: An Introduction', in A. Ryall, J. Schimanski and H. H. Wærp (eds), *Arctic Discourses*. Newcastle: Cambridge Scholars Publishing.
Schubart, Rikke (1993), *I lyst og død: Fra Frankenstein til splatterfilm* [*Through Lust and Death: From Frankenstein to Splatter Films*]. København: Borgen.
Sharrett, Christopher (1984), 'The Idea of Apocalypse in *The Texas Chainsaw Massacre*', in B. K. Grant and C. Sharrett (eds), *Planks of Reason: Essays on the Horror Film*. Lanham: Scarecrow Press.

Sjögren, Olle (1993), *Inte riktigt lagom? Om 'extremvåld', filmcensur og subkultur* [*Not Quite Right? On 'Extreme Violence', Censorship and Subculture*]. Uppsala: Filmförlaget.
Skal, David J. (2002), *Death Makes a Holiday: A Cultural History of Halloween*. New York and London: Bloomsbury.
Smith, Greg M. (1999), 'Local Emotions, Global Moods, and Film Structure', in C. Plantinga and G. M. Smith (eds), *Passionate Views: Film, Cognition, and Emotion*. Baltimore: The Johns Hopkins University Press.
Smith, Murray (1995). *Engaging Characters: Fiction, Emotion, and the Cinema*. Oxford: Clarendon Press.
Smith-Isaksen, Marte (2013). 'Så videovold – ville drepe.' Videolovgivningen i Norge i perioden 1976–1999 ['Saw Movie Violence – Wanted to Kill.' Video Legislation in Norway 1976–1999]', in O. Solum (ed.), *Film til folket: Sensur og kinopolitikk i 100 år* [*Film to the People: A Hundred Years of Censorship and Cinema Politics*]. Bergen: Fagbokforlaget.
Solum, Ove (1997), 'Veiviserne [Pathfinders]', in G. Iversen and O. Solum (eds), *Nærbilder: Artikler om norsk filmhistorie* [*Close-ups: Articles on Norwegian Film History*]. Oslo: Universitetsforlaget.
Solum, Ove (2016a), 'What is it about Nordic Noir?', in J. Lothe and B. Larsen (eds), *Perspectives on the Nordic*. Oslo: Novus Press.
Solum, Ove (2016b), 'Nordic Noir: Populærkulturell suksess og velferdssamfunnets mørke bakside [Nordic Noir: Popcultural Success and the Dark Side of Welfare Society]', in E. Oxfeldt (eds), *Skandinaviske fortellinger om skyld og privilegier i en globaliseringstid* [*Scandinavian Stories of Blame and Privilege in an Era of Globalisation*]. Oslo: Universitetsforlaget.
Spoto, Donald (1983), *The Dark Side of Genius: The Life of Alfred Hitchcock*. Boston and Toronto: Little, Brown and Company.
Staiger, Janet (2005), *Media Reception Studies*. New York and London: New York University Press.
St.meld. nr. 22 (2006–7). *Veiviseren: For det norske filmløftet* [*Pathfinder*, a government white paper on Norwegian film policy]. Oslo: Ministry of Culture.
Sørensen, Øystein (1998), 'Når ble nordmenn norske? [When did Norwegians become Norwegians?]', in O. Sørensen (ed.), *Jakten på det norske* [*The Search for Norwegianness*]. Oslo: Ad Notam Gyldendal.
Tudor, Andrew (1989), *Monsters and Mad Scientists: A Cultural History of the Horror Movie*. Oxford and Cambridge: Basil Blackwell Ltd.
Tudor, Andrew (2002), 'From Paranoia to Postmodernism? The Horror Movie in Late Modern Society', in S. Neale (ed.), *Genre and Contemporary Hollywood*. London: BFI.
Vaage, Margrethe Bruun (2010), 'Fiction Film and the Varieties of Empathic Engagement', in *Midwest Studies in Philosophy*, 34, pp. 158–79.
Vidler, Anthony (1992), *The Architectural Uncanny: Essays in the Modern Unhomely*. Cambridge and London: The MIT Press.
Vogt, Eskil and Joachim Trier (2017), *Thelma: Screenplay*. Oslo: Tiden Norsk Forlag.
Waade, Anne Marit (2017), 'Melancholy in Nordic Noir: Characters, Landscapes, Light and Music', in *Critical Studies in Television: The International Journal of Television Studies*, 12:4, pp. 380–94.
Wells, Paul (2000), *The Horror Genre: From Beelzebub to Blair Witch*. London: Wallflower.
Wolff, Cynthia Griffin (1983), 'The Radcliffean Gothic Model: A Form for Feminine Sexuality', in J. E. Fleenor (ed.), *The Female Gothic*. Montréal and London: Eden Press.

Wood, Robin (1979), 'Introduction', in *The American Nightmare: Essays on the Horror Film*. Toronto: Festival of Festivals.
Wood, Robin (1986), *Hollywood from Vietnam to Reagan*. New York: Columbia University Press.
Wood, Robin ([1986] 2003), *Hollywood from Vietnam to Reagan . . . and Beyond*. New York: Columbia University Press.

ONLINE RESOURCES

Andresen, Christer Bakke (11 September 2018), 'Analysen: *Skjelvet* [Analysis: *The Quake*]': https://montages.no/2018/09/analysen-skjelvet-2018/ Accessed 9 November 2021.
Berglund, Nina (5 February 2018), 'Norway is now the Richest Country in the World': https://www.newsinenglish.no/2018/02/05/norway-is-now-the-richest-in-the-world/ Accessed 3 June 2020.
Bredeveien, Jo Moen (22 November 2019), 'Vi som drømte om Sverige [We who dreamed of Sweden]': https://www.dagsavisen.no/debatt/kommentar/2019/11/22/vi-som-dromte-om-sverige/ Accessed 1 November 2021.
Brown, Todd (28 June 2010), 'Pål Sletaune talks *Babycall*': https://screenanarchy.com/2010/06/pal-sletaune-talks-babycall.html Accessed 4 July 2020.
Budalen, Andreas (29 January 2012), 'Spilte inn huldrefilm i iskald kjeller [Shot Hulder-film in freezing basement]': http://www.nrk.no/nordland/silje-29-debuterer-som-hulder-1.7973724 Accessed 4 July 2020.
Corrigan, Gemma (12 April 2017), 'Lessons from Norway, the world's most inclusive economy': https://www.weforum.org/agenda/2017/04/lessons-from-norway-the-world-s-most-inclusive-economy/ Accessed 3 June 2020.
Ekeberg, Øivind and Hem, Erlend (2019), 'Hvorfor går ikke selvmordsraten ned i Norge? [Why is there no Decline in Norwegian Suicide Rates?]': https://tidsskriftet.no/2019/07/kronikk/hvorfor-gar-ikke-selvmordsraten-ned-i-norge Accessed 3 June 2020.
Film & Kino (2010, 2012, 2013, 2014, 2015), 'Official Collections of Statistics from the Norwegian Cinema Association': https://www.kino.no/incoming/article1294921.ece Accessed 6 June 2021.
Folkvord, Glenn (29 March 2018), 'Bloody Easter: The Origins of Norwegian Holiday Crime Fiction': https://www.thelocal.no/20180329/bloody-easter-the-origins-of-norwegian-holiday-crime-fiction/ Accessed 6 June 2021.

Gitmark, Hannah (26 July 2021), 'Ulikheten øker [Inequality increases]': https://www.dagsavisen.no/debatt/kommentar/2021/07/26/ulikheten-oker/ Accessed 20 September 2021.

Iversen, Gunnar (15 June 2015), 'Filmen ved siden av – norsk films nye randsoner [Cinéma bis – new borderlands in Norwegian cinema]': https://rushprint.no/2015/06/filmen-ved-siden-av-norsk-films-nye-randsoner/ Accessed 12 October 2021.

Knutsson, Johannes (7 November 2014), 'Skal vi la politiet bestemme? [Should we let the police decide?]': https://www.nrk.no/ytring/skal-vi-la-politiet-bestemme-1.12031458 Accessed 12 June 2020.

Lorch-Falch, Sophie and Tomter, Line (15 August 2021), 'Når hver krone teller [When every penny counts]': https://www.nrk.no/spesial/nar-hver-krone-teller-1.15551896 Accessed 20 September 2021.

Müller, Reidar (30 August 2018), 'Forskere og institusjoner forsøker å sko seg på *Skjelvet* [Researchers and institutions attempt to profit from *The Quake*]': https://www.aftenposten.no/meninger/kronikk/i/kajA3v/forskere-og-institusjoner-for soeker-aa-sko-seg-paa-skjelvet-reidar-mu Accessed 9 November 2021.

Nes, Ragnhild Bang et al (17 December 2021), 'Livskvalitet i Norge [Quality of life in Norway]': https://www.fhi.no/nettpub/hin/samfunn/livskvalitet-i-norge/ Accessed 20 December 2021.

Reiersen, Tonje Skar (14 October 2011), 'Analysen: *Babycall* [Analysis: *The Monitor*]': http://montages.no/2011/10/analysen-babycall-2011/ Accessed 4 July 2020.

Ritman, Alex (3 March 2021), 'Berlin Hidden Gem: Norwegian Supernatural Thriller *The Innocents* Asks if Children Can Be Genuinely Evil': https://www.hollywoodreporter.com/movies/movie-news/berlin-hidden-gem-supernatural-thriller-the-innocents-asks-if-children-can-be-genuinely-evil-4141982/ Accessed 26 August 2021.

Schubart, Rikke (26 January 2010), 'Norsk slasher-serie [Norwegian slasher series]': http://videnskab.dk/blog/norsk-slasher-serie Accessed 4 July 2020.

Sletaune, Pål (10 March 2005), 'Sletaune går inn i marerittet [Sletaune Enters the Nightmare]': http://www.nrk.no/kultur/sletaune-gar-inn-i-marerittet-1.539485 Accessed 4 July 2020.

Statistics Norway (14 September 2018), 'Formuesulikheten øker [Wealth inequality increases]': https://www.ssb.no/inntekt-og-forbruk/artikler-og-publikasjoner/formuesu likheten-oker Accessed 7 September 2021.

Statistics Norway (9 April 2019), 'Minste antall straffedommer på 30 år [Lowest number of convictions in 30 years]': https://www.ssb.no/sosiale-forhold-og-krim inalitet/artikler-og-publikasjoner/minste-antall-straffedommer-pa-30-ar Accessed 10 June 2020.

Statistics Norway (24 September 2020), 'Ulikheten – betydelig større enn statistikken viser [Inequality – significantly bigger than statistics show]': https://www.ssb.no/inntekt-og-forbruk/artikler-og-publikasjoner/ulikheten-betydelig-storre-enn-statis tikken-viser Accessed 6 August 2021.

Thompson, Bill (25 December 2013), 'Wide World of Horror: *Naboer* (*Next Door*) – the Mind is a Dangerous Place to be': http://www.soundonsight.org/wide-world-of-horror-naboer-next-door-the-mind-is-a-dangerous-place-to-be/ Accessed 4 July 2020.

Thorkildsen, Joakim (16 September 2014), '- At det er litt norsk aksent gjør ingenting [- A little Norwegian accent is fine]': http://www.dagbladet.no/2014/09/16/kultur/filter/film/dod_sno_2/tommy_wirkola/35299156/ Accessed 4 July 2020.

United Nations Development Programme (2020), Human Development Index Ranking: http://hdr.undp.org/en/content/latest-human-development-index-ranking and Norway Human Development Indicators: http://hdr.undp.org/en/countries/pro files/NOR Accessed 10 June 2021.

INTERVIEWS CONDUCTED

Pål Sletaune: 20 January 2016
Martin Sundland: 16 November 2015
Roar Uthaug: 19 November 2015
Eskil Vogt: 23 August 2021
Pål Øie: 18 October and 25 November 2015

INDEX

Note: Page numbers in *italics* refer to figures

12th Man, The (Zwart), 128

action films, 22–3, 97, 111, 128
a-ha, 11
Aliens (Cameron), 45, 60
All Must Die (Greni), 67, 153, 163
American action heroes, 119
American crime films, 11, 73
American horror films, 21, 64, 111
American slasher films, 36, 41, 44, 48
   cinematic space, 69
   early v. late, 51
   final girl, 67
   water, 33
Americanisation, 5, 23, 122, 123, 151
Amityville Horror, The (Rosenberg), 69
Antichrist (von Trier), 12
Antuñes, L. R., 26, 130
apocalypse, 142–52
   Catching the Flame (Øie), 144–5
   The North Sea (Andersen), 149–50, 151–2
   The Quake (Andersen), 148–9, 150–1
   The Tunnel (Øie), 145

The Wave (Uthaug), 146–8
Arctic, 10, 13, 19, 25–7, 130–1, 146, 157
Atlantic Crossing (Eik), 127, 128
Aune, V. T., 151

Bachelard, G., 19, 26, 27, 129, 130
Bergman, K., 10
Black Death, 3
black metal music, xiv
Bloody Water (Nordås), 67, 153, 162
bodily empathy, 95
Bodom (Mustonen), 13–14
Bondevik, K. M., 24
borderline images, 101
Botting, F., 86
Burger King, 151

Carpenter, J., 37
Catching the Flame (Øie), 144–5
Cave (Dahlsbakken), 162
censorship law, 14, 24–5, 36, 74–5, 113
children's films, 109
Christmas Blood (Kiil), 44, 68, 153, 163

cinematic space, 69, 74
Clocks by Moonlight (Bergstrøm), 28, 159
Clover, C. J., 55
  cinematic space, 69
  Cold Prey (Uthaug), 40
  final girl, 44–5, 47, 67
  Others, 57
  revenge, 55
  slasher subgenre, 16, 35, 36, 48
  technology, 63
  'Terrible Place', 42
Coates, K., 131
Cold Prey franchise, 70, 151, 157
Cold Prey II (Stenberg), 58–62, 63, 67, 68, 122, 160
Cold Prey III (Sandemose), 62–7, 68, 151, 161
Cold Prey (Uthaug), 35–6, 39–47, 160
  and American remakes, 52
  apocalypse, 144
  Easter holidays, xiv
  emotion markers, 42, 54, 70
  empathy, 95
  generic expression, 31
  marketing, 151
  novelty value, 66
  rural setting, 53, 54, 63, 68, 69
  ticket sales, 122
  water, 103, 129
  young people, 49
comedy *see* horror comedy
Craven, W., 69
crime thrillers, 9, 28, 73, 115, 156

Dahlsbakken, H. M., 116
Danish authors, 8
Danish cinema, 6
Danish horror films, 12–13, 14
Dark Souls (Péteul and Ducasse), 117, 118, 122, 153, 161
Dark Woods 2 (Øie), 17, 22, 84, 125–7, 128–9, 152, 162
Dark Woods (Øie), xii, 18, 22, 28–34, 53, 160
  apocalypse, 144
  Easter holidays, xiv
  Nazism, 10
  water, 103, 129, 131, 133
Day, W. P., 81
Dead Snow 2 (Wirkola), 26, 115–16, 161

Dead Snow (Wirkola), 26, 112–15, 144, 160
dead water, 17, 19, 124
  Dark Woods 2 (Øie), 125–6, 128, 129
  Dark Woods (Øie), 32, 129, 131, 133
  Lake of Death (Robsahm), 138, 141
  Lake of the Dead (Bergstrøm), 27, 32, 132
  The Monitor (Sletaune), 130
  Thelma (Trier), 130
Denmark, 3, 4, 11, 24, 143
Detour (Eskeland), 7, 62, 160
digital technology, 122, 154
Dika, V., 36, 38, 41, 46, 48, 68
disaster films, 17, 141, 142, 145–52
  The North Sea (Andersen), 149–50, 151–2
  The Quake (Andersen), 148–9, 150–1
  Troll (Uthaug), 152
  The Tunnel (Øie), 145
  The Wave (Uthaug), 146–8
dual identities, 83

earthquakes, 148–9, 150–1
Easter holidays, xiii, xiv, 39
elsewhen, 69, 74, 87–8
emotion markers, 33, 65–6
  Cold Prey III (Sandemose), 64
  Cold Prey (Uthaug), 42, 54, 70
  Dead Snow (Wirkola), 115
  Hidden (Øie), 83
  The Innocents (Vogt), 101
  The Monitor (Sletaune), 89
  Next Door (Sletaune), 89
emotional abuse, 98
empathy, 95–6, 97, 98, 101
end of the world *see* apocalypse

Fantefilm, 120, 121–2, 146, 147, 149–52, 153
feminism, 50
film festivals, 9, 19–20, 99, 124, 153
film genres, 19, 22–5; *see also* horror genre
film noir, 11
film politics, 15, 23–5, 32–4, 74–5, 113
Films on Ice (MacKenzie and Stenport), 26
final girl, 16
  American slasher films, 67
  Cold Prey II (Stenberg), 60
  Cold Prey III (Sandemose), 66

175

final girl (*cont.*)
   Cold Prey (Uthaug), 40, 41, 42, 44, 52, 68
   Friday the 13th (Cunningham), 47
   Friday the 13th Part II (Miner), 48, 51
   Halloween (Carpenter), 38, 49, 52
   legacy of, 47–52
   The North Sea (Andersen), 150
   The Texas Chain Saw Massacre (Hooper), 37
   The Texas Chainsaw Massacre (Nispel), 51
Fincher, D., 9
Finland, 11, 13–14
Finnish horror films, 13–14, 14
Forshaw, B., 11
Freeland, C. A., 20, 22, 38, 54, 82, 92, 131
Freud, S., 134
Friday the 13th (Cunningham), 21, 33, 38, 47, 48, 57, 67
Friday the 13th (Nispel), 51
Friday the 13th Part II (Miner), 38, 48, 51, 52
Frostbite (Banke), 12

gender, 49, 135, 136
genre crossbreeds/hybrids, 16, 106–7, 122–3, 153
   Dark Souls (Péteul and Ducasse), 117, *118*, 122, 153, 161
   Dead Snow 2 (Wirkola), 26, 115–16, 161
   Dead Snow (Wirkola), 26, 112–15, 144, 160
   Project Z (Dahlsbakken), 116, 153, 163
   Ragnarok (Sandemose), 119–21, 144, 161
   Thale (Nordaas), 118–19, 161
   Troll Hunter (Øvredal), 107–12, 122, 144, 161
genre fiction, 106
genres, 19, 22–5; *see also* horror genre
German expressionist cinema, 20–1
German invasion *see* Nazi invasion/occupation
Gjelsvik, A., 119
global streaming services, 154
gothic
   definition, 20, 86
   The Monitor (Sletaune), 86–93

New American Gothic, 88
rural, 56
gothic literature, 21, 91
gothic tales, 125
Greenland, 3, 13
Gunning, T., 63, 110
Gypsy (Ibsen), 5

Haakon VII, 3, 7, 127
Håkon IV Håkonsson, 3
Halloween (Carpenter), 21, 31, 37–8, 44, 49, 50, 52
Halloween (Zombie), 51–2
Halloween II (Rosenthal), 38, 58
Hansen, M. N., 103
Harper, J., 50
Haunted (Raabe), 163
health care, 102
Heavy Water War, The (Sørensen), 127
Hidden (Øie), 83–4, 160
Hill, D., 37
historical dramas, 144–5
Hjort, M., 6
Hollywood, 5, 12, 122
   action films, 22–3
   horror films, 21, 69
   Norwegian directors in, 155–8
   Norwegian horror cinema, 123
horror comedy, 115–16
   Dead Snow 2 (Wirkola), 26, 115–16, 161
   Dead Snow (Wirkola), 26, 112–15, 144, 160
   Project Z (Dahlsbakken), 116, 153, 163
   Troll Hunter (Øvredal), 107–12, 122, 144, 161
horror film festival, 19–20, 124, 153
horror genre, 19–22, 25, 27; *see also* Nordic horror cinema; Norwegian horror cinema; Norwegian horror films; psychological horror films; slasher films
House, The (Kiil), 75, 83, 153, 162
hulder, 118
humour, 113; *see also* horror comedy
hunters, 56; *see also* masked killer
Hutchings, P., 49, 83

Ibsen, H., 5, 122, 132
Ibsen, T., 5, 123
Iceland, 11, 13, 14

INDEX

imaginary empathy, 95
income distribution, 102
independent films *see* low-budget independent films
Innocents, The (Vogt), 71, 84, 99–101, 103, 104, 163
Insomnia (Skjoldbjærg), 9, 73
Isle of Darkness (Diesen), 28, 159
isolation, 68, 73, 82
  Cold Prey franchise, 41, 46, 63
  Next Door (Sletaune), 72, 76, 77
Iversen, G., 5, 11, 47, 56, 64, 153, 154

Julsrud, K., 31

Karlyn, K. R., 50
Kendrick, J., 72, 87, 91
Keskitalo, E. C. H., 26
Kiil, R., 154
King's Choice, The (Poppe), 127
Kittelsen, T., 110
Klevberg, L., 156
Kurt Josef Wagle and the Legend of the Fjord Witch (Wirkola), 161
Kurt Josef Wagle and the Murder Mystery (Henriksen), 163

Lake of Death (Robsahm), 1–2, 135–41, 163
Lake of the Dead (Bergstrøm), xii, xiii, 1, 28, 53, 132–5, 159
  dead water, 27, 32
  v. *Lake of Death* (Robsahm), 139–40
Last Voyage of the Demeter (Øvredal), 157
Let the Right One In (Alfredson), 12
Little Horror? A (series), 153
location *see* rural setting; urban setting
Loen disasters, 146
Louder Than Bombs (Trier), 99
low-budget independent films, 15, 21, 28, 142, 153, 154; *see also Dark Souls* (Péteul and Ducasse); *Lust* (Eskeland); *Texas Chain Saw Massacre, The* (Hooper)
Lust (Eskeland), 62, 82–3, 162

mainstream horror, 153–5
Manhunt (Syversen), 54–8, 65, 76, 89, 144, 160
marketing, 151–2
masked killer, 16, 35, 142

Cold Prey (Uthaug), 35, 40, 44
The Texas Chain Saw Massacre (Hooper), 37
see also hunters
Max Manus (Rønning and Sandberg), 127, 155
melancholy, 10–11, 13, 61
Méliès, G., 20
Millennium (Larsson), 8, 9, 10, 143
mirror motif, 139, 140, 141
mobile phones, 33, 63, 114
Monitor, The (Sletaune), 86–93, 161
  dead water, 130
  empathy, 97
  setting, 100
  social-democratic nightmare, 103–4
  ticket sales, 84
  unreliable narrator, 98–9
  window motif, 78
monster horror, 13, 107, 120, 122
monsters, 112, 115, 117, 122
mood cues, 33, 42
MovieMaker Magazine, 19
Murder of Engine Maker Roolfsen, The (Hansen), 9
'Murders in the Rue Morgue, The' (Poe), 9
My Bloody Valentine (Mihalka), 38
Myling (Thorvaldsen), 75, 135, 153, 162
Myrstad, A. M., 4

narrators, 72
national identity, 47
national romanticism, 4–5, 61, 69, 70, 110, 144
nature, 15–16, 17, 32, 124, 130–1
  Cold Prey (Uthaug), 47
  Dark Woods 2 (Øie), 128
  Dark Woods (Øie), 18, 129
  see also Arctic; rural setting
Nazi invasion/occupation, 7, 10, 113–14, 127, 128, 132
Nazi zombies, 114, 115
Neale, S., 37
neoslasher films, 51–2
Nesbø, J., 8, 9
Netflix, 152, 154, 156
New American Gothic, 88
news coverage, 54
Next Door (Sletaune), 74–81, 160
  apocalypse, 144
  emotion markers, 89

Next Door (Sletaune) *(cont.)*
  social-democratic society, 104
  spatial disorientation, 81–2, 93
  ticket sales, 84
  unreliable narrator, 72, 88
Night of the Living Dead (Romero), 112
Nightmare, The (Rasmussen), 164
Nightmare on Elm Street, A (Craven), 21, 38, 51, 67, 69, 137
Nine Lives (Skouen), 128
Nordic crime literature, 8–9
Nordic folklore, 107, 118; *see also* Norse mythology
Nordic horror cinema, 8–14; *see also* Norwegian horror cinema
Nordic noir, xiv, 8–14, 134, 143
NORSAR, 150
Norse mythology, 39, 112, 120, 121; *see also* Nordic folklore
North Sea, The (Andersen), 149–50, 151–2
northern-ness, 26
Norway
  geography, 25–6
  history, 3, 7, 17, 127 (*see also* Nazi invasion/occupation)
  national romanticism, 4–5, 61, 69, 70, 110, 144
  quality of life, 2
  social-democratic ideal, 61, 79, 143
  social-democratic society, 101–5
  social-democratic welfare state, 2–3
  suicide rates, 6
Norwegian apocalypse, 142–52
  Catching the Flame (Øie), 144–5
  The North Sea (Andersen), 149–50, 151–2
  The Quake (Andersen), 148–9, 150–1
  The Tunnel (Øie), 145
  The Wave (Uthaug), 146–8
Norwegian cinema, 4–6, 22–5, 122–3; *see also* Norwegian horror cinema
Norwegian condition, 157
Norwegian crime fiction, 9
Norwegian Film Institute, 31, 33
Norwegian film politics, 15, 23–5, 32–4, 74–5, 113
Norwegian Film School, 24, 39
Norwegian horror cinema, 25, 26–7, 33, 104–5, 130–1, 143
Norwegian horror films, 21–2, 101–5,

157–8; *see also* psychological horror films; slasher films

oil industry, 117, 149–50
old community, 56
Oslo bombing, 7
Others, 56, 57
Øvredal, A., 107, 111, 156–7

Petridis, S., 47, 48, 50, 51
plague, 3
Poe, E. A., 27
Polanski, R., 73
police officers, 7
Possession (Dahlsbakken), 116, 164
product placement, 151
Project Z (Dahlsbakken), 116, 153, 163
Psycho (Hitchcock), 36–7, 43
psychoanalysis, 134
psychological horror films, 16, 21–2, 71–4, 85
  Hidden (Øie), 83–4, 160
  The Innocents (Vogt), 71, 84, 99–101, 103, 104, 163
  Lake of Death (Robsahm), 1–2, 135–41, 163
  Lust (Eskeland), 62, 82–3, 162
  The Monitor (Sletaune), 86–93, 161: dead water, 130; empathy, 97; setting, 100; social-democratic nightmare, 103–4; ticket sales, 84; unreliable narrator, 98–9; window motif, 78
  Next Door (Sletaune), 74–81, 160: apocalypse, 144; emotion markers, 89; social-democratic society, 104; spatial disorientation, 81–2, 93; ticket sales, 84; unreliable narrator, 72, 88
  social-democratic nightmares, 101–5
  Thelma (Trier), 84, 93, 94–9, 103, 130, 144, 162
unhomely spaces, 81–4
Punter, D., 20, 88

Quake, The (Andersen), 148–9, 150–1

racism, 64
Radcliffe, A., 44
Ragnarok (Sandemose), 119–21, 144, 161
Ramaskrik Oppdal, 19, 20

INDEX

rape, 64–5, 82, 88, 139
Rare Exports (Helander), 14
realistic horror, 54
Reiersen, T. S., 88
religion, 94, 97, 98
Repulsion (Polanski), 73, 81, 92
return of the repressed, 81, 87, 134
Reykjavik Whale Watching Massacre (Kemp), 13, 33
Robsahm, N. B., 135
Rønning, J., 155
rural gothic, 56
rural setting, 31–2, 53–8, 63, 65, 68–70, 112, 148

Saboteurs, The (Sørensen), 127
Sandberg, E., 155
Sandemose, M. B., 120
Sauna (Annila), 13, 14
Schubart, R., 70, 112
Scream (Craven), 16, 47, 48, 49–50
Second World War, 10, 113–14, 127, 128
setting *see* rural setting; urban setting
sexual violence, 75, 76–7, 78–80, 82; *see also* rape
Shape of Water, The (del Toro), 20
Sharrett, C., 144
Shining, The (Kubrick), 46–7, 73, 81, 92
Sixth Sense, The (Shyamalan), 87
slasher films, 16, 21–2, 36–8, 72, 136–7
  basic structure, 48
  Cold Prey II (Stenberg), 58–62, 63, 67, 68, 122, 160
  Cold Prey III (Sandemose), 62–7, 68, 151, 161
  Cold Prey (Uthaug), 35–6, 39–47, 160: and American remakes, 52; apocalypse, 144; Easter holidays, xiv; emotion markers, 42, 54, 70; empathy, 95; generic expression, 31; marketing, 151; novelty value, 66; rural setting, 53, 54, 63, 68, 69; water, 103, 129; young people, 49
  final girl legacy, 47–52
  Manhunt (Syversen), 54–8, 65, 76, 89, 144, 160
  rural setting, 31–2, 53–8, 63, 65, 68–70
  slasher killers, 44, 59, 60; *see also* masked killer

Sletaune, P., 22, 75, 77
Smith, G. M., 33
snuff movies, 62
social-democratic ideal, 61, 79, 143
social-democratic nightmares, 101–5
social-democratic welfare states, 2–3, 10, 61, 79
Something Completely Different (Kolstad), 153, 159
soundscape, 101
spaces, 77, 81–4, 92; *see also* cinematic space
spatial constructs, 131
Spielberg, S., 119, 121
Stoltenberg, J., 23, 24
streaming services, 154
suicide, 6, 91–2
Sundland, M., 36
supernatural powers, 71, 85, 142
  The Innocents (Vogt), 99, 100
  The Monitor (Sletaune), 87
  Thelma (Trier), 93, 94, 96, 98
Sweden, 3, 4, 143
Swedish authors, 8
Swedish horror films, 11, 12, 14
'Sycamore Leaves' (a-ha), 11
Syversen, P., 156

technology, 63, 122
television series, 9
'Terrible Place', 42–3, 69
Texas, Norway, 56, 64, 89
Texas Chain Saw Massacre, The (Hooper), 37, 56, 144
Texas Chainsaw Massacre, The (Nispel), 51, 52
Thale (Nordaas), 118–19, 161
Thelma (Trier), 84, 93, 94–9, 103, 130, 144, 162
Thompson, B., 77
time, 92
Toft, M., 103
Tomb Raider (Uthaug), 155
torture porn, 55
Train to Bergen Was Robbed Last Night, The (Grieg and Lie), xiii
transcendence, 142
transgression, 142
Trier, J., 93–4
Troll (Uthaug), 152
Troll Hunter (Øvredal), 107–12, 122, 144, 161

179

Troll: The Tale of a Tail (Munroe and Kamp), 109
trolls, 107
Tudor, A., 60, 69
Tunnel, The (Øie), 145
twins, 1, 132, 133, 136, 139, 140–1
Tyldum, M., 155–6

uncanny, 82
unhomely spaces, 81–4
United Nations, 2
unreliable narrator, 72, 98–9
urban setting, 77, 78, 89–90, 148
urban-no-particular-place, 89, 90, 91, 92, 130
Uthaug, R., 31, 36, 39, 52, 155
Utøya massacre, 7, 66

Vaage, M. B., 95
Valley of Shadows (Gulbrandsen), 153, 162
Vidar the Vampire (Berg and Waldeland), 153, 163
Viking Age, 3
Viking Wolf, The (Svendsen), 164
Vogt, E., 99
von Trier, L., 12
Vreid, xiv

Waade, A. M., 10
war genre, 106, 127–8; *see also* Nazi invasion/occupation
war history, 17; *see also* Nazi invasion/occupation
water, 26, 27, 32, 33, 129, 139; *see also* dead water

Water and Dreams (Bachelard), 27
'Water Sprite' (Kittelsen), 6
Wave, The (Uthaug), 106, 146–8
wealth distribution, 102
welfare states *see* social-democratic welfare states
What Happened to Monday (Wirkola), 115, 156
White Zombie (Halperin), 112
wilderness *see* nature; rural setting
Willoch, K., 102
window motif, 78, 90, 92, 93, 101
Wirkola, T., 112, 156
Wolff, C. G., 44
Wood, R., 37, 81
World Bank, 2
World Economic Forum, 2
World War II, 10, 113–14, 127, 128
Worst Person in the World, The (Trier), 99

young community, 41, 56, 57
young people, 49

zombie films
    Dark Souls (Péteul and Ducasse), 117, *118*, 122, 153, 161
    Dead Snow 2 (Wirkola), 26, 115–16, 161
    Dead Snow (Wirkola), 26, 112–15, 144, 160
    Project Z (Dahlsbakken), 116, 153, 163
    White Zombie (Halperin), 112
Zwart, H., 155